SERIAL KILLERS

SERIAL KILLERS
Understanding Lust Murder

Phillip C. Shon
Dragan Milovanovic

CAROLINA ACADEMIC PRESS
Durham, North Carolina

Library of Congress Cataloging-in-Publication Data

Shon, Phillip C.

Serial killers : understanding lust murder / by Phillip C. Shon and Dragan Milovanovic.

p. cm.

Includes bibliographical references and index.

ISBN 1-59460-178-X

1. Serial murderers. 2. Serial murders. I. Milovanovic, Dragan. II. Title.

HV6515.S545 2006

364.152'3--dc22

2006010127

Carolina Academic Press
700 Kent Street
Durham, North Carolina 27701
Telephone (919) 489-7486
Fax (919) 493-5668
www.cap-press.com

Printed in the United States of America

TABLE OF CONTENTS

Part II
Paraphilias and Lust Murder

Chapter 1

Introduction

Phillip C. Shon and Dragan Milovanovic

Serial murderers, their methods of operation, and their victims have been a fruitful topic for "true crime" writers and the producers of fictional and documentary programming on television and film, especially in the past fifteen years. Recently, however, scholarly works have moved away from the popularized accounts of serial murder, and have treated the topic from a theoretically diverse and interdisciplinary perspective, drawing on disciplines such as criminology/criminal justice, psychology, forensic sciences, and geography. A growing body of literature has also indicated that the label "serial killers" encompasses a variety of forms of expression. In this book, we are especially concerned with homicides that are sexually motivated—"lust homicide."

Lust Homicide

"Lust homicide" forms of serial killing have only been recently defined (Hazelwood and Douglas 1980), although attempts at definition can be traced back several decades (Jesse 1924). Sometimes referred to as "sexual serial murders," these forms of horrific violence have captured the imagination of the public through movies such as *Silence of the Lambs* (released in 1991). The perpetrators of these types of crimes have come from various backgrounds, both deprived and well-to-do. For instance, Dennis Rader, the BTK predator ("bind, torture, and kill") was raised by a loving mother and a "tough but decent and strict father." He was a Boy Scout, U.S. Air Force veteran, home alarm installer, a father with two children, the president of a local church, and a code-enforcement official (Zandt 2005). That is, he was hardly the stereotypical predator one would envision for the secretive and gruesome ten homicides that he committed over thirty years. Others, however, have come from families that have been abusive, unloving, and dysfunctional. Appearances, too, are deceiving. Jeffrey Dahmer, Ted Bundy, and Dennis Rader, for example, hardly fit the stereotype of lust homicide predators.

While homicides that are sexual in nature have existed for quite sometime, only recently have we begun to see a body of knowledge being developed on this topic, one that is theoretically cogent. Still, much is still of the journalistic variety or media driven (see Fuller, Chapter 8; Kudlac, Chapter 9). In this book we explore the various dimensions of lust homicide. We will first outline the rise of serial killers, the prevalence of female serial killers (a topic not fully developed in this book), definitional issues, motivational theories, and the role of paraphilia. We will conclude with a brief summary of each chapter.

This book assembles a range of writers, from practitioners and decisionmakers for the release of sexual predators from confinement, to commentators of media presentations and academicians. It also indicates some similarities in the phenomenon outside of the United States. The book will appeal to students of violence, policing practitioners in the field, decisionmakers in psychiatric institutions, treatment professionals, academicians (both theoretically and empirically oriented), and media analysts.

Rise of Serial Killers

There is historical evidence to suggest that serial homicides have been slowly rising since the 1970s. For instance, the increase in the number of homicide cases in which the relationship between the victims and the offenders remains unknown to police—strangers killing strangers—is often cited as a reflection of a disturbing trend in the rising number of serial homicides in the United States (Lane 1997).[1] This, in combination with the declining trend in the clearance rates of homicides, points to a disquieting pattern of murder in America.

Just as disquieting as the declining trend in the clearance rates of murder is the number of serial killers that are currently active in the United States. Estimates have been as low as 200 and as high as 300 (Holmes and Holmes 1994). A recent study, however, presents an up-to-date and methodologically sound estimate of the frequency of serial sexual homicide victimization in the United States. To estimate its prevalence, McNamara and Morton (2004) compiled their data from several sources. In order to calculate the number of serial sexual murderers in Virginia over a ten-year period, they collected homicide records from the databases of Virginia State Police (VSP), the Federal Bureau

---

1. Not withstanding the critique concerning the dark figure of crime. Official statistics only deal with "crimes known to the police."

of Investigation's (FBI) Violent Criminal Apprehension Program (ViCAP), the VSP ViCAP, the Virginia Homicide Investigators Association (VHIA), Virginia Division of Forensic Science (VDFS), and the media coverage in LEXIS/NEXIS that might have been reported but missed in official records.

McNamara and Morton (2004) noted a total of 5,183 homicides in Virginia from 1987 to1996, and concluded that the frequency of serial sexual homicide victimization was less than one percent (.5 percent). Extrapolating from the Virginia study, they estimated that the total number of victims of serial sexual killers in the United States was "one-half of one percent of all victims or approximately 750 serial sexual murder victims per year" (McNamara and Morton 2004, p. 4). They did, however, caution that the estimate from the Virginia sample might not be valid since Virginia was not representative of the U.S. population.

In the ten-year period McNamara and Morton (2004) examined there were six serial sexual killers that emerged from their study; five out of the six were known to the police, along with the number of victims each killed; but what is noteworthy is that their study illuminated generic portraits of the killers and the type of victims each killer chose. For instance, offender 1 in the study was a black male who targeted adult men, both black and white; offender 2 was an Asian male who attacked and killed young white females; offender 3 (white male) was caught after one offense; offender 4 was a black male who primarily attacked middle-aged white females, along with a young Asian girl; offender 5 targeted pre-pubescent and pubescent females. Offender 6 was not identified, but was linked to four victims, all white females between the ages of 55–84. All of these cases included a "sexual" element, such as the victims' state of undress, lewd posing, or evidence of sexual assault. While the aforementioned cases fall under the broad definitional umbrella of serial homicide, they are unique due to their specifically sexualized components. This book offers a conceptual grounding of such phenomenon, and links the occurrence of such crimes within the existing research on dangerous sexual paraphilias (see Hickey 2006b).

There have been some, however, who argue serial killers are a myth, mere fictional accounts (Rhodes 1999, pp. 211–213; see also Jenkins 1994), more a manufactured category responding to perceived threats to civilization. Jenkins traces the origins of the term "serial killers" to the Behavioral Sciences Unit of the Federal Bureau of Investigation which was initiated in the early 1970s for the purpose of establishing profiles of violent offenders. By the early 1980s a hysteria emerged as to the dangers to children "from pornographers, satanic clubs, lethal day care centers and kidnappers," which was further encouraged by the Behavioral Sciences Unit in its input to the media (Rhodes 1999, p. 211). By the 1990s, Rhodes tells us, this hysteria took even greater momentum. The image of "irrational, predatory serial killers was widely acknowledged, not least because it fit so many social, political, cultural, and bureaucratic agendas, including those of family-value and law-and-order conservatives, antipornographers, feminists, homophobes, federal law enforcement agencies, child-victim advocates and Christian fundamentalists." We cannot discount this thesis in the production of serial killers. However, in making their point, Rhodes and others in this tradition understate an emergent form of homicides that has recurrent themes and predators. Jenkins's study downsizes the number of serial killers, but still acknowledges its prevalence. Nor can we discount Rhodes's as well as Jenkins's thesis of fiction creating, for we have seen much media fascination with crime and the serial killer, especially since Jonathan Demme's film in 1991, *The Silence of the Lambs* (see also Chapters 8 and 9, respectively by Fuller and Kudlac on the relation between the media, the serial killer, and the public).

Female Serial Lust Homicide

In this book we are primarily concerned with male serial killers. Due to page length consideration, the issue of female serial killers of the "lust" variety should be addressed another day (a starting point could consult Hickey 1997; Schechter 2002, pp. 31–41; Manners 1995; Segrave 1990; Jones 1996; Michael and Kelleher 1998). We make no pretenses that we have come to an understanding of female homicide (so-called "angels of death," "black widows"), which may very well follow different dynamics. For example, some literature does suggest that female serial killers follow some traditional gender distinctions. Thus the use of poison is often associated with conventionalized gender roles, such as the mother (cook) and caretaker (nurse). Hickey's (1997, pp. 223–24) empirical study of 399 serial killers from 1800 to 1995, with a data set of 62 women, concluded that many of the female serial killers appeared more centered on "financial security, revenge, enjoyment, and sexual stimulation." Schechter (2002, p. 31) provides another view:

> brutal penetration is not what turns them on. Their excitement comes —not from violating the bodies of strangers with phallic objects— but from a grotesque, sadistic travesty of intimacy and love: from spooning poisoned medicine into the mouth of trusting patient, for example, or smothering a sleeping child in its bed. In short, from ten-

derly turning a friend, family members or dependent into a corpse—from nurturing them to death.

Some literature also indicates that the female serial killers often emerge in historical settings based on crime scares. Schechter (2002, pp. 174–179) looked at the late 1800s during which women were organizing and demanding equality that produced anxieties in men. This along with media generated stories of women, "in the guise of loving housewives, mothers, and caretakers," produced images of rampart killing of close ones. The literature also indicates considerable sadistic forms of female serial killers: Mary Ann Cotton killed thirty-three people; Jane Toppan, thirty-one; Amy Archer-Gilligan, forty; and a group of Hungarian women called the "Angel-makers of Nagyrev" who killed over one hundred (Schechter 2002, pp. 307–308). And some of these were sexual in nature: Jane Toppan, after killing the mom, took her ten-year-old son to bed.

Understanding lust homicide by women could also productively consider Lacan's notion of sexuation (1998, pp. 78–89). What Lacan was to show in his theory of sexuation is that even though discursive subject positions are normatively established in culture—a discursively constructed space in discourse in which a coherently appearing "I" can take up residence to speak—and embedded in the unconscious (in the Other), nevertheless, a woman can occupy both the traditionally defined position, or can occupy that of a "man's" discursive subject position. In the latter case, the very dynamics developed throughout this book on lust serial killers can be applied. Conversely, where a person occupies the discursive subject position of woman, a different dynamic is suggested by Lacanian analysis. In other words, we would need to study the various identifications, conflicts, fantasies, resolutions, etc., quite differently in the one case as opposed to the other. Alternatively, it may be that this "essentialism" may not do, and that a very different dynamic exists, perhaps following such theorists of the body as Gilles Deleuze (1988, 1989; see also Grosz 1994). This should certainly be taken up in a future book.

Defining Sexual and Serial Homicide

Serial murderers are so defined if they have killed three or more victims, on separate occasions, in a thirty-day period. This broad definition has been the object of criticism as well as debate (see Ferguson et al. 2003). The debate centers around the constitutive elements of serial murder, factors such as the number of homicide victims that have to be present in order to be counted as a serial offense, the numbers ranging from two to ten (see Dietz 1986; Egger 1984). Furthermore, broad definitions such as the one provided earlier assume the crime to be the work of a solitary offender, operating in a "comfort zone," punctuated by "cooling periods" between offenses. As Harbort and Mokros (2001) point out, however, these types of definitional constraints make classification of certain cases problematic, such as those involving two completed offenses and one attempted murder, the status of the offender as being mentally ill, the presence of multiple offenders in one incident. As a result of these potential problems, Harbort and Mokros (2001, p. 313) proffer a revised definition of serial murder: "the fully or partially culpable perpetrator commits alone or with accomplice(s) at least three completed murders, each of which have to be premeditated and characterized through a new, hostile intent." The legal issues involved in the definition of murder and responsibility are developed by Kohut and colleagues in Chapter 2. Various defenses are also explained in this chapter.

A subset of serial murder, one explicitly addressed in this book, is serial murder that is sexual in nature (Carich and colleagues differentiate sexual homicide from serial sexual murder in Chapter 3): "In sexual murder the goal is to kill the victim as part of a ritualized attack. For this type of offender the primary motivation is acting out the sexual fantasy that has preoccupied him for some period of time" (McNamara and Morton 2004, p. 2). Sexually motivated homicides involve cases where victims are sexually assaulted, tortured, mutilated, and their body parts displaced in a way that is meaningful only to the killer (Geberth 1996; Money 1990). Researchers have shown that sexually motivated homicides—lust murders—are tinged with an expressive orientation rather than an instrumental one (e.g., killing in the course of a robbery, killing as a way of covering up rape) since the former are guided by the expression of primal emotions while the latter are dictated by their cool yet calculated character (Douglas and Olshaker 1999). Furthermore, it has been argued that a lust murderer's sadistic torture, ritualistic assault, and lewd posing of victims serve to ultimately control the victims by humiliating and degrading them (Keppel and Birnes 1997).

In addition to the psychological degradation of victims, there are other features that warrant elaboration, such as the insertion of foreign objects into the various orifices of the victim, the use of instruments that may prolong the pain and suffering, evidence of sexual activity on or near the victim (e.g., presence of semen near the victim), the use of restraints, mutilation of body parts, and posing (Santilla et al. 2001). To appreciate the relative rarity of aforementioned events, it is worthwhile to compare patterns found in sexual homicides with the "typical" murder. For instance, the analysis of homicides in the state of Washington from 1981–2000 (N=5224) revealed that only .3 percent (14) cases involved "posing" of victims (Keppel and Weis 2004). Posing entails the "deliberate positioning of victims' body" and is done to shock the police and for the killer's own pleasure. Keppel and Weis (2004) speculate that posing is highly suggestive of a serial (sexual) killer at work since seventy-one percent of posed victims indicated evidence of sexual assault. Sexual homicides of the serial type thus combine physical assault with sexual elements that are quite unlike other forms of murder (Geberth 1996). Moreover, these types of behaviors have been found to occur with some regularity in this type of offender; and it is these types of sexual serial killers who have received much attention in the popular and academic literature.

Recent work suggests the presence of psychological imprints of sexually motivated killers in the "signatures" they leave at crime scenes (Keppel 1995, 2000; see also Woods, Chapter 6). A signature refers to the enduring aspects of a murderer's crimes, those that are present across crimes, and needed for a killer's sexual gratification. It is comparable to a behavioral fingerprint that is unique to a killer in that the crime scenes concurrently embody and reflect a killer's idiosyncratic expression—"personal style." These signatures are unique because they are ritualistic expressions of often violent fantasies that have been festering in the offender's mind. Hence, they occur with regularity and differ from an MO (modus operandi) since the latter is situationally determined, to a certain extent, shaped by the reciprocating actions on the part of the victim and the circumstances (Keppel 2000). Thus, there is no reason to presuppose the endurance of an offender's MO given that it may be modified to meet the situational exigencies of the next offense. As Keppel (1995, p. 670) notes, "the MO of the killer includes actions necessary to commit the murder and change over time as the killer discovers that some things he/she does are more effective." Signatures, however, remain constant despite alterations in MO since they represent an "obsessive" element to them, one that fulfills a "primal psychological need."

Scholars have also observed that when this "psychological need" manifests in the details of the crime, two principal "styles" emerge, the *organized* versus *disorganized* offender (Douglas and Olshaker 1999; Ressler et al. 1988). These two signatures represent two opposing ends of the unique behavioral patterns that are seen across the crime scenes of serial killers. Organized offenders are the paragon of rationality and calculation in that they assume a deliberate and orderly approach to their selection of victims, method of torture, kill, and disposal of bodies (see Holmes and Holmes 1994). Thus, rather than attacking a stranger with brute force, they are likely to employ a sophisticated verbal ploy or a cunning ruse to gain a momentary trust of their victims (Keppel and Birnes 1995); in that regard, they possess a certain amount of eloquence and deceptive grace. After they have killed, they are likely to transport the body from the actual kill site to a different dump site to minimize their discovery, therefore showing a high degree of mobility (Keppel and Weis 1994). Furthermore, they are less likely to leave physical evidence at the scene than the disorganized type (Harbort and Mokros 2001).

Disorganized offenders on the other hand leave a plethora of evidence since their assault and kill is marked with impulsivity, spontaneity, and immaturity rather than the product of rational calculation (McCrary and Ramsland 2003). Rather than bringing weapons to the scene, they are more likely to use weapons that are available on scene to complete the murder, and rather than transporting the body from one location to the next, they are more likely to leave the victims as they fell when they killed them, without concealment. Experts agree that the crime scenes in these types of cases are "messy": the offenders do not show much awareness or knowledge of forensic techniques, often leave evidence behind, do not clean up after themselves as organized offenders do, often intimating a violent and often "uncontrolled" assault on the victim (Safarik et al. 2002).

While this primary classification has been successfully applied to serial homicide offenders, recent work has attempted to reconcile the study of crime scenes and the concomitant characteristics of offenders in more mundane homicides (e.g., Salfati 2003). This emerging trend in the literature draws upon a distinction that is well established in the homicide studies since the pioneering work of Marvin Wolfgang (1958). For instance, Wolfgang (1958, p. 109) wrote: "homicide is generally committed against persons who are relatively close friends or relatives, and the opportunities for such personal contacts are probably much greater during the leisure hours of evenings and weekends." The cast of characters involved in this type of "mundane" homicides, along with the time and setting, indicate that homicides of this fabric are a culmination of a confrontation that is anchored in sociality; that is, homicide is the fatal outcome of related but lesser offenses that are mediated by luck, chance, and opportunity (Block and Block 1992). These types of homicides are expressive in that they can be characterized by their impulsivity and spontaneity. Thus, echoing Wolfgang (1958), Block and Block (1991, p. 40) note that "expressive violent acts tend to begin as a fight, brawl or argument that occurs relatively spontaneously with little rational planning." The aim of this type of aggression is simply to hurt the other.

Instrumental violence, on the other hand, is predatory: it is highly premeditated and carefully planned, exemplified in the acquisitive character of the act. Simply put, the aim of instrumental violence is to acquire material gain. Hence, instrumental homicides are marked by the rational calculation of maximal utility, prototypically committed by strangers against strangers, the weaponry chosen to maximize victim compliance (Block and Block 1992; Wolfgang 1958). For investigators, instrumental homicides are more difficult to solve precisely because of the anonymous character of the participants involved; expressive homicides on the other hand are relatively easier to solve since the participants share an emotional, social, and dramaturgical foci (Regoeczi et al. 2000; Puckett and Lundman 2003).

This difference between expressive and instrumental homicides has been examined in the context of crime scene behavior, as an effort to reconcile the innovative work done in the area of crime scene analysis and profiling and the extant structural work on homicides (Salfati 2003; Salfati and Haratsis 2001). This avenue of inquiry suggests that crime scenes and the behavior of offenders in such scenes demonstrate a clear logic of aggression, emotion, and rationality. Thus, expressive homicides are marked by extreme physical attacks, a historical and social relationship between victims and offenders, impulsive with little planning, show a "frenzied" attack, and a conspicuous absence of attempts to destroy evidence (Safarik and Jarvis 2005). Instrumental homicides on the other hand evince motivation that is not expressive but related to a nefarious ulterior aim; these scenes show meticulous organization, evidenced by the relative lack of forensic evidence, theft of property from the victim, and the transportation of the murder weapon to the scene. And rather than leaving the victim where s/he fell, homicide offenders in this type are more likely to transport the body to a dump site away from the primary murder site. Furthermore, homicides of this type are likely to involve the use of restraints and postmortem sexual activity (Santilla et al. 2001).

A more theoretically cogent and parsimonious dichotomy of serial sexual killers and violence in general can be found in the work of Robert Keppel (1992, 1995) and his signature theory of murder (see Keppel and Weis 1994). Keppel's (1995) signature analysis indicates that sadistic and sexually motivated killings, in addition to the organized versus disorganized distinction, can be primarily classified into two distinct signatures: (1) anger-retaliation (2) anger-excitation. These two principal categories reflect the diverging objectives of each type of killer, and illuminate how those primal aims are translated and embodied in the general behavior of offenders at crime scenes.

The anger-retaliation signature describes killers who seek out symbolic victims, that is, "stand-ins," for particular people who are thought to be responsible for their misfortune in life. These symbolic figures can be the proverbial domineering mother or a tyrannical female boss, the victims selected by the anger-retaliation signature killer because there is some cosmetic resemblance, or because the victim is accessible and convenient. In a sense, the killers see themselves as "administrators" of justice since they are simply operating in accordance with the principle of desert and their self-righteous attitude is evident in their behaviors found in crime scenes. Keppel and Birnes (1997) note that these types of scenes reflect a certain amount of control, but the central psychological makeup that scribes the retaliation killer is embodied in his experience of shame after the attack. Thus, rather than leaving the victims where they fell or lewdly posing them, the killers often take the time to cover the bodies and faces of the corpses (see also Keppel and Weis 2004).

Anger-excitation killers, on the other hand, have transformed their anger into a sexually titillating experience, hence, rather than seeking retribution on symbolic representatives of their deep-seated hatred toward a class of victims, they use that anger as impetus for sexual thrill and gratification in the sadistic pain they inflict on their victims (e.g., binding, biting, burning). For Keppel and Birnes (1997, p. 187), this predator "converts his anger into sexual excitation and kills for the sexual thrill, not merely to dispense revenge." But the key sign of the excitation killer lies in the way he disposes of his victims, in plain view, without concealment, and in the positioning of the victims in sexually degrading ways (Keppel and Weis 2004).

The parsimony of signature theory lies in the fact that, while it is possible to illuminate the behaviors of sadistic sexual killers, it is also able to explain a range of behaviors that parallel them; furthermore, since signature theory places murder in the midpoint on the violence continuum rather than the end, it is also able to cogently account for the behaviors that precede and follow the homicidal act. Hence, in this framework, paraphilias such as voyeurism and garment fetishes do not merely constitute "harmless" sexual deviancies; instead, they are symptomatic of far more insidious behaviors to follow, as do offenses such as breaking and entering, cruelty to animals, and cat-burglary since these offenses portend the escalation in violence that is likely to emerge in the future.

What is analytically relevant is that signature killers do not begin as experts but become so in the way they learn and refine their techniques, and this evolution is demonstrable in the crime scene behaviors themselves. According to the tenets of signature theory, a sexual homicide offender is not born as much as he evolves into existence, shaped by a constellation of unique socio-historical factors, as well as the trial and error method of self-instruction. In this sense, the signature killer undergoes a developmental process much like any other identities; and even here, there is no assurance along the way that the initially developed anger will necessarily manifest in homicide, let alone serial homicide. The literature in the field is incapable of predicting precisely who will become, and who will not become a predator of the lust homicide form, since, many have similar developments as serial killers and do not engage in homicide. At best, we can attempt to find commonalities in the developmental process and perhaps suggest probabilities of occurrence, without precise specification as to who will or will not complete the process. Consider the following account from Ted Bundy, told in the third person:

> Then another night he was a woman walking home—late at night, or early in the morning. He followed her home, looked into the windows, and watched her get ready for bed. And he did this on several occasions, for this was a regular kind of thing. Eventually he created a plan where he would attack her, in the house. And early one morning, uh, he snaked into the house, through a door he knew was open, and entered the bedroom. And implementing a plan based somewhat on fantasy—based, you know, on anything but personal knowledge—uh, uh, he jumped on the woman's bed and attempted to restrain her. But all he succeeded in doing was waking her up and, uh, causing her to panic and scream. He left very rapidly (Michaud and Aynesworth 2000, pp. 75–76).

In this brief excerpt, we can see the self-correcting ways of a serial killer in the fledgling stages of his career; notice the trial and error method of instruction and the auto-learning that takes place in the education of a serial sexual killer. In a previous discussion (not included) he relates how he had attempted to attack a woman in the street, only to lose sight of her in the darkness; after that initial failure, he tries attacking a woman as she is walking into her house, only to have her scream aloud when he strikes her; then, in a moment of epiphany, he realizes that it would be tactically advantageous to attack a victim inside her home. That revelation is made possible from the zen-like practice of voyeurism and stalking that he has practiced for years; and when looking is no longer to sufficient to satisfy his fantasies, he desires to touch his victims (Hickey 2006c). This leap is not a giant one, almost anticipatable and expectable, since he only has to extend his already occurring behavior. Consequently, he moves the location of his offense from outdoors to indoors, conducts intelligence gathering missions to learn the victim's habits and routines as well as security flaws in the target's residence. He then attempts to restrain, only to fail again. This time, rather than waiting six months to recover from the shock of his own behavior, only three months pass before he is able to do it again, but realizes that the victim will need to be rendered helpless (with blows) before using restraints. These types of MOs are gradually altered and modified over time, and signature theory provides a cogent theoretical framework to collate and account for these types of recurring behaviors (see also Woods, Chapter 6). The explanations as to why sexual killers kill have been as diverse as the disciplines themselves.

Motivational Models

Each discipline begins with an *a priori* set of unexamined and presupposed axioms prior to any empirical expatiation. For instance, a psychologically rooted theory of sexual homicide—and violence in general—maintains that the compulsion to kill arises from the internal conflict in one's psyche; hence, in a particularly Freudian vein, a killer's aggression is thought to be the expression of instincts that are inherently in place—the projection of one's primal tendencies onto others (DeHart and Mahoney 1994). Alternatively, in a revisionist Freudian approach exemplified by Jacques Lacan (1977a, b), we see the central place played by fantasy—its construction within the imaginary, its tracing to identifications, conflicts, and resolutions. It also includes the notion of "crime as a mode of subjectivization" (Salecl 1994) whereby the commission of crime provides grounds for the development of subjectivity.

A biologically oriented theory of murder and aggression posits that the injuries sustained to the head, consequently, causing damage to the frontal lobe and impairing the ability to control one's impulses, are causal factors that compel aggression (Pincus 2001). Sociologists, however, have attempted to view such crimes as revolutionary acts against the prevailing social structures, a function of population density, and the absence of inhibitors against those acts. The integration model combines the significant features of the aforementioned theories, explaining sexual homicides as a function of insufficient socialization during a killer's formative years, child abuse, negative parenting, unresolved conflicts, and facilitators such as alcohol, drugs, and pornography that exacerbate the dispositions already cultivated by biological, social, and environmental conditions (McCrary and Ramsland 2003; Ressler et al. 1988).

An alternative approach roots the phenomenal experience of lust homicide in edgework literature (for a background on edgework, see Lyng 2005; see also Shon and Milovanovic, Chapter 10). "Edgework" recalibrates the boundaries of order and chaos, excitement and sheer terror, and provides a theoretically novel way to digest various forms of voluntary risk taking behavior. Many studies in the literature implicitly and even explicitly indicate how excitation plays a crucial role in lust homicide. Consider, for example, Schechter (2002,

p. 325): "lust-killing often becomes an addiction. Like heroin users, they not only become dependent on the thrilling sensation—the rush—of torture, rape, and murder; they come to require ever greater and more frequent fixes."

The theoretical nexus that binds the range of sexually deviant and homicidal behavior is the need to exert control over the lives of others that satiates either the retributive allure that the symbolic victims possess or the sexual gratification that a killer might be able to taste through sadistic corporeal control. Again, the parsimony, as well as the explanatory breadth, of signature theory hinges in its ability to recontextualize "nuisance" antemortem offenses and dangerous postmortem offenses into one cogent, yet expansive, theoretical infrastructure. In addition to its capacity to account for the aberrant as well as the ordinary and the mundane, signature behavior model offers a unique perspective on the etiology and the manifestation of a range of pathological human behaviors through a critical dissection of the personality structures of signature killers and abusers.

According to signature theory of serial murder (see also Woods, Chapter 6), sexual killers are motivated by the need to instill a sense of dread, dependency, and degradation. That is, signature killers accomplish this objective by forcing the victims to rely on the killer for basic sustenance (dependency), thereby compelling a realization of the victim's own impotence and helplessness: the victim realizes the humiliation and degradation of being dependent on another for life's most rudimentary elements; the victim that is held captive in the killer's cellar, handcuffed and chained to an iron-post, without any connection to the outside world except her captor, or begging for mercy as the killer binds her hands and feet behind her back—all function to intercalate pure terror and dread into the psyche of the victim. The sense of dread, dependency, and degradation that the killer wishes to exert bears an uncanny resemblance to the ritualistic and ceremonial aspects of religious worship—theological—for the sense of the awesome and the majestic that such power and control wields borders on the divine (Eliade 1957).

Keppel and Birnes (1997) maintain that the underlying pattern of behavior in signature killers and signature abusers is their common personality structure. That is, signature behavior model is not merely applicable to serial murderers, but to ordinary behavior as well, since the need to control, dominate, and degrade others embodies gradient—and different—forms. Keppel and Birnes point out that this signature abuse can be seen in the workplace in the supervisors who maniacally control their employees and subordinates with excessive, almost unrealizable demands and tasks, the professors who humiliate and psychologically abuse their students while currying sexual favors, in the bosses and coworkers who serially manipulate their subordinates and colleagues into a sense of dependency in a guile of friendship only to stab them in the back. What the signature abusers and killers have in common is that they are not able to think about others except themselves; and much like the children who have no siblings to socialize them into the interactional order of compassion, turn-taking, and "otherness," they live their lives chanting the mantra "me, me, me"—in a word, "self-indulgent" (Keppel and Birnes 1997, p. 291).

Signature theory of behavior asserts that this self-indulgence is a byproduct of a socialization that is entirely devoid of primary intersubjective relations between a subject and the primary caretakers as a function of parental neglect; furthermore, even if a subject is situated in a family, there is a perception of being least favored (rejection) and being an outsider in the family. As a result of this exclusion and rejection, Keppel notes that such a subject retreats into a world of fantasy, becoming over-reliant in its use as a coping mechanism, thereby effectively cutting off further emotional and social development, resulting in a silent but pervasive anger that suffuses the personality of such a person. The development of anger as a result of subjects' perception of being least favored can be witnessed in some of the well-known biblical narratives:

Excerpt 5 (Genesis 4:1–7) (*New International Version*)
Now Abel kept flocks and Cain worked the soil. In the course of time Cain brought some of the fruits of the soil as an offering to the Lord. But Abel brought fat portions from some of the firstborn of his flock. The Lord looked with favor on Abel and his offering, but on Cain and his offering he did not look with favor. So Cain was very angry, and his face was downcast. Then the Lord said to Cain, "Why are you angry? Why is your face downcast? If you do what is right, will you not be accepted? But if you do not do what is right, sin is crouching at your door; it desires to have you, but you must master it." Now Cain said to his brother Abel, "Let's go out to the field." And while they were in the field, Cain attacked his brother Abel and killed him.

Excerpt 6 (*Genesis 27: 1–10*)
Isaac said, "I am now an old man and don't know the day of my death. Now then, get your weapons—your quiver and bow—and go out to the open country to hunt some wild game for me. Prepare me the kind of tasty food I like and bring it to me to eat, so that I may give you my blessing before I die ... Now Rebekah was listening as Isaac spoke to his son Esau. When Esau left for the open country to hunt game and bring it back, Rebekah said to her son Jacob, "Look I overheard your father say to your brother Esau, 'Bring me some game and prepare me some tasty food to eat, so that I may give you your blessing in the presence of the Lord before I die.' Now, my son, listen carefully and do what I tell you: Go out to the flock and bring me two choice young goats, so I can prepare some tasty food for

your father, just the way he likes it. Then take it to your father to eat, so that he
may give you his blessing before he dies."

Excerpt 7 (*Genesis* 37: 3–18)
"Now Israel loved Joseph more than any of his other sons, because he had been born
to him in his old age; and he made a richly ornamented robe for him. When his
brothers saw that their father loved him more than any of them, they hated him
and could not speak a kind word to him (Gen. 37: 3–4) … his brothers were jeal-
ous of him" (Gen. 37: 11) … they saw him in the distance, they plotted to kill him."

In all three of the cases noted above, one brother is favored by a paternal
authority figure, and out of envy the spited sibling(s) conspires to murder his
brother (two attempted, one completed). But before envy turns into homicidal anger, the alienated ones undergo a profound humiliating experience of
rejection. Hence, Cain feels rejected by God; Esau feels excluded because his
father blesses his brother Jacob; Joseph receives special treatment from Israel
because he is born to him at an old age through sheer chance and luck, and
his brothers writhe in fury as they see their father doting on the youngest. But
these fraternal rivalries also exemplify the primacy of envy as a social emotion,
one that precedes anger, envy which paves the emotional road for anger to follow, and the levy that is paid in the currency of blood. Notice that envy starts
Cain's emotional engine, and anger is its product: "Cain was very angry, and
his face was downcast."

Anger is a moral emotion that travels upward (Katz 1988). In Cain's case his
countenance (perhaps even his spirit) goes down—ontologically lowered—as
a result of the initial rejection—degraded, humiliated, and put down; and it is
that humiliation that accompanies rejection which is converted into rage, similar to the way oppressed and angry people "rise up" against their oppressors,
and the way silver-spooned college students "stand up" to their professors. The
fraternal rivalry in the stories of Joseph and his brothers, Jacob and Esau, and
Cain and Abel also illustrates the moral dynamics of signature theory in another
important way. The gain that is sought by offenders is not instrumental. What
Esau, Joseph's brothers, and Cain desire is recognition. It is only when they are
denied this valued commodity that they experience another fundamental
human emotion—envy, and it is that which ignites the homicidal spark of rage.

In the above cases, an authority figure (e.g., parent, God) displays favoritism
towards one brother, which creates a perception of being least favored, and that
feeling of being "outside" breeds envy and hatred. Consequently, the spited siblings conspire to eliminate their rival. So what is it about 'recognition' that is
so fundamental? The recognition is not simply cosmetic; it is metaphysical and
ontological. Being recognized as a subject—*being*—capable of recognizing oth-

ers and having that capacity reciprocated lies at the fundamental root of agency (Lacan 1977a). Subjectivity is constituted through a dialectical and intersubjective process, via dialogue or through scopic interactions (Lacan 1977b). In other words, a central role is played by various conflicting identifications, with their attendant pleasures and aggressivities. If recognition is such an integral process in the moral development of the human psyche, then it follows that those whose development is thwarted at such a primal level will manifest disturbances, of which murderous impulses are but one.

But notice that despite the rejection, and even after the initial favoritism, the killer's desire is not immediately to kill his rival brother, but, as best reflected in Esau's words, to request a redistribution of affection and recognition according to a principle of equality and fairness: "Do you have only one blessing, my father? Bless me too, my father!" (Gen. 27: 38). Rejected ones simply want to be treated as the favored one has been treated. But when that is not forthcoming, they choose the path to murder. And consistent with precepts of signature theory, those who have been socialized at the fringes of families as outsiders and least favored children have lost the chance to be adept at relating to the world socially; in a way, the logical outlet (fantasy) becomes a liability in that it thwarts his capacity to be a social being in an absurdly circular way, resulting in greater isolation, alienation, and self-indulgence.

More recently, integrative theories are being developed. Two leading approaches are represented in this book. Carich and colleagues, in Chapter 3, integrate a lifestyle and mind-body developmental approach. Arrigo and Purcell, in Chapter 4, develop a "motivational-trauma control" theory.

Carich et al.'s integrative theory in Chapter 3 focuses on how serial killers enter "dissociative states" whereby the predator detaches himself emotionally from "reality." In this state, the predator sees himself watching himself committing the crime ("hidden observer") with little sensitivity or emotionality. They then focus on how the serial killer developmentally constructs his reality. This process entails the development of an "implicit theory" (see also Fisher et al., Chapter 5) from early childhood. As they say, "these implicit theories function like scientific theories and are used to explain empirical regularities (e.g., other people's actions) and to make predictions about the world. They are relatively coherent and constituted by a number of interlocking beliefs and their component concepts and categories." These are, in short, more hidden frames of references, narratives, that we all develop and make use of in our everyday activities. The lust serial killer is no different. Carich and colleagues make use of five implicit theories identified in the literature and show how the predator makes use of particular conceptions of women, male sex drives, entitlement, and a world view. They then situate this development in the context of biological functioning of the hypothalamus limbic system of the brain in indicating a biological-socio-psychological contributions for explaining sexual homicide.

Arrigo and Purcell, in Chapter 4, below, integrate a "motivational model" and a "trauma control" model. The motivational model employed is derived from Burgess et al. (1986) and focuses on cognitive and psychosocial factors. The trauma control model is derived from Hickey (1997, 2001). His focus was on predisposing factors and "facilitators." Predisposing factors are biological, sociological, and/or psychological. Thus traumatic events, esteem issues, deviant fantasies, dissociation, and rejection can all co-develop in complex ways. In context, these can be "triggers" for subsequent behavior. In addition, "facilitators" such as alcohol and drugs can contribute to increasingly violent predispositions. Arrigo and Purcell then integrate these two approaches. They argue that their integrative model is focused on "triggering factors" such as rejection, isolation and ridicule, which "are stressors, constraining or thwarting one's capacity to adequately cope with the strain of everyday life." (In Chapter 10, Shon and Milovanovic suggest such a starting point in the context of Halleck's theory of functional adaptations in indicating the milieu from which the serial killer develops, although they focus more on a phenomenological and existential understanding than etiology.) Arrigo and Purcell then suggest that feedback loops are established which then escalate the dynamic. The end result may become sadistic, predatory behavior.

The Role of Paraphilia in Lust Murders

It is self-indulgence, coupled with the inability to relate to and empathize with others, establish bonds, and a pervasive sense of insecurity, and absent self-esteem that is related to the attraction to objects rather than persons (Hickey 2006b, d). What differentiates lust killings from "typical" homicides is that there is a wide range of deeply pathological behaviors that precede and follow the homicide. For instance, killing someone during the course of a robbery is instrumental since the gain is material; killing someone during the course of an argument is expressive since the gain is moral; but killing someone and hiding the body in a secluded dump site for necrophilic purposes, or butchering the remains for consumption iterates the truly abysmal facets of human behavior, one that transcends the traditional expressive/instrumental distinction. And just as researchers have long observed that homicide is not one crime but many (Block and Block 1992), sexual murders can be conceptualized in a similar way, with a constellation of cognate offenses that precede them.

The behavioral link between sexual paraphilias and lust homicides is consistent with extant research. The pioneers of behavioral science profiling (Federal Bureau of Investigation's Behavioral Sciences Unit) noted that serial murderers had certain traits in common: bed-wetting, fire-setting, and cruelty to animals (Ressler et al. 1988). If sexual paraphilias such as necrophilia, vampirism, and cannibalism lie on the far end of the continuum of violence that motivate and follow lust murders, then the range of "normative" paraphilias that antecede murder also warrant an explanation since they constitute antemortem offenses in the continuum of violence (Keppel and Birnes 1995).

Fisher et al., in Chapter 5, Carich et al., in Chapter 3, and Arrigo and Purcell, in Chapter 4 have identified other traits: Fisher et al., posit, for example, implicit theories that belittle women, offer an excuse of male sex drive as uncontrollable, pronounce entitlement, and posit a dangerous world; for Carich et al., lifestyles (lack of empathy and remorse, narcissistic themes, dysfunctional emotional attachments, isolation, alienation; implicit theories objectifying targets and constructing devious world views); for Arrigo and Purcell, traumatic events in early childhood, facilitators (drugs, alcohol), and ineffective social environment.

Thus, offenses against objects (non-humans), such as fetishism, fire-setting, cruelty to animals, destruction of property, and "boundary crossing" offenses (e.g., trespassing) represent the formative precursors to interpersonal crimes since objects do not possess the capacity to retaliate, whereas crimes such as physical abuse, bondage, and torture represent a pathological escalation given that the offender has transcended the moral boundary between objects and persons (Keppel and Birnes 1997).

There is also consensus amongst practitioners and theorists that normative paraphilias are consistently preceded and motivated by an intrapsychic process that functions as a blueprint for the behaviors to come. There seems much agreement that fantasy plays a central role in lust homicide (see, for example, Schechter 2002, p. 260; Ressler et al. 1988). Reviewing the theoretical literature, beyond descriptive or sensationalist approaches, we can see the relevance of Jacques Lacan's work (1997; for an accessible introduction, see Haute 2002), since in his revisionist Freudian approach he posits a central role of fantasy in the very constitution of subjectivity. In his decentered subject of Schema L, for example, we see two primary dimensions or axes constitutive of the subject.

The imaginary axes concerns the relation of the ego (e) to the other [i(o)]. The ego is constituted through its relation to the other. This mirroring is both a basis of a fundamental coherence and aggressivity since the ego both embraces the image of the other as constitutive of a coherent recognized self, and as the target of hostility since it is perceived as overdetermining in its separateness and equivalence. The second axes critical for the constitution of the subject is the symbolic axis. Here, the axis concerns the relation of the Other—the sphere of the unconscious and its ongoing forms of semiotic production, most often hidden to the subject—and its relation to the "I."

The "I," the appearance of the centered subject, the individual, arises, in the Lacanian model, as a marker, filled in by the workings of desire. Moreover, the "I" takes on specific form in particular discourses which offer subject positions with which to identify and develop narrative constructions. Thus in the Lacanian model, both the imaginary and symbolic axes are constitutive of subjectivity. Fantasy, or phantasy (Lacanians do make a distinction), [2] then, plays a pivotal role in this operation. This theoretical orientation along with empirical studies of early socialization could shed light on how various adjustments are made including aberrant forms.

In a second depiction of the subject, the "graphs of desire," Lacan (1977) shows how the constituted ego (ideal ego) is also brought into conflict with the ego ideal. Whereas the former is the imaginary construction of self, the latter concerns how the subject symbolically identifies with particular traits ("trait unaires") within the Other. These traits are signifiers, or markers with which the subject forms a primordial bond—anchors of sorts—that bear on subsequent identifications and constitutions of the self. We will have occasion to see how various trophies and souvenirs collected by the predator become such forms; we also shall see how the targeted victims often reflect one of these elements. In short, along with the tension found between the ego and the other, we see an additional tension between the ideal ego and the ego ideal. It is within these irresolvable and ongoing tensions, Lacanians would tell us, that behavioral styles become stabilized, including the perversions of the lust homicide predator.

Fantasy in other literature has been depicted as an avenue of escape from boredom, monotony, and impotence prior to actual violence; and the ontogenesis of paraphilias necessitates the formation of and reliance on fantasy as a coping mechanism to a perceived sense of powerlessness (Pincus 2001; Ressler et al. 1988). It has been observed that pre-adolescents in particular use fantasy as a way of coping with severe trauma (e.g., psychological, physical, and sexual abuse), developmental and interpersonal failure, and perceived rejection from authority figures (Peven 1993). Consequently, individuals who

---

2. Lacanians use the word "phantasy," and some argue that it differs from the everyday imagination, or "fantasy" (see Harari 2001). According to Harari, phantasy is more closely related to masturbation and orgasm, and to how the subject anticipates. In this book, for lust homicide predators, fantasy is being employed in the more psychoanalytic form of phantasy where it is connected with sexual crimes.

excessively rely on fantasy sever their ability to cope with reality, resulting in further social isolation, and this serves as a catalyst for a vicious circular re-production of violent tendencies. Fantasies are generally harmless but have the potential to incite serious offenses, especially if combined with images of sexual violence and chronic masturbation (Arrigo and Purcell 2001). Consider the following account from a convicted serial pedophile: "My initial attempts at masturbation were purely physical acts that resulted in my feeling pleasure. To the best of my recollection, when I began doing this, my actions were not brought about, or accompanied by, any type of sexual thoughts or fantasies … I've often tried to figure out at what age I reached this point of being fixated, but about the best I can come up with is at the point when I joined my use of fantasies as a means of escape with my use of sexual stimulation as a source of physical pleasure" (Alan, in Hammel-Zabin 2003, pp. 45–46).

In this account, parallels in the anteceding behaviors that a serial sex offender shares with serial rapists and sexual murderers are evident (see also Carich et al., Chapter 3). Whether the initial childhood trauma is physical/sexual abuse or the perception of being different and rejected by the primary caretakers or a cohort of peers, the use of fantasy as a way of controlling the chaotic and uncontrol-lable external reality progresses along a continuum of violence, portending things to come. For instance, Alan introspectively recalls masturbating as a purely physical form of self-gratification, but when that is not enough, he in-corporates fantasies (molesting younger children) into his cognitive repertoire to sustain the level of sexual stimulation necessary to achieve orgasm. When fan-tasy no longer provides stimulation, he graduates into manipulating actual vic-tims as a way of fulfilling his fantasy-driven quest for control. In a later account, Alan describes how he escalated his risk-taking behavior to heighten his sexual arousal, such as molesting kids in their homes while parents were in another room, and molesting multiple victims concurrently (see Hammel-Zabin 2003).

In short, the structure of fantasy is a key component in understanding lust homicide. Key theoretical analysis, then, must engage this construction for any bona fide analysis of lust homicide. Jacques Lacan is uniquely situated for pro-viding one direction in this theoretical development, but its basic flaw, many recent theorists would argue, is that it is fundamentally built on a notion of de-sire that is based on inherent "lack," a tension-reduction model. An alternative model might consider the work of Gilles Deleuze (1988, 1989) and Elizabeth Grosz (1994) on the body and a desire not based on "lack" but on production.[3]

---

3. For Deleuze, fantasy is not a separate realm; it is part of the "virtual" where images, flows, intensities, forces are interconnected and achieve temporary stability with effects. Lacanians would argue that there are clearer separations among the imaginary, symbolic,

What the existing research supports, then, is that while the primary incit-ing incident in the evolution of a sexual killer is moored in fantasy, homicide is not the next logical process or the culmination of violence, but at a cross-road in the meandering road of violence.[4] In other words, unlike a linear de-velopmental model, we must entertain the idea that non-linear change, sin-gularities, and unintended results are integral to the development, as dynamic systems theory (chaos theory) would suggest (see also Cahill et al., Chapter 7). As Keppel and Birnes (1997) note, for some anger-retaliation killers, mur-der is only the beginning of more deeply pathological and sexually deviant acts to come. In this sense, murder is incidental and instrumental since it merely gives the killers access and outlet for their dangerous sexual paraphilias. It also provides, especially in the anger-excitement model (ibid.), a sense of excite-ment, adrenaline rush, intense emotional arousal. Keppel and Birnes (1995) note that sexual murderers do not just commit one crime (murder), but en-gage in a host of antemortem offenses such as stalking, trespassing, breaking and entering, retaliation-free offenses, and verbal and physical assault prior to their involvement in murder. Consider the following account from a noto-rious serial sexual killer:

> Say he was walking down the street on one occasion, one evening, and just totally, uh, by chance looked up into the window of a house and saw a woman undressing ... And he began, with some regular-ity, with increasing regularity, to, uh, canvass, as it were, the com-munity he lived in. By peeping in windows, as it were, and watching a woman undress, or watching whatever could be seen, you know, during the evening, and approaching it almost like a project, throw-ing himself into it, uh, literally for years (Michaud and Aynesworth 2000, p. 68).

This account, offered in the third person by Ted Bundy, one of the most prolific sexual killers in U.S. history, illustrates the incremental character of sexual deviance and crime, along with a snapshot of a serial killer in evolu-

---

and real orders and each undergoes a different development. See, for example, his work on the borromean knots. Grosz, on the other hand, has integrated and synthesized the two and indicated how the inside (psychic structure) and outside (body) are interconnected by the twist as in the moebius strip.

4. The BTK ("bind, torture, kill") killer, Dennis Rader, in an interview (Zandt 2005) of his killing of Mrs. Otero, her husband and two children, said: "I was really on a, not a sexual high. I was just scared high ... Very nervous. Not like a master criminal at all. This is my first time that I'd ever crossed that barrier."

tion. First, notice that the voyeurism begins as a byproduct of chance. His involvement in this rather common "nuisance" sex crime begins not as a constitutional defect, but as the result of sheer luck. Second, this incidental event is transformed into a substantive paraphilia in that it becomes the basis for a persistent fantasy, compelling the subject to restructure his life to accommodate his newfound habitual nocturnal activity (excerpt not included), and the sexual excitation becomes a conditioned response as he masturbates to this fantasy; third, he employs non-consenting partners as objects of sexual gratification, thereby substituting the representation for the actual object. Fourth, Bundy's initial involvement in this "nuisance" sex crime leads to other more predatory offenses. Keppel notes that Bundy was a master burglar, one that was historically related to his experience and knowledge about the habits of residents at home. Fifth, when eyes no longer suffice to sustain his fantasy, he begins to encroach into the personal space of his victims, later taking steps to physically acquire his victims in the flesh. Thus, merely classifying voyeurism as a nuisance sex crime does injustice to its seriousness. Voyeurism almost serves as a "training offense" for more lethal offenses to emerge.

And that's what this book attempts to do: it treats those "training" offenses before the actual murder, and the ones that occur after it as justifiable topics in their own right. This book explicitly addresses the sexually deviant behaviors associated with sexual homicide, thereby differentiating the current work from others. Furthermore, rather than relying on case studies and devoting specific chapters to notable serial killers, this book offers a theoretically cogent view of lust killings, their etiology, legality, and public perceptions mediated through the mass media. We now turn briefly to the media influence

Media, Lust Serial Killers and the Public

The very appearance of the word "serial killer" generates much media attention since it stirs the public's curiosity and fears; this public clamor is fueled by the popularity of movies such as the *Red Dragon*, *Manhunter*, and *The Silence of the Lambs*, which have seeped their way into the public discourse in art, music, film, and literature with noticeable frequency (Schechter 2003, pp. 369–402; Egger 2002, pp. 100–110; see also Chapters 9 and 10). Egger (2002, p. 100) concisely sums up this media driven process when he refers to serial killings as a "growth industry." Serial killing, indeed, is a booming business, often launching the careers of law enforcement personnel involved in the investigation, courtroom professionals involved in its adjudication, reporters covering the case, and the peripheral classmates, "friends," and acquaintances who appear out of the bushes to soak up their fifteen seconds of fame in order to relate their "encounters" with the killer; this, notwithstanding the "star-like" status of the killers themselves. That is, everyone in the serial killing business profits, except the victims, their families, and other close ones.

But as repulsive as this phenomenon is, Egger (2002, p. 103) notes that the " ... roots of the glorification process are deeply ingrained in the American psyche. The United States has long made legends of outlaws. American history is full of the folklore of killers." At this point in time, serial killers just happen to be in the spotlight. This fascination is compounded by the fact that now, just about anyone can get his/her dosage of serial killing on the web (see Chapter 10, note 17). It would seem that the phenomenon of serial killing, particularly of the lust homicide form will remain a central interest to the public for some time to come—until some new form of murder replaces it.

Fuller notes that (Chapter 8) serial killing "has been elevated to celebrity status by media looking for sensational stories and a public with an insatiable appetite for the lurid, grotesque, and blood." That is, the media is not just a neutral entity that simply reports the news; Fuller argues that the media actively creates the public's understanding and perception of the phenomena, thereby significantly shaping what it means to be a serial killer. And as Kudlac states, why some serial killers become media darlings while others, despite having killed more victims, are treated like unwanted stepchildren depends on social structural factors such as race, class, and gender of victims, almost more than the body count. Then there are the likes of *The Son of Sam*, the *BTK* killer, and *The Zodiac Killer* who play to the media, using them as a public message board to taunt the police, in the process, satiating their need to exert control and dominate in another facet of existence. And when the public learns that the captured killer is a law student with a long history of civic participation, a pudgy mailman who resembles the class dork, and the president of a local church, the public is left scratching their heads, shocked to see the middle-class face of terror.

In a classic study, *Using Murder: The Social Construction of Serial Murder* (1994), Jenkins argued that the imagery we develop of serial murder can be attributable to three factors: popular culture, news media, and law enforcement agencies. The interaction of these three groups, even though not conspiratorial, nonetheless produces a particular image of the predator and a picture of the threat society faces in the serial killer (see also Rhodes 1999, pp. 211–213; Surette 1998). According to Jenkins, the hysteria surrounding serial killers also allowed various "claim-makers" to attach several other compelling social concerns, from missing children to racism (see also Surette 1998, p. 14).

As to whether the media (a "social construction engine" according to Surette, 1998) is a "cause" of crime more generally, Surette (1998, p. 235) dismisses a "primary causal model" that links the media directly to crime, and advocates a more indirect relation, the "negligible cause model." He concludes that "the media plays a role in the generation of predisposed people" (Surette 1998, p. 235) and that "by [the media] providing live models of violence and creating community and home environments that are more inured to and tolerant of violence, violent behavior also helps to create more violently predisposed individuals in society" (Surette 1998, p. 236). Thus, no direct effects exist, but the media's influence is to contribute to a feedback mechanism sustaining ever higher forms of violence.

Kudlac, in Chapter 9, describes in great detail the coverage of serial killers all the way through to their conviction and punishment. He shows that once the serial killer garners media attention, the public hankers on any detail whatsoever having to do with the alleged killer. This tendency is demonstrated in the case surrounding Aileen Wuornos, a celebrated female serial killer convicted of killing six people. She pleaded self defense and no contest pleas. She was offered numerous movie and book contracts. She was eventually executed. For Kudlac, it was particularly noteworthy to see the minimal concern raised by the media about capital punishment in each of the cases he examined. Both Kudlac and Fuller provide insightful commentary about the morbid relation between the public's hidden desires and the predator's existence. In studying the serial killers, we uncover some of the deeper secrets in our own lives.

On the other hand, lust serial murderers such as Dennis Rader have provided, in their very own explanations, some direct linkages between their activity and the media. In 1979 Dennis Rader had "retired" after killing seven people, but media revival was to have an effect.

> That really stirred it. I read that in the paper and I always thought, you know, I'd like to bring this back out again, but should I? And I think I've reached the point in my life—the kids were gone. Not really bored, but kind of bored ... Eventually I was going to tell the story in my terms and not his terms. They already had the killings, so that's factual. But they didn't know how I worked and moved around the projects, the haunts, how I picked my victims. They didn't know how that worked. I could just really stir the hornet nest up with the media by just showing them pictures and puzzles and playing a game with them.

Thus, twenty-five years later, stirred by an anniversary article about the BTK killer in the *Wichita Eagle*, he became re-inspired and "re-invented" himself by killing three more (interview reported in Zandt 2005). Rather than dealing with the empty nest syndrome and the vacuity of middle age by buying a sports car or having an affair with a twenty-something clerk at a national coffee chain, he rekindled his proclivities by obtaining sexual release through binding, torturing, and killing—the paradigmatic example of an excitation killer. Others have noted that the loss of a job, the departure of an intimate partner, or rejection from a woman serve as stressors that trigger the sequence of events (see Chapter 10); with BTK, the editors were unwittingly complicit in the chain of events.

Organization of Chapters

Our book includes ten chapters. We have assembled a range of writers from practitioners to academicians (both theoretically and empirically driven). Our book is not only intended in bringing the phenomenon within a more keen theoretical and empirical investigation, shedding more scholarly insights for the student of the phenomenon, but also to be suggestive for developing research hypotheses for academicians and for further insights for practitioners in the field. Our book is divided into three parts: Part 1 is entitled "Theory of Sexual Homicide and Sexually Violent Predatory Laws"; Part 2, "Paraphilias and Lust Murders"; and Part 3, "Media Influence and Edgework."

Accordingly, Chapter 1, the Introduction, sets out some broad themes of sexual/lust serial homicide. We include a discussion of history, definitions, motivational models, the role of paraphilia, and female lust homicide. Chapter 2, "They Must Be Crazy … Aren't They? Legal Issues With Sexual Serial Murderers," by Kohut, Carich, and Stanislaus, spells out legal definitions, competency to stand trial issues, insanity defenses, "designer defenses," and famous fakers.

Chapter 3, "Sexual Murder and Sexual Serial Killers: Towards a Mind-Body Developmental Theory," by Carich, Fisher, and Kohut, develops a motivational model for serial killing. They focus on four areas: distinguishing between the rapist and sexual serial killer; personality and lifestyle themes; mind-body developmental process; and the implications for treatment of violent offenders. They also comment on the notion of "implicit theories" that are said to be operative at the more unconscious level of the predators.

Chapter 4, "Sexual Homicide, Serial Murder, and Lust Killings: Theoretical Integrations and Practical Limitations," by Arrigo and Purcell, focuses on developing an integrated model to explain sexual homicide and serial killing. This model assimilates the insights of a motivational model and a trauma control model. The integrative model is then applied specifically to Jeffrey Dahmer to indicate practical implications. These suggestions are particularly directed toward law and public policy, police administration/management, and criminal and clinical psychology. The authors also note the limits to their integrative model and suggest further theoretical and empirical work in this area.

Chapter 5, "Sexual Homicide: A British Investigation of Motivation and Implicit Theories," by Fisher, Beech, Carich, and Kohut, draws from empirical investigation conducted by Dawn Fisher and Beech et al. (2005) in Britain. The latter consisted of intensive interviews of twenty-eight incarcerated sexual killers. The authors of this chapter are interested in understanding why a sexual killer makes the decision to kill and the treatment implications for the violent sexual killer. They draw from the notion of "implicit theory" literature which suggests the constitutive role of more hidden narratives that underlie motivations to engage in lust homicide. They review five forms of these implicit theories and apply it to the empirical findings (intensive interviews of twenty-eight incarcerated sexual killers). In the final section, they suggest how each group identified with a particular implicit theory may benefit from a particular form of treatment.

Chapter 6, "Piquerism: The Investigative Challenge of Serial Murder" by Woods, investigates the MO (method of operation) of serial killers, the training of investigators, "signatures" of serial killers, and overkill. He pays particular attention to piquerism as one subcategory of "signature murder," that deals primarily with sexual arousal connected with serial homicide. Piquerism entails stabbing, cutting, jabbing, slashing, and gouging the victim for sexual arousal. Cutting instruments are the focus. The author concludes with suggestions for a successful investigation of serial murder cases.

Chapter 7, "A Synthesis and Reinterpretation of Necrophilia in the Context of Lust Murders: The Role of Fate," by Cahill, Dickey, and Shon, discusses a particular practice of some lust homicide predators—the practice of engaging sexual intercourse with a corpse. It reviews and conducts a critical re-reading of the literature and the links to lust homicide. It specifically looks at the role of chance and situational factors in the etiology of necrophilia. It concludes with a comparison of necrophilia to other paraphilias.

Chapter 8, "The Portrayal of Extreme Crime by the Media: Reflecting or Creating Fear," by Fuller, examines lust homicide and the reasons it causes the extent of fear and fascination with the public. It argues that the media has elevated the lust homicide predator to celebrity status. The media is said to be driven to materializing sensational stories connected with the public's "insatiable appetite for the lurid, grotesque, and bloody." To this end, Fuller first explains three forms of extreme violent crimes that are particularly interesting for the media: serial murder, mass murder, and lust murder. He then focuses on Ted Bundy as a case in point in media attention. Fuller concludes with a discussion of the "chicken-and-egg" dilemma as to the level of attention of this crime: does the media lead in the public display of lust homicide predators or does the event itself lead to media preoccupation. He responds that it is a bit of both.

Chapter 9, "High Profile Serial Killers and Capital Punishment 1977–1994," by Kudlac, explains the media's attention to serial homicide. He investigates the reportage of serial killing from 1977 to 1994. The *New York Times*, *Time* and *Newsweek* magazine, and HBO, in the early 1980s were to portray the rampart nature of serial killing. Stereotypes of the serial killers began to take form. An increasingly exaggerated nature of its prevalence was also developing. Kudlac looks especially at the coverage of several serial killers: Ted Bundy, John Wayne Gacy, Richard Ramirez, and Aileen Wuornos. He also looks at the "unattractive" serial killers—Gerald Stano, Randy Kraft and Ronal Simmons and asks why they were not extensively covered in the media, even though the number of homicides inflicted were equally large (Stano allegedly killed 49; Kraft, 16; Simmons, 14). Kudlac notes that it was not only the number of victims involved, but their characteristics (race, class, and gender) that were also an important component of why some and not other serial killers were given much publicity.

Chapter 10, "Crime, Subjectivity and Edgework: The Case of Lust Homicide," by Shon and Milovanovic, develops a phenomenological and existential account of lust serial homicide. They are less focused on etiology than the meaning constructed by lust serial killers. Accordingly, they look at serial killing as an adaptive mechanism (following Halleck's theory), as a mode of subjectivization, the ritualistic and ceremonial rites of sacrifice of serial killers, and lust murder as a form of "edgework." The role of fantasy has been shown to be of considerable value in understanding the developed scripts for lust homicide. Similarly the role of mutilation, sacred places, trophies and taunting of police is developed. The lust killer, too, can be brought within the literature of "edgework" in understanding the important component of excitement, adrenaline rush, and approaching of boundaries. Here, a five-dimension framework is offered that integrates Lacan and Deleuze with the edgework literature.

Part 1

Theory of Sexual Homicide and Sexually Violent Predatory Laws

Chapter 2

They Must Be Crazy ... Aren't They? Legal Issues with Sexual Serial Murderers

Margaret R. Kohut, Mark S. Carich,
and Angeline Stanislaus

"I was born with the devil in me. I could not help the fact that I was a
murderer, no more than the poet can help the inspiration to sing."

—Dr. H. H. Holmes
Confession, 1896 (Larson 2003)

Introduction

Jerry Brudos abducted, tortured, killed and mutilated at least four young
women in his garage. His wife and children lived in the adjoining home and
never knew what Jerry was doing in his "workshop."

Ted Bundy raped and murdered at least forty known victims, preferring
pretty girls with long hair parted in the middle. After dumping their bodies
in rural areas, he often returned to the dump site and applied cosmetics to the
dead girls' faces, then had sex with their decomposing bodies.

Ken Bianchi and his cousin Angelo Buono killed at least ten young women
after first torturing them by electrocution and asphyxiation; they then bound
the women and brutally raped them repeatedly before strangling them to
death. They dumped their bodies along hillsides in California.

Joel Rifkin was a quiet young man who killed seventeen women. He had an IQ of 130 but no social skills. When stopped for a traffic offense, police discovered Joel had a corpse in his trunk that had been there for several days.

Jeffrey Dahmer lured boys and young men to his apartment to supposedly drink beer and pose for sexually explicit pictures. Instead, he drugged them, killed them, and had sex with their corpses. He stored human remains (primarily heads and genitalia) throughout his apartment, including his refrigerator, freezer, and barrels of acid.

John Gacy was regarded as a conscientious, community-minded businessman who dressed as a clown to entertain sick children. He raped, tortured, and murdered thirty-three young men and then buried them in the crawl space under his house.

Albert Fish resembled a kindly grandfatherly gentleman who would harm no one. But he lured fifteen children into his home, raped them, killed them, and ate them. At the time of his arrest, Fish had frozen strips of human flesh in his freezer. He liked to experiment with seasonings that helped bring out the wonderful flavor of children's flesh, especially their buttocks.

Joseph Kallinger claimed to hear voices and have visual hallucinations instructing him to kill three billion people—including his own son. So he killed his son, along with many others. He said he was followed by a disembodied human head named Charlie, who told him what homicides to commit.

Reclusive farmer Ed Gein had a fascination with dead bodies. In 1957, he became a suspect in the disappearance of a local woman in Plainfield, Wisconsin. Entering his house, police made an incredible discovery. Junk and rotting garbage covered nearly every surface of the house. A decapitated, disemboweled female corpse was found hanging in the kitchen—the missing local woman. The ramshackle house was filled with human remains: wastebaskets, an armchair, and lamps all made of human skin; skulls made into bowls; an entire human suit made of victims' skin; female genitalia kept in a shoebox; a belt made of nipples; a human head; four noses; and a human heart.

How can there be any element of rational thought in these crimes, and so many others? How can anyone who commits these horrific crimes *not* be insane? Only someone severely mentally ill would do these things. "Normal" people just don't commit crimes like these—it's just impossible. Because we live in a society with laws and rules of social conduct, we mistakenly assume that everybody who is emotionally healthy conforms to these standards of decency towards others. Homicide, especially sexual homicide, baffles us, intrigues us, and scares us. First, murder is the only crime in the nation with no legal statute of limitations. Second, sexual homicide is all the more repugnant because it brings not only death to the victim, but it also humiliates, dominates, and violates the victim in the worst ways possible. Victims of sexual murder aren't real people to the killers; they're just objects to satisfy the killers' need to completely control another person. While their crimes are repugnant to us, they also fascinate us. Our ambivalence toward serial sexual killers probably began in London's East End slum, Whitechapel, in 1888. Jack the Ripper's identity remains unknown, but his name still evokes that combination of fear and fascination. Today, Jack would be considered a "light-weight wannabe" since he killed and sexually mutilated only five women. Until FBI agent Robert Ressler coined the term "serial killer" in 1972, we weren't sure what to call the perpetrators of serial homicide. Today they are also called "psychopaths," "sociopaths," and "antisocial personalities." In defining serial murder, Egger (1990a) stated: "A serial murder occurs when one or more individuals commit a second murder and/or subsequent murder, is relationshipless (no prior relationship between victim and offender), is at a different time and has no apparent connection to the initial murder, and is usually committed in a different geographical location. Further, the motive is not for material gain and is believed to be for the murderer's desire to have power over the victims. Victims may have symbolic value and are perceived to be prestigeless, powerless and/or lower socio-economic groups." And with very few exceptions, which are discussed later in this chapter, they are legally sane.

To better understand how our criminal justice systems copes with serial sexual murderers, we need to first look at some basics of American criminal law (i.e. defining the elements that constitute this crime; determining if the accused is competent to stand trial; deciding if the accused should be held legally liable for the homicide; and how to cope with deviant sexual killers in sentencing and then in correctional facilities or maximum security psychiatric hospitals).

Defining Criminal Sexual Homicide

Among law enforcement and others who work in the criminal justice system, sexual homicide is defined as murders with evidence or observations that indicate the murder had some sort of sexual component. In identifying a sexual homicide, forensic scientists examine such things as the victim's clothing or lack of clothing, exposure and/or mutilation of the victim's genitalia, insertion of objects into the victim's vagina or anus, and evidence of substitute sexual activity (e.g. masturbation), sexual interest, or sexual fantasy (Ressler et al. 1992). While at first glance these homicides may seem random and unorganized, to the trained eye, their true nature is revealed.

Every crime, whether a felony or misdemeanor, has certain elements that must be present in order for a prosecutor to prove, beyond a reasonable doubt, that a crime was in fact committed and that the defendant committed the crime. First, there must be a criminal act, or *actus reus,* that violates a law of the jurisdiction where it was perpetrated. In sexual homicides, the *actus reus* is the physical element of the crime that resulted in the victim's death. Second, the act must be intentional, committed with *mens rea,* or "guilty mind." The *mens rea* is the mental element of the crime of sexual homicide, including purpose, knowledge, recklessness or negligence. Since we cannot see into an offender's mind, and since sexual serial homicides are seldom witnessed by others unless two killers act in congress, confessions are the only sure way to identify *mens rea.* The defendant's true intentions must be proved by his actions that provide circumstantial but incontrovertible proof of the necessary *mens rea.* Putting these elements together indicates that for a defendant to be held criminally liable for homicide the prosecutor must prove the existence of *actus reus, mens rea,* circumstance (death occurred unlawfully), causation (the unlawful act triggered a chain of events that caused the victim's death) and the end result—the death of another person (Samaha 2005a). Homicide is a "capital" felony, meaning that it is punishable by death or life in prison without parole. Criminal homicide, then, is homicide that is *not* justified or excused by concepts like self-defense and legal insanity; it includes intentional purpose, or knowledge that an action could cause death, or reckless behavior that a reasonable person would know could cause death, or negligence by a person who has a legal obligation towards the victim whose negligent act caused the death of the victim. In the past decade, criminal sexual statutes have been expanded to embrace a wider range of nonconsensual penetration and contact that now includes any type of unlawful touching for sexual gratification.

The legal definition of murder is that the crime involved the killing of another person with malice aforethought—a carefully planned homicide where the perpetrator intends for his acts to cause death to the victim. Most states recognize three types of criminal homicide, based upon the *mens rea* involved (Samaha 2005a):

1. First-degree murder (with malice aforethought).
2. Second-degree murder (in the heat of passion).
3. Felony murder (death occurs during the commission of another felony).

Using sex offenses as an index crime, the following are real-world exemplars of the three types of murder:

Ted Bundy planned his crimes with precision and a very cool head. He took the passenger seat out of his Volkswagen to allow for the presence of his incapacitated victim. He kept what police call a burglary kit in his car (e.g. tire irons, hammers, ropes, saws). He lured at least two of his victims to his car by putting his arm in a sling and asking the victims to help him load his sailboat onto his car. After raping and killing his victims in a remote area, he carefully concealed their bodies to avoid detection. Bundy's acts clearly demonstrated the *mens rea* of first degree murder.

Homicidal drifter Henry Lee Lucas was badly abused, physically and emotionally, by his alcoholic mother, a prostitute who often made Henry watch while she had sex with numerous men. One day he and his mother had a fierce argument; Lucas struck out in anger and impulse and killed his mother. Lucas did not have the *mens rea* to be convicted of first degree murder since it was not committed with malice aforethought. Lucas was convicted of second degree murder "in the heat of passion." His other sexual crimes, after his release from prison, were first degree murder because they had the necessary *mens rea*.

What plagued Dahmer throughout his life was a devastating sense of loneliness. After having sex with his victims, he did not want them to leave. Abandonment and rejection were intolerable to him. To alleviate his loneliness, Dahmer attempted to create love slaves of some of his victims by drilling holes in their heads and pouring muriatic acid into their brains. As any reasonable person would deduce, several victims died immediately after this crude lobotomy. One victim supposedly functioned minimally for a few days before dying (CourtTV 2005; Kohut 2005). Dahmer's actions with these victims illustrate the crime of felony murder. Simply put, felony murder occurs when an accidental death happens during the commission of another felony. Dahmer did not have the *mens rea* in these deaths for them to be considered as first degree murder; the last thing he wanted was for the young men to die and leave him alone again. However, drilling holes in people's heads and putting acid into their brains constitutes the felony of battery, defined as "offensive bodily contact" (Dix 2002; Samaha 2005a). Felony murder rarely applies to sexual serial killers since their crimes demonstrate the *mens rea* of first degree murder; they intend for their victims to die.

A defendant's *actus reus* becomes critical when either the judge or the jury determines whether a first degree murder warrants the death penalty or life in prison without parole. Capital punishment is much more likely to be invoked if the homicide was especially heinous, atrocious or cruel; torture murders that cause a lingering, agonizing death for the victim is much more likely to result in execution.

Since first and secondary degree homicide are distinguished solely on the basis of the *mens rea* of the killer, courts have had to determine if the homicide was overtly premeditated (first degree) or if the killer had adequate time to cool off before the murder. How much time has to elapse between the provocation and the homicide? The landmark case of *Macias v Arizona* (1929) set the precedent for distinguishing between first and second degree murder: "There need be no appreciable space of time between the intention to kill and the act of killing. They may be as instantaneous as successive thoughts of the mind. It is only necessary that the act of killing be preceded by a concurrence of will, deliberation, and premeditation on the part of the slayer, and if such is the case, the killing is murder in the first degree." Pursuant to this ruling, there is no set time limit that must pass between the alleged sudden provocation and the killing. This is a decision that must be made in each individual case by the trier of fact—the judge or the jury.

The murders committed by Aileen Wuornos are legally unique in two ways: First, she was a female serial killer. Not the only one, certainly, but it is generally assumed that serial murderers, especially a sexual murderer, is male. Second, Wuornos made no attempt to claim legal insanity under any of the accepted definitions. Instead, she pled not guilty to multiple charges of first degree murder under the legal definition of self-defense. In every jurisdiction, if a person has a "reasonable and prudent belief" that he/she is in imminent danger of grievous bodily injury or death at the hands of another person, the endangered person may legally use whatever force is necessary to prevent being harmed—even deadly force if the situation calls for it and there is no other way. The legal catch, however, is that the endangered person *must*, before using deadly force, make every reasonable effort to flee from his/her attacker (Samaha 2005a).

Aileen Wuornos was a prostitute who "worked" an interstate highway. Sexually abused as a child, Wuornos hated men and maintained a mental construct that all men would harm her if they had the opportunity. Going to a secluded area with her highway pick-ups in their cars, Aileen believed that the men were not going to pay for her services, that they, in essence, would or did rape her. Wuornos shot and killed these men. At her trial for the first degree murder, the judge instructed the jury to consider whether or not a reasonable and prudent person in Wuornos' situation would believe that she was in danger of imminent bodily harm or death and could not flee to safety. The jury's verdict was guilty of first degree murder; Wuornos failed the reasonable and prudent person test that is a cornerstone of the self-defense argument.

Pre-Trial Assessment and Competency to Stand Trial

A sexual homicide has occurred. Maybe more than one—perhaps a serial sexual killer has been apprehended. The crimes are inexplicable, horrific, and repulsive to society. The alleged perpetrator's competency to stand trial is an issue usually raised before the trial, and is most often made by the defendant's attorney. However, if a defendant's bizarre behavior occurs during a trial, the presiding judge or even the prosecutor may raise the issue; judges and attorneys typically do not wish to have to re-try a case if it is overturned on appeal because the defendant's competency was not addressed.

A competency to stand trial issue occurs if:

1. A defendant has extensive past psychiatric history, including hospitalizations, suicide attempts, and history of lengthy mental health care.

2. A defendant has been very difficult to manage while incarcerated prior to trial (e.g. violence towards inmates and staff, repeated self-injury, throwing urine or feces on self and others).

3. A defendant makes multiple requests to the trial judge (e.g. requesting to change/fire the defense attorney; making lengthy and frivolous trial motions; stating a plan to call as witnesses famous people, government officials, and deceased people).

4. A defendant exhibits cognitive deficiencies that may be the result of mental retardation, learning disabilities, severe head injuries, dementias or other medical conditions involving the central nervous system.

A forensic behavior examiner (a psychologist or psychiatrist) must conduct a clinical study to determine if the defendant is competent to stand trial. Forensic assessment instruments are used to determine the defendant's intelligence, personality, degree of psychopathy or psychosis, and his ability to understand the proceedings and take an active part in his defense (Arrigo and Shipley 2005). Assessment instruments include the Competency Screening Test, the Competency Assessment Instrument, the Georgia Court Competency Test, and the MacArthur Competency Assessment Tool—Criminal Adjudication (Rosner 2003). The evaluator should first discuss the defendant's case with the referring attorney or judge while also examining arrest and investigators' reports and the defendant's medical/mental health records. The evaluator's examination consists of two parts: (1) The defendant is examined for any current mental disorders, cognitive deficiencies, and the need for psychological testing and (2) The defendant is asked to describe the reasons for his arrest and the charges pending against him, his understanding of how the criminal justice system works, and how he will be able to assist in his own defense.

Competency to stand trial is *not* the same question as whether or not the defendant was insane at the time the homicide was committed. Is the defendant competent *at the time of the trial?* Pretrial assessments must adhere to both legal and ethical parameters of this sole question. The results of the forensic assessment to determine competency to stand trial must be communicated in a manner that is understandable to non-mental health professionals (e.g. attorneys, judges, and juries).

In the Home Box Office prison drama, "Oz," one of the prisoners, Cyril, is portrayed as mentally retarded and possibly mentally ill. Cyril is incarcerated for murder. His brother Ryan, also a homicidal inmate, has a ferocious fight with another prisoner. Cyril kills the prisoner who he thought was going to kill Ryan. In the real world, this occurrence would raise three questions: was Cyril insane at the time of the killing, and is he currently competent to stand trial? Only a forensic specialist can make this judgment, usually with the administration of psychological testing such as the MMPI-2 and the Millon assessment instruments, and a thorough clinical interview. A third question would be: Can Cyril be legally excused for the killing because he reasonably believed he was defending his brother's life? This is an issue for the trier of fact to determine—the judge (in a bench trial) or the jury.

Black's Law Dictionary (Garner 1996, p. 117) defines competency to stand trial as "the mental ability to understand and make decisions." One of our rules of law and of moral standards is that a defendant should not be subjected to the process of the criminal justice system if he is unable to understand the nature and purpose of the proceedings (Wrightsman et al. 1994). This safeguard not only protects the due process rights of defendants who are presumed innocent until proven guilty, but it also protects our society by ensuring accurate results from the trial, maintains the dignity of the justice system, and justifies the imposition of punishment. It is certainly possible that an accused sexual serial killer was legally sane at the time of his crime(s), but for some reason is not competent to stand trial. In 1960, the Supreme Court ruled in the case of *Dusky v United States* that a defendant must have (1) sufficient present ability to consult with a lawyer with a reasonable degree of rational understanding and (2) rational as well as factual understanding of the proceedings. *Weiter v Settle* (1963) cast further light on the criteria for competence to stand trial: the defendant must be mentally well-oriented; understand that he is charged with a criminal offense; understand the role of the judge, jury, and attorneys; must understand how his attorney will represent him; and have the ability to understand and remember all these issues.

An alleged killer who is found not to be competent to stand trial does not gain the freedom to return into society. He is confined in a maximum security mental health facility and receives psychiatric care until his competency to stand trial is restored (Grisso 2003). This process takes many months, perhaps even years. Many family members who await the trial of their loved-one's murderer grow impatient with this system, feeling it is a way for the defendant to avoid trial, conviction and sentencing as long as possible. But from a legal point of view the alleged perpetrator has not been convicted of any crime, but is still virtually incarcerated. The answer to this frustrating question is that, according to the U.S. Constitution, a defendant does have a right to a speedy trial, but that trial must be a fair and impartial one, protecting the defendant's right to due process. The Supreme Court's decision in *Jackson v Indiana* (1972) placed limits on the amount of time an incompetent defendant could be confined before trial. "A reasonable period of time necessary to determine whether there is a substantial probability that he will attain competence in the foreseeable future" stated the Court's decision. In some cases, depending upon the seriousness of the charges, if a defendant is unlikely to regain competency to stand trial in the near future, the charges against him might be dropped—the district attorney does not, and will not, have a case he/she can win. This most often means that the accused killer will spend much time in a forensic psychiatric facility with only the slimmest chance of being released into society. Lest the public have the misconception that defendants found incompetent to stand trial get off easy, it is essential to understand that these alleged criminals—who are presumed innocent—often spend more time in forensic hospitals than they would have spent in prison for their offense. It is not uncommon for a defendant charged with murder(s) to be found incompetent to stand trial and be court-ordered into a secure mental health facility for such a lengthy period of time that a defense attorney must file a *writ of habeas corpus* ("release the body" or "you have the body") to ensure that his/her client is not confined to the hospital for an unreasonably lengthy period of time. In the vernacular, a *writ of habeas corpus* can be interpreted as "You have the body. Now release my client and let him go free, or show cause why he should be denied his freedom." This type of writ is rarely used by attorneys for serial killers; if a judge grants the writ, and the suspected killer is released from the hospital it would mean the defendant is deemed competent to stand trial for murder. If convicted, lethal injection could be the end result. But even with suspected sexual serial killers, time passes—evidence disappears, witnesses re-locate or die, and victims no longer wish to testify, having moved on with their lives. Knowing that the prosecutor can no longer sustain the burden of proof (beyond a reasonable doubt) required for first degree murder, the defense attorney may file a *habeas corpus* motion, and the charges against the suspected serial killer will be dismissed for lack of evidence. As abhorrent as this may appear on the surface, an attorney's sworn code of ethics requires him/her to *vigorously represent the client.* To do otherwise is a serious breach of ethics for any attorney that could lead to censure or even disbarment. The "Miranda Warning" rights provided to every defendant who is charged with a crime, requires that an attorney must be appointed at no charge if the accused cannot afford legal representation. This applies to suspected serial sexual killers; *the law must apply to everyone, or it applies to no one.*

The Insanity Defense

Jerry Brudos was a mild, pudgy, socially awkward man who was both a husband and a father. He also had a sexual fetish for women's shoes and underclothing that began in his adolescence. At age seventeen, Jerry abducted and beat a woman, was apprehended and spent nine months in a psychiatric hospital with a diagnosis of "possible onset of schizophrenia." In the late 1950s and 1960s, Jerry murdered at least four women, quite possibly many more. He strangled them in his garage workshop and liked to leave their bodies dangling from a rope and pulley so he could observe them. Jerry had a large collection of women's shoes and underclothes; he liked to dress the corpses in these clothes, place them in sexually explicit poses, and have sex with their bodies. He had deviant fantasies about putting women's corpses in his freezer. He cut the breasts off one victim, and the foot off another. He kept the foot for quite some time, putting different shoes on it and taking photographs. Jerry also enjoyed dressing himself in women's underclothes. Although he was married, Jerry went to the local college grounds and tried to meet young women, claiming he was a lonely Vietnam veteran looking for companionship. One of these women found Jerry to be very strange, and told the police about him. A search of his property told the entire story, and the whole nation became acquainted with "The Fetish Killer." Jerry pled not guilty by reason of insanity, blaming everything from his mother's lack of love for him to blackouts of unknown origin, to hypoglycemia for his actions. Charged with four first degree murders, seven psychiatrists examined Jerry extensively. All found him legally sane and competent to stand trial, assuring the district attorney that Jerry knew right from wrong and describing him as "arrogant" and having antisocial personality disorder. Jerry also had a paraphilia (i.e. a fetish for women's shoes and underclothes). Fetishes are fairly commonplace and harmless unless they infringe upon the rights of others. Many people find fetishes weird, but having one in no way excuses deliberate homicide. Having failed in prevailing with an insanity defense, Jerry pled guilty to four murders and was sentenced to consecutive life sentences. Although he has been eligible for parole, he has been denied repeatedly despite being a "model prisoner." Jerry now states that he did not commit these sexual homicides. He was again denied parole in 2005.

In American jurisprudence, there are probably no topics more hotly debated than the insanity defense and capital punishment; these two topics are frequently intertwined. The insanity defense, in its purest form, is seldom utilized, and is even more seldom successful. Although this defense has been a part of American culture since the Constitution was framed, it came under heated scrutiny when John Hinkley Jr. was found not guilty by reason of insanity (NGRI) for the attempted assassination of President Reagan in 1981. He was confined to a mental health institution, where he remains to this day. His goal in assassinating the President was to obtain the attention of actress Jodie Foster. No doubt he was successful, but far from the way he intended. After his trial, America rebelled. "No more excuses! Hold people fully accountable for their actions!" became our society's rallying cry. In 1982 Harvard criminal law professor Charles Nesson wrote: "Lots of people have tough lives, many tougher than Mr. Hinkley's and manage to cope. The Hinkley verdict let those people down. The Hinkley verdict is demoralizing, an example of someone who let himself go and who has been exonerated because of it" (*New York Times* 1982). In the case of Jerry Brudos and many more serial sexual killers, the insanity defense is just as despised, just as controversial as one-time violent acts such as that committed by Hinkley.

Lorena Bobbit was found to have been "temporarily insane" when she cut off her sleeping husband's penis after being sexually abused by him. The trial of Lorena Bobbit was watched by millions via Court TV; testimony indicated that John Bobbit, the victim, wasn't a very nice guy. Although many felt that Bobbit "had it coming," for being abusive to his wife, this is not the legal issue. If Mrs. Bobbit had marital problems, she could have left her husband at any time she chose (CourtTV 2005). The law does not sanction assault and battery, regardless of the personal character of the victim. Finding Lorena Bobbit temporarily insane at the time of her illegal act is an example of what has long been known as "jury nullification." In this action, a jury returns a verdict that does not hold the defendant accountable for his crime even though it is glaringly obvious that the defendant did commit the crime. The classic example of jury nullification is when a man discovers that his child is being sexually molested by a neighbor; he goes to the abuser's home and shoots him dead. The jury finds him not guilty by reason of temporary insanity because

"He had it coming. I would do the same thing." This type of frontier justice is not often seen in the modern age, but still pops up from time to time, as it did in the Bobbit case.

Insanity is a legal term, *not* a psychiatric term or a clinical diagnosis. Mental health professionals diagnose patients using the standard guidelines of the *Diagnostic and Statistical Manual of the American Psychiatric Association (Version Four*, Revised). In terms of the law, "mental defect" as defined in the insanity defense is a "retardation" that affects a defendant's ability to form the prerequisite *mens rea* of homicide, and the inability to exercise rational will that prevents him from performing the *actus reus* of homicide. "Mental disease" in legal terms refers to a psychosis that also prevents the defendant from forming the necessary *actus reus* and *mens rea* for first degree murder. Therefore, legal insanity is understood as a condition that excuses the defendant from criminal liability because of mental disease or defect (Samaha 2005a). An insanity defense is based upon the idea that what the defendant did was a crime, but because he is legally insane he is not held accountable for his actions.

No matter how atrocious the crime, the law presumes that a defendant is legally sane, of normal intelligence, and possesses a healthy mind. It falls to the defense to prove that this is not the case; the insanity defense is known as an "affirmative defense" because it is the burden of the defendant to take action to prove that he was insane at the time he committed the crime by clear and convincing evidence. The burden of proof then shifts back to the government to prove that the defendant was not insane at the time of the offense. Then the "battle of the experts" begins; each side calls forensic mental health experts to testify to their particular point of view—sanity vs insanity. It is ultimately the jury who weighs the credibility of each expert witness to arrive at a verdict. Unfortunately, there is no uniform standard in all fifty states that precisely defines "legal insanity." So what is insane in one state may not be insane in another state. Adding to this confusion are the many definitions of legal insanity, which follow.

The M'Naghten Rule of 1843—also called the "right-wrong test"—is the prevailing definition of legal insanity in twenty-five states (Samaha 2005a). The Rule originated in England, where defendant M'Naghten shot and killed the secretary of the Prime Minister, although his intention was to kill the Minister himself. In this case the precedent was set that focuses on two necessary elements: (1) The defendant had a mental disease or defect at the time of the offense, *and* (2) The disease or defect caused the defendant not to know either the nature and quality of his acts, or that what he did was wrong/unlawful. This defense focuses on the defendant's ability to reason—

the ability to discern right from wrong. Gary Ridgeway, the Green River Killer, dumped the bodies of his victims in remote, isolated areas. He did not want them to be discovered, and he wanted to avoid detection. This implies that he had no mental disease or defect that prevented him from knowing his actions were wrong.

The "Product of Mental Illness" test, also called the Durham Rule of 1954, is not widely used. The Rule states that acts which are the products of mental disease or defect excuse the perpetrator from criminal liability. The concept of insanity is stretched beyond purely intellectual knowledge and into deeper areas of cognition and will. Critics of the Durham Rule say that it makes legal insanity the same thing as mental illness (Samaha 2005a).

The "Irresistible Impulse" test of sanity evolved from an 1877 case, *Parsons v State*, and was used successfully in John Hinkley's trial. The court ruled in this case that society can neither blame nor deter people who, because of mental disease or defect, lose their self-control and are unable to conform their actions to the confines and standards of the law. Defendants can be found NGRI if their disease or defect damages their volition, or intention, to commit a crime; the required *mens rea* is absent. This test is made up of three legal questions: (1) At the time of the crime, did the defendant have a mental disease or defect? (2) If so, did the defendant know right from wrong regarding the crime? If not, then the defendant is excused from criminal liability. (3) If the defendant did have such knowledge, he can still be excused from liability *if* the disease caused the defendant to lose the power of control to understand right from wrong to avoid committing the crime, and the disease was the sole cause of his act (Samaha 2005a). So unpopular was the Hinkley decision that most states have abolished the Irresistible Impulse rule, and it has been entirely abandoned by the federal court system.

The "Substantial Capacity" test of sanity emphasizes both the qualities of insanity that affect the defendant's legal culpability: the ability to reason, and self-will (Samaha 2005). In 1985, the American Law Institute formed the *Model Penal Code*, which was intended to unify criminal liability and criminal procedures. This Code's definition of insanity specifies that "a person is not responsible for criminal conduct if, at the time of such conduct, he suffers from a mental disease or defect that causes him to not to have the substantial capacity to either appreciate the criminality (wrongfulness) of his conduct or to conform his conduct to the requirements of the law" (*American Law Institute Model Penal Code* 1985, p. 163). The Substantial Capacity test specifically excludes psychopathic/antisocial personality types. In fact, Black and Larson (1999) stated: "antisocial psychopaths fail every legal test designed to pardon defendants who are truly psychotic." However, it is possible that a defendant with marked antisocial personality traits can also be psychotic to the point that he is legally insane.

With the "Diminished Capacity" test, the defense alleges that the accused has a mental disease or defect that diminishes his capacity, but not enough to make him legally insane. Not many states use this test, and those that do tightly restrict its use (Samaha 2005). In *Dial v Washington State* (2003), this test was given this definition: "To maintain a diminished capacity defense, a defendant must produce expert testimony demonstrating that a mental disorder, not amounting to insanity, impaired the defendant's ability to form the specific intent (*mens rea*) to commit the crime."

Should the insanity defense be abolished completely? Again, our society is divided. One position is that people who commit horrific crimes such as serial sexual homicide will never be able to function in society. Finding them insane doesn't help them—it merely means the offender will spend his life in a maximum security forensic hospital. The defendant should be punished by going to prison, not coddled in a hospital. Murderers who are insane are not that much different from sane murderers; both will be indefinitely incarcerated. The opposite position supports the idea that although there are many abuses of the insanity defense, when it is properly applied it ensures that defendants who are legally insane and not responsible for their actions are provided treatment, not punishment for revenge. Our society should be above seeking revenge, and should recognize that some people are simply too mentally ill to stop what they're doing and behavior in legally acceptable manners.

Hare (1993) emphasizes that psychopaths/sociopaths/antisocials know right from wrong, but this knowledge fails to deter them from their murderous actions. They are woefully deficient in the ability to translate this knowledge into compliance with the rules of law in our society. "Legal insanity" vs "moral insanity" is a test sexual serial killers will always fail.

"Designer" Defenses

There's an old saying among lawyers: "When you've got the facts on your side, you pound the facts. When you've got the law on your side, you pound the law. When you have neither the law nor the facts on your side, you pound the table."

Most Americans would agree that there's way too much table pounding going on in our criminal justice system. In the past two decades, it seemed nobody was responsible for anything. The defendants clearly committed the crimes, but somehow it just wasn't their fault. They weren't legally insane, but they still wished to be excused of criminal liability due to any number of mitigating "syndromes" that do not constitute mental disease or defect, but in some mysterious way caused the defendant's criminal act (Dershowitz 1994; Kirwin 1997). Sexual serial killers are particularly notorious for this kind of "designer defense," but other violent crimes fall prey to many legal shenanigans as well. Sometimes these defenses actually prevail. The original concept of the "designer defense" dates back to Chicago, 1924, in one of the most famous murder trials in our nation's history. Nathan Leopold and Richard Loeb were very bright young men who came from prominent affluent Chicago families. However, their college classes were not stimulating enough for them. So they planned the perfect murder, just for the fun of it and to demonstrate their intellectual superiority. They kidnapped a twelve-year-old boy named Bobby Franks. Leopold and Loeb drove Bobby to a secluded area and beat him to death. Next, they contacted Bobby's father and demanded a $10,000 ransom for the boy's safe return. To their disbelief, they were apprehended when a police detective discovered a pair of men's glasses next to the body. The specific description of the glasses matched that of Nathan Leopold.

The families called in the top defense attorney of that time, and perhaps of all times, Clarence Darrow, to save their boys from the death penalty. Darrow was a curious sort of lawyer; he was an avowed atheist, but also a vehement crusader against the death penalty's inhumanity. Under his direction, Nathan Leopold and Richard Loeb pled guilty to the murder of Bobby Franks and Darrow argued to spare their lives with what was probably the first designer defense. Freudian psychoanalysis was just coming into vogue at this time, and various newspapers offered to pay Sigmund Freud himself any price he named to psychoanalyze the two defendants. Dr. Freud declined the offers. Leopold and Loeb were examined by no less than six alienists, as forensic psychiatrists were known in those days, to examine the killers to see if they suffered from what the Chicago journalists called "the new-fangled mental psychosis" condition. They did not, according to the alienists; both young men were found to be legally sane under the M'Naghten standard. However, Darrow's flawless defense brought forward several mitigating circumstances in the young men's lives that called for life in prison, but not capital punishment. Darrow cited Leopold and Loeb's childhood sexual fantasies, their alleged molestation by governesses, and (for the 1920s) a few vague references to what might have been homosexual tendencies between the young men. Darrow's closing argument is one that is still studied in law schools around the nation, a brilliant oratory of pounding the table. "I am arguing for a time in the future," he said, "where all life is worth saving, and mercy is the highest attribute of man" (Kirwin 1997). Darrow's defense prevailed; Leopold and Loeb were sentenced to life plus ninety-nine years in prison for the kidnapping and murder of Bobby Franks.

The number one entry on today's "it ain't my fault" defense list is the "I was abused as a child" defense. It was used (unsuccessfully) by Lyle and Eric Menendez, Susan Smith, Ken Bianchi, John Gacy, and many, many others. While our society certainly condemns and abhors the physical, sexual and emotional abuse of children, it is difficult to understand why such abuse should be a legal excuse for murder, especially serial sexual murder. Jeffrey Dahmer was not abused; far from it, he grew up in a stable home in a solid economic status. Ted Bundy was not abused; he was loved by his mother and stepfather. It's certain that Henry Lee Lucas and John Gacy were both physically and emotionally abused. The legal issue for the trier of fact to determine is whether they should be excused from criminal liability because of their past abuse. To our society's detriment, child maltreatment occurs at an alarming rate. Yet the vast majority of survivors who suffered abuse as children do not commit violent crimes as adults. They themselves know that murder is wrong, so why should Lucas, Gacy, and others literally get away with murder because they were abused? (Dershowitz 1994; Kohut 2004a).

Another "designer defense" that pops up from time to time is post-partum depression and psychosis. This tragic condition is unfortunately very real. It is also often abused. Ann Green was a nurse on a maternity ward. Her co-workers found it pitiable that she continued to work in this ward after two of her own children died from SIDS only days after birth. On the same day that she brought home her third child, a neighbor came to her home and witnessed Ann putting a pillow over the infant's head to smother him. Ann was charged with the second degree murder of her first two infants and the attempted murder of her third child. Her attorney argued that Ann was suffering from post-partum psychosis/depression; Ann was found not guilty. She stayed in a psychiatric hospital less than thirty days and was then released (Kirwin 1997).

Sexual serial killer Joel Rifkin claimed the "I was adopted as a child" defense. Rifkin, who had already been convicted for one of his seventeen sexual homicides, claimed during a subsequent murder trial that he felt rejected by his birth mother and this made him feel rage towards women. The popular quasi-mental health catch phrase "failure to bond" could have been argued to excuse Rifkin's serial sexual murders. On impulse, Rifkin changed his mind and pled guilty to the other murders attributed to him (Kirwin 1997).

Excessive fascination with pornography is another designer defense. For example, before his execution, Ted Bundy claimed that pornography had a powerful influence on his life and his crimes; he speculated that sexually explicit material may have been a factor in his crimes by creating within him deviant sexual fantasies that took a homicidal turn. By this time, with his date with the electric chair looming, Bundy would have, and did, say anything to keep him out of the chair. Pornography is a multi-billion dollar business in America. Numerous men (and some women as well) look at pornographic material and do not commit sexual serial homicide. Perhaps Bundy had it backwards: pornography may indeed catch the interest of serial sexual killers, but pornography does not *create* such killers, and Bundy himself stopped short of saying that his sexual homicides were *caused* by pornography (CourtTV 2005; Hazelwood and Michaud 2001).

Post-traumatic stress disorder is an actual mental disease, classified as such by the DMS-IV-R. It is seen most often in combat veterans, battered women, abused children, adult survivors of abuse, assault victims, victims of natural disasters, and others who experienced a horrific emotional and/or physical experience. PTSD can be successfully treated with therapy and medication. However, juries have not tended to excuse from criminal liability those who commit violent crimes and claim that PTSD caused their actions.

And then there's "black rage," as claimed by Colin Ferguson, the Long Island Railroad shooter. Ferguson, who conducted his own defense, testified that he was so angry at "white America" and how badly Caucasians treated African Americans that he should be excused from criminal murder and attempted murder because he was unable to contain that rage. Ferguson told his jury that he had been charged with 93 criminal counts because the year was 1993, and he wanted to call the President of the United States as a witness (Kirwin 1997). Ferguson was found guilty of first degree murder and attempted murder.

How about sleepwalking? Too much violence in movies and on TV? Repressed memories? Graves' disease (a thyroid condition that can cause erratic/violent behavior)? Pre-menstrual syndrome? Excessive testosterone? All these designer defenses have been tried, and routinely fail. The trial that stands out in American legal history is the "Twinkie Defense" in the 1979 trial of Dan White. White, a city supervisor in San Francisco shot and killed Mayor George Moscone and city supervisor Harvey Milk over their political disagreements. White claimed insanity because, on the day of the murders, he had consumed large amounts of Coca Cola, chocolate cupcakes, and Twinkies. His elevated blood sugar, his lawyers and several mental health professionals argued, caused impairment in his ability to know right from wrong—to form the required *mens rea* of homicide. White was acquitted of first degree murder and was convicted merely of manslaughter. This verdict was distinctly unpopular with citizens, attorneys, judges, and law enforcement personnel nation-wide. White served five years and was paroled. Within months of his release from prison back into a society that felt his punishment was far from adequate, White committed suicide (Kirwin 1997).

In pondering the insanity defense and the designer defenses, it must be said that there are truly mentally ill people who commit violent crimes, including serial sexual homicides. While their illness may excuse them from criminal liability, these defendants are not excused to such a degree that they wander freely amidst society, untreated, to perhaps cause more harm to innocent victims. The American criminal justice system has come a long way, making huge strides in rendering verdicts that fit the crime. To illustrate this point, legal history verifies that Lizzie Borden, clearly guilty of the axe murders of her father and stepmother, was acquitted in 1892 because her all-male jury simply could not believe that a woman was capable of that kind of violent crime.

Famous Fakers

It can be difficult to prove that a criminal defendant is faking mental illness to avoid conviction and sentencing. It is easy to feign psychotic symptoms like auditory or visual hallucinations. Objective changes in behavior and deterioration of functioning is required to diagnose a true mental health disorder. It is important, then, for the forensic examiner to obtain collateral reports from family members, prior mental health providers, and records from the jail staff. Because of the often beguiling demeanor of the sociopathic killer, it is sometimes perplexing for forensic behavioral specialists to deduce if the defendant is mentally ill or merely doing a good job of feigning illness that will relieve him of criminal liability. The examiner will need to ponder the defendant's alleged history of psychiatric symptoms. Inconsistency in the history and observed behaviors is a tip off to the examiner that the defendant may be faking a mental health disorder. Ken Bianchi, who, along with his cousin Angelo Buono, committed the "Hillside Strangler" serial sexual homicides, not only successfully fooled mental health professionals into believing that he was hypnotized, he also faked having a multiple personality named Steve Walker. It was Steve, said Bianchi, not he, who committed these truly appalling crimes. Steve even "came out" during a hypnosis session. When a doubting and clever forensic examiner told Bianchi that most people with multiple personality disorder have more than one alternate personality, Bianchi, right on cue, promptly came up with yet another ego state! Caught in his ruse, Bianchi admitted that on the night before his first session supposedly under hypnosis, he had watched the movie "Sybil," about a woman with multiple personality disorder (CourtTV 2005).

David Berkowitz, the Son of Sam killer, attempted to feign psychosis by telling examiners that his neighbor Sam's barking dog was sending him messages to shoot people. Berkowitz said he was just doing what the dog told him to do. And besides, he belonged to a murderous Satanic cult that commanded him to commit the homicides of random strangers. Berkowitz was found to be legally sane and is serving a life sentence in prison (CourtTV 2005).

John Gacy, the Killer Clown, tried his best to convince forensic mental health professionals that he, like Ken Bianchi, had a murderous alter-ego named Jack Hanley. Jack "took control" if Gacy drank too much alcohol, and it was Jack who killed thirty-three young men. Gacy did not pursue the insanity defense when forensic examiners unanimously disbelieved his claim of mental illness (CourtTV 2005).

It's a mistake to believe that this type of fakery is a product of recent society. If Jack the Ripper set the prototype for serial murder in 1888, Dr. H.H. Holmes was his American contemporary. Until Eric Larson's best-selling book *The Devil in the White City* was released in 2003, Holmes' name was virtually unrecognized. Today the exact number of his victims is unknown; he took that secret to the grave with him. It is certain he killed at least nine people, but modern researchers put his actual body count as at least fifty victims.

Holmes (real name—Herman Mudgett) was a physician and pharmacist who killed for fun and profit. He is often counted among sexual serial killers because some of his female victims were also his lovers. But mostly, Holmes just liked murder. He profited by his many homicides through taking possession of land the victims had deeded to him prior to their murder and collecting on insurance policies he had taken out on the victims before he killed them. He turned quite a profit by selling the cadavers and skeletons of his victims to medical schools that were desperately in need of them—no questions asked. Holmes committed his crimes against the back-drop of the 1893 Chicago World's Fair—called "The White City." He constructed a special "castle" that contained rooms for fair visitors, office space for fair venders, and specially designed rooms for torturing and killing his victims, most of whom were women visiting the fair. During the six months of the fair, Chicago was deluged by so many out-of-towners that no one even missed Holmes' victims. Later, when there were inquiries made about some of the vanished women, Holmes fled, taking the three children of his assistant in murder, Benjamin Pitezel, with him for some bizarre reason. Not only did Holmes kill Pitezel, he killed the children as well. After his apprehension, Holmes claimed that he had a homicidal alter ego named Edward Hatch; it was Hatch who killed the children. This insanity defense didn't work for Holmes in 1896 any better than it worked for Bianchi and Gacy a century later. Awaiting trial for first degree murder, Holmes insisted that his physical body was actually changing to re-semble the Devil, who, he said, had "been with me from birth" (Larson 2003). Holmes may have been the first killer to try "the Devil made me do it" designer defense.

Conclusion

"I'm the most cold-blooded son of a bitch you will ever meet. I just loved to kill."

—**Ted Bundy** (CourtTV 2005)

Jerry Brudos, Ken Bianchi, Joel Rifkin, David Berkowitz, and Henry Lee Lucas are still in prison. Albert Fish died in prison of natural causes. Jeffrey Dahmer was killed in prison by another inmate. H.H. Holmes, Ted Bundy, John Gacy, and Aileen Wuornos were executed. Though their crimes were particularly heinous, and perhaps to the public seemed like acts only a severely mentally ill person would do, these serial killers were found competent to stand trial and legally sane. Each of these murderers failed to meet the legal definition of insanity under the M'Naghten test, the Substantial Capacity test, the Diminished Capacity test, or the Durham test. They were found to meet the *mens rea* (guilty mind) and committed the *actus reus* (guilty act) standards necessary to be convicted of first degree murder.

Joseph Kallinger's sanity is still debatable; he has spent time both in forensic hospitals with a diagnosis of paranoid schizophrenia and in prison. The criminal justice system remains uncertain if Kallinger is legally insane or if he should be held fully liable for his murders. Kallinger once stated that if he is ever released from custody, he believes he will kill again (CourtTV 2005).

Ed Gein was found not guilty of murder by reason of insanity. Mental health professionals were of the opinion that he suffered from necrophilia and an unspecified psychotic disorder. He spent the rest of his life in a forensic hospital (CourtTV 2005). Using Gein as one of the few serial killers who prevailed in pleading insanity, it is helpful to review this chapter's current legal sanity tests that have widespread use.

Gein met the requirements of the M'Naghten Rule: he had a mental disease at the time of the offenses *and* because of this disease he did not understand that his actions were wrong. This inability to comprehend that his acts were unlawful is evidenced by the overwhelming evidence found in his home; he made no attempt to conceal his crimes. Gein met the requirements of the

Substantial Capacity test: he had a mental disease at the time of the offenses *and* the disease caused him not to have the substantial capacity to conform his actions to the requirements of the law. Gein lived as a hermit in an isolated farmhouse. He compulsively robbed graves to obtain corpses in a nearby cemetery and was unable to stop himself from either killing or from stealing corpses, two activities that were both unlawful and abhorrent. Finally, Gein met the requirements of the Durham test: he had a mental disease that amounted to legal insanity, thus he was not legally responsible for his actions.

The mostly abandoned Irresistible Impulse test would not have applied to Gein; his crimes, from grave robbing to murder, occurred over a period of several years—hardly the spur-of-the-moment actions of an impulsive killer. Nor would the Diminished Capacity test have been applicable to Gein; he had a mental disease, specifically his psychotic illness, which diminished his capacity to know right from wrong. However, this condition *did* render him legally insane as opposed to suffering from a mental disease that failed to meet the criteria in this test as insanity.

Are some people born to be bad? Or are serial killers created through a process of failed socialization as exemplified by Charles Manson and his "family"? (Lanier and Henry 2004). During his murder trial, Manson screamed at the courtroom "These children that come at you with knives ... that's what you deserve!" (Bugliosi and Gentry 1974). While the psychogenesis of sexual homicide is still largely unknown, there is one thing that is certain: serial killers are walking among us undetected, concealed by a "mask of sanity." By the time they are identified and apprehended, they have committed so many murders and destroyed so many lives, that our criminal justice system and our mental health practitioners are overwhelmed with the problem of what to do with them. H.H. Holmes committed most of his crimes between 1892 and 1893; he was apprehended in 1894 and executed in 1896. Today, it is the norm for convicted murderers to sit on death row for a decade or more before their death sentence is carried out, awaiting the outcome of appellate procedures. On 2 December 2005, Kenneth Lee Boyd was executed by lethal injection in Raleigh, North Carolina. He was the 1,000th murderer to be executed since the re-instatement of capital punishment in 1977. Boyd was incarcerated for seventeen years; he requested clemency from the Supreme Court because of his military service in Vietnam where he was "shot at daily, which contributed to his crimes" said Boyd's attorney Thomas Maher. Although Boyd never denied killing his estranged wife and her father, his designer defense failed (CourtTV 2005). On the same day, in Sarasota, Florida, another designer defense was ineffective in preventing a jury from sentencing Joseph Smith to death for the kidnapping, rape, and murder of eleven-year-old Carlie Brucia in 2004. Smith's attorney was unsuccessful in convincing the jury to recommend that he be sentenced to life without parole; Smith was addicted to cocaine, heroin, and narcotic painkillers at the time of the offense, and suffered from chronic back pain and depression. As discussed in this chapter, voluntary intoxication is not a legal defense. As jury foreman Reverend Ron Kruzel recommended the death sentence, a man in the courtroom jumped to his feet and shouted, "Let's string him up now!" (CourtTV 2005). America seems disenchanted with the endless designer defenses.

With very few exceptions, sexual serial killers are both competent to stand trial and are legally sane and responsible for their actions. For them, involvement in the criminal justice systems begins when law enforcement personnel pursue them—sometimes for months or even years—apprehend them, and remove them from society. The system is completed when the killer is convicted and sentenced. This chapter has explained the legal necessity of proving the elements of homicide, competency to stand trial, the insanity defense, and the designer defenses. Using real-world examples, this chapter illustrated how the criminal justice system *does* succeed in permanently removing the sexual serial killer from our midst.

Chapter 3

Sexual Murder and Sexual Serial Killers: Toward a Mind-Body Developmental Theory

Mark S. Carich, Dawn Fisher, and Margaret R. Kohut

Introduction

Sexual murders and sexual serial killers have always been of interest to the public. Professionals are still mystified as to why sexual killers commit the "ultimate crime" of both sexual assault and homicide. Questions also emerge as to why some sexual offenders kill once whereas others many times. It has long been understood that the vast majority of sexual offenders, such as pedophiles and adult rapists, do *not* kill their victims. The purpose of this chapter is to explore serial sexual murder in terms of both theoretical and clinical parameters in an attempt to understand why these types of offenders commit the ultimate crime. We will also examine the similarities and differences between serial sexual murderers and typical rape offenders who do not kill their victims. Using real-life examples of well-known serial killers, we will compare the "theoretical" with the "practical": what happened, why it happened, and what we may be able to do about it. The authors of this chapter present two perspectives: (1) a developmental motivational view as to why serial killers commit these homicides and (2) implications for treatment of violent offenders. To adequately present these perspectives, we must look at four distinct areas: (1) differentiating between the two types of lust murderers (i.e. rapists and sexual serial killers), (2) examining personality or lifestyle themes, (3) exploring the mind-body developmental process, and (4) treatment applications for violent offenders.

Definitions of Sexual Murder versus Serial Sexual Murder

Sex offenses can be viewed along a continuum, from non-contact or covert offenses, to contact or overt offenses. The ultimate contact offenses include sexual murder and serial killings that also result in cannibalism and necrophilia. The dynamics of one-time murderers are much different from those of serial sexual killers who commit repeated crimes as part of their offense pattern. The one-time murderer is governed by the situation or circumstances of the offense, while the serial killer maintains a continuous offense pattern with a "cooling-off" period between murders (Ressler 1992, 1997).

It is essential to differentiate between sexual serial murderers and serial rapists. Both are violent contact offenses. Proulx and colleagues (2002) found that in terms of personality profiles, rapists and sexual murderers have more similarities than differences. Ressler and colleagues (1988) found that both types of offenders often experienced childhoods of physical and emotional abuse, caretaker instability, and perceptions of unfair treatment within the family. In unique populations such as the United States armed forces, offenders who are incarcerated for sexual aggression against women report thoughts, behaviors and personality styles similar to civilian sexual serial killers. This problem has become exponentially compounded since the number of female U.S. service members has risen so rapidly in the past decade (Kohut 2004b). Proulx (personal communication with second author, April 2003) makes the crucial point that the differences between sexual murderers and rapists may lie in the situation where the offense took place and in the particular circumstances of the offense rather than in any underlying differences in offense-related thought process.

The Lifestyle of a Sexual Serial Killer

The "lifestyle" concept originated from Alfred Adler (1941) and expanded by Dreikurs (1950) and Mosak (1979). Lifestyle refers to the related themes and patterns of an individual's daily life, including behavioral patterns, personal characteristics, and life themes. Adler (1941) proposed that everyone has a distinct lifestyle pattern and serial killers are no exception. This chapter attempts to summarize previous observations about lifestyle themes, including those of serial killers. We can expand Adler's original concept to include ego states or contextualized behavioral patterns along with other commonly found personality themes easily identified in the lifestyle of serial sexual killers.

An examination of lifestyle themes includes dissociative ego states, antisocial traits, narcissistic traits, schizoid traits, and borderline personality traits. Sexual serial killers do not necessarily have all of these themes and/or personality traits, except for dissociative and ego-state phenomena. Likewise, the themes and traits may differ in degree and specificity. These were adapted from Carich and Adkerson (1995, 2003), Carich and Calder (2003), and Carich et al. (1996). The themes are discussed below.

In the commission of their crimes, serial killers appear to enter into dissociative states (Carich et al. 1996). Dissociation refers to a sense of detaching emotionally from current reality while also maintaining contact with external reality (Carich and Metzger 1999, 2004; Carich and Calder 2003; Lankton and Lankton 1983; Yapko 1984, 1995). Dissociative behaviors take the form of deviant fantasies and other forms of covert arousal. Hypnotic trance states occur when the offender exhibits intense concentration and is completely absorbed in the commission of his crime in which immediate awareness is temporarily suspended. The killer is usually oblivious to his external surroundings. This is not a psychotic state, however, but is simply a level of unconscious awareness. Dissociation is considered to be a form of hypnotic behavior because hypnosis or trance-like states do require some form of dissociation.

The trance state phenomena is similar to the concept of the "hidden observer," or the dissociative hypnotic behavior of a killer observing himself from an emotional distance or imagining himself engaged in some violent or deviant act while detached from his current surroundings (Yapko 1984). During confessions, treatment sessions, mental health evaluations, and court proceedings, many serial killers describe feeling "unreal" as they sexually assault and kill their victims, as if they were watching someone else commit the act. Again, this dissociation is not a psychotic state and therefore cannot be used as a legal defense. Chapter 2 in this book discusses the legal aspects of serial homicide, as well as the oft-tried (but seldom successful) "insanity defense." The killer maintains full knowledge that his acts are illegal, and he could conform his actions to the requirements of the law if he wished.

Watkins and Watkins (1997) took the concept of the hidden observer and developed ego states. The sexual serial killer's lifestyle involves ego state phenomena. For some offenders this involves generalized behavior such as that demonstrated by Ted Bundy whose crimes were committed in a definite identifiable pattern. Bundy even generalized his choice of victims (i.e. targeting girls with long hair parted in the middle). Other killers may literally switch ego states. The legendary classic example of this phenomenon is Robert Lewis Stevenson's *Dr. Jekyl and Mr. Hyde*, in which, through some ill-advised biochemical experiments, the "good" Dr. Jekyl unleashed his brutal and evil "dark twin," Mr. Hyde. Stevenson's portrayal of the dual nature of ego states was far ahead of its time; modern sexual serial killers like John Gacy maintained several conscious ego states including rapist, killer, family man, and community leader. In sexual serial murder, the killer's ego states contain well-defined sexual "scripts" or templates as described by Ward and Hudson (2000). Such templates are blueprints or internal maps and belief systems including core schemas that guide the killer's decision-making patterns. These offenses, then, can be viewed as a state of contextualized behaviors. The killer simply accesses state dependent memory, learning and behaviors (SDML&B) systems which may be in the form of ego states as defined by Rossi (1993, 2002). SDML&B systems appear to be the common denominator of dissociative trance behavior and Rossi (1993, 2002, 2003) emphasizes that behavior is *state dependent* and learned in contexts, or states. Learning is a psycho/physiological process housed in the hypothalamus limbic system of the brain. Thus, sexual scripts are ingrained throughout the mind-body process as discussed later in the chapter. Similarly, other lifestyle themes that play a role in deviant behavioral choices are state dependent. Other lifestyle themes include personality traits of antisocial, narcissistic, schizoid and borderline characteristics found in the DSM-IV-R (APA, p. 280). A brief description follows below.

Antisocial (Psychopathic) Themes

Without a doubt, sexual serial killers have antisocial, or psychopathic, lifestyle themes as indicated by their high level of violence and their seeming complete lack of conscience and empathy. Although there are different views of antisocial/psychopathic personality characteristics, the primary theme centers around lack of empathy and remorse; exploiting others to meet their own needs; victimization; manipulation; failure to learn from mistakes; and an uncanny ability to blend into society, chameleon-like, to avoid suspicion and capture (Carich and Calder 2003). Ted Bundy, John Gacy, Gary Ridgeway, (The Green River Killer), Albert DeSalvo, Ken Bianchi, and Angelo Buono (the Hillside Stranglers), and Jeffrey Dahmer all led rather "normal" exterior lives with no observable hints of the sexual psychopathology that lurked deep in their subconscious minds. Hare (1993) considered psychopathy and the antisocial personality disorder as separate entities, while others view these behaviors on the same continuum (Marshall, W.L. personal communication with first author, 2001). These behaviors occur in degrees. For example, not all serial killers engage in their psychopathic state continuously, while others do. Bundy earned a degree in psychology, attended law school, and worked as a volunteer in various political campaigns. Henry Lee Lucas and his sometime-partner Ottis Toole, however, could not hold jobs, made money by stealing, kept themselves well hidden from mainstream society, and heavily abused substances. Lucas regularly engaged in necrophilia with the bodies of his victims and, with Toole, sadistic homosexual behavior. Bundy, Ridgeway, and Dahmer also practiced necrophilia—the ultimate form of power and control.

Narcissistic Themes

Antisocial/psychopathic serial killers and sexual serial killers display significant degrees of narcissistic traits, being self-centered with marked feelings of entitlement (Carich and Adkerson 1995, 2003; Carich and Calder 2003). In addition to these two traits, other narcissistic themes of grandiosity (e.g. exaggerated vicious behavior and feelings superiority towards others, especially law enforcement officials who are unable to capture them). Charles Manson not only thought of himself as a gifted musician, he also managed to convince his followers that he was the new Jesus Christ, specifically referring to his last name and adopting the interpretation that he is "The Son of Man" (Bugliosi and Gentry 1974). This grandiosity is not the same thing as normal, healthy, realistic self-esteem. In reality, these killers typically feel quite inferior to others in a number of areas in life including their own "core" self-view. Thus, they compensate for their perceived inferiority by behaving as if they are superior to others, including their victims. These killers enjoy grabbing newspaper headlines and thrive on publicity. Many relish grandiose thoughts of outsmarting law enforcement. After his capture, Lucas stated that being a notorious serial killer is "just like being a movie star." He confessed to hundreds of murders and thoroughly enjoyed his notoriety. In reality, Lucas is thought to have killed only two people—his mother and his teenage girlfriend. Ottis Toole was convicted of another homicide. Law enforcement officials are certain that Toole's most infamous murder was that of six-year-old Adam Walsh, son of "America's Most Wanted" host John Walsh. Toole never confessed to this crime but thrived on tormenting the victim's family with innuendos about Adam's murder until his own death in prison of AIDS (CourtTV.com 2005; Walsh 1997).

Borderline Themes

Most serial killers have underdeveloped or dysfunctional emotional attachments to others (Carich et al. 1996). Their detachment in relationships is especially found all types of sexual offenders (Carich and Adkerson 1995, 2003; Carich and Calder 2003; Marshall 1996, 1999). Sexual serial killers have very superficial interpersonal relationships, at best. However, many seem to maintain an ability not to allow others into their deviant world. Many have families, raise children, and relate well to employers and fellow workers. Others, like Bundy, Richard Ramirez (The Night Stalker), and Tex Watson (Manson Family killer) go so far as to marry while they are incarcerated for murder. They are the ultimate emotionally distant partner, and seem to attract women who, for unfathomable reasons, choose this type of unstable, chaotic relationship. Gary Ridgeway, thought to be the most prolific serial killer in America with as many as ninety victims over a twenty-year period, married three times and had a son; all of these relationships were chaotic and superficial (Arts and Entertainment network series "Biography," 2005). Sexual serial killers display the borderline personality behavior of numerous dysfunctional relationships, poor mood regulation skills and persistently unstable affect, poor impulse control (inability to refrain from deviant behavior), and jealousy, possessiveness and a need to be in total control of relationships. Many killers form relationships via fantasies, and then project these fantasies onto their victims. These characteristics often seem to project a psychotic dimension, when in fact, most are not psychotic states.

Schizoid Themes

Sexual serial killers have significant intimacy defects and most are unable to form "connected" relationships. They may prefer to remain isolated and alienated from others. The schizoid theme consists of avoiding intimate relationships, and a flat, restricted affect. Bundy and Gacy, for example, had good external social skills that they used to lure their victims into trusting them. Conversely, Dr. Theodore Kaczynski (the Unabomber), isolated himself in a remote mountain shack in Montana. He had no neighbors, no telephone, and no automobile. Although he was highly intelligent, he had no social skills and never had meaningful, intimate relationships—not even with his mother and brother. Kaczynski even killed from a distance, sending his cleverly constructed explosive devices to carefully selected targets through the mail. Sexual serial killers with schizoid personality features tend to exploit their victims but never attempt to become emotionally intimate with them.

The Developmental Process: A Proposed Theory of Mind-Body Development

Life is a constant state of emotional and social evolution and development. All people, including sexual serial killers, remain within a developmental process. This section discusses this process including specific motivational factors that propel a killer to sexually assault and murder his victims. Several theoretical assumptions are discussed followed by an etiological developmental process entered through the mind-body SDML&B system. The premise of this chapter hinges upon these basic assumptions: constructivism, self-determination, teleogy, holism, and evolution.

Constructivism

This perspective is based on the view that people construct, or create, their own internal reality (Bateson 1978; Carich 1999b, 2002; Kelley 1963; Mahoney 2003; Rychlak 1981). Constructivism stems from Plato's idealistic philosophy in which external reality doesn't exist and Kant's critical realism in which external reality does exist—however, given the human perceptual filtering system, we may never know it (Rychlak 1981). Constructivism encompasses both individual and societal constructs. The latter refers to the constructed social realities created by groups of people. This concept is crucial to fully understanding the serial killer's motivations and developmental experiences and the symbolic meanings of their sexual assaults and homicides. Mahoney (2003) acknowledges the internal self-organizing processes along with the biological processes of the human system, including individual differences and our birthright of being able to make choices in our behavior. He points out that the principle of constructivism is that we are active participants in our own lives. We all make choices, and those choices make important differences in our lives and the lives of all with whom we are connected. Relationships, in Mahoney's viewpoint of constructivism, are critical to our development. Constructivism emphasizes the developmental process. Thus, sexual assaults and murders have different meanings and purposes among killers that highlight individual differences among offenders (Burgess et al. 1986; Egger 1990a).

Teleological Perspective

The teleological perspective proposed by Adler (1941) is that human behavior is goal-oriented and serves purposes within the system (Dreikurs 1950, 1967; Mosak 1979). This perspective encompasses purposeful, goal-oriented behavior; sexual assaults are goal-driven. This is evident in clinical work with offenders. For example, one offender related a theme or factor as to why he raped and killed his victims; he has a small penis and feared he would be rejected by a consensual sexual partner. Through sexual assault and homicide, this offender gets many of his need met besides sexual gratification (Carich and Calder 2003; Carich et al. 1996; Ward and Stewart 2003). Most of these needs involve power and control over their victims.

Self-Determinism

According to Adler (1941), this is a concept that emphasizes that individuals make conscious decisions and choices. Decisions to rape and/or murder are complex choices made at all levels of awareness, including a variety of experiential domains (Carich and Metzger 1999, 2004; Carich and Calder 2003). The act of entering a deviant cycle, accessing deviant sexually violent scripts and ego states requires a sense of decision-making. For example, a serial rapist told this chapter's first author that at night as he was driving down a street near his house, if he turned right he would go to his home, and if he turned left he would rape and possibly kill a victim. Fortunately for the intended victim, he turned right and went home. Another serial child molester and rapist of adolescents and adults consciously made a decision one night to rape or not when he spotted a female potential victim who was using the phone near a gas station. As she drove away, he decided that he would indeed kidnap and kill her. Again, this victim was spared when she left the gas station and unknowingly escaped her would-be killer. These offenders describe themselves and their behavior as "being on autopilot," but they are making both conscious and unconscious decisions.

Holistic View

This view encompasses the whole-person concept, including the mind-body process (Adler 1941; Dreikurs 1950, 1967; Keeney and Ross 1983; Mosak 1979). This view has been adapted to include sexual offenders and serial killers (Carich and Calder 2003; Longo 2002; Carich and Stone 1996). For many, deviance is only one part of themselves. Of course, other sexual offenders and killers are consumed with deviancy. Dennis Rader held jobs, had a family, and was very active in his church. People who thought they knew him were astonished when he was arrested as the BTK killer. Danny Rowling, however, was a drifter living in the Florida woods in a tent and was obsessed with thoughts of rape and murder (CourtTV.com 2005). The concept of "self" can be subdivided into experiential domains: the cognitive (perceptual) domain, the affective (mood) domain, the behavioral (overt activity) domain, the social (interpersonal) domain, the biophysiological (internal body processes) domain, and the contextual (environmental) domain. Emphasis in this chapter is placed on the mind-body connection along cognitive-affective domains involving the developmental encoding processes through developmental experiences.

Developmental Patterns and Processes

The premise of this chapter emphasizes developmental patterns. It is widely accepted that individuals and their social systems evolve through time (Erickson 1963; Carich 1985). Developmental processes are demarcated into patterns and tracks with stages arbitrarily assigned. Similarly, the serial killer moves through these evolutional processes and patterns. The typical sexual killer does not randomly simply decide to rape and murder; this decision requires a developmental process. Deviant offending patterns and processes emerge. Based upon clinical observations, serial killers offend in a pattern often referred to as cycles, pathways or processes (Carich and Stone 1996, 2001; Carich et al. 2001; Carich and Calder 2003; Laws 1995, 1999; Ward and Hudson 1998; Bays and Freeman-Longo 1990). These patterns can be demarcated into arbitrarily selected stages or specific behavioral steps. They evolve through time and incorporate developmental experiences. The serial killer's behavior can clearly be tracked. Both Dahmer and Ridgeway began to commit violent crimes while still in adolescence, beginning with the killing of animals. Ridgeway was an arsonist by the time he graduated from high school. In tracking the stages of these killers' developmental processes, it is clear that they both experimented with dealing in death as young men, graduating to full-blown sexual serial homicide in their twenties. Studying the violent forensic behavior in children that develops into antisocial psychopathology in adults, the term *superpredator* is often used in the vernacular to describe children who exhibit the "terrible three" traits of a conduct disorder in their early years: cruelty to animals, fire-setting, and bed-wetting. Whether or not early intervention with these children will deter them from developing violent behavior as adults is yet to be proven.

The Etiological—Telelogical Mind-Body Developmental Process

This process emphasizes the mind-body process via SDML&B systems described by Rossi (1993, 2002) and was applied to sexual offenders by Carich and Parwatikar (1992, 1996). This concept is the key to understanding the learning and decision-making processes. Etiological factors refer to both generic (global) and specific developmental events and experiences, while telelogical factors refer to specific needs, goals and purposes, otherwise known as motivational factors. As the serial offender develops or evolves through life, he/she experiences a number of developmental events and incorporates these internally through the mind-body process, or SDML&B systems.

The developmental perspective is supported by Burgess et al. (1986), who explain the role of these formative events: "The developing child encounters a variety of life events, some normative, and others non-normative.... One assumption regarding early traumatic events is that the child's memories of frightening and upsetting life experiences shape the child's developing thought patterns. The type of thinking that emerges develops structured, patterned behaviors that in turn help generate daydreams and fantasies." Burgess et al. (1986) maintain that traumatized children remain fixated on those events. "Early traumatic events such as direct sexual and physical abuse are influential in the child's social development ... concurrent with the abusive event, the child may experience a sustained emotional/physiological arousal level. When this sustained arousal level interacts with repetitive thoughts about the trauma, the child's perceptions and patterns of interpersonal relations may be altered." Female serial killer Eileen Wuornos was raped at an early age. Declaring herself to be a lesbian who hated men, she earned money through prostitution and ended up murdering her customers because she perceived that they had attempted to rape her. Her early sexual trauma resulted in the development of her perception that all men are bad, all men are rapists.

Developmental information is encountered, processed and interpreted by the sexual offender as he develops. Interpretations are guided by current frames of reference, based upon multiple levels of cognitive-emotional structures including beliefs and core schemas as described by Polaschek and Ward (2002). The filtering process, the intensity of the experience, determines the interpretation of the experience and defines various issues, needs and core beliefs. The interpretation of the experience leads to specific core issues and needs, and perhaps reframes core beliefs. Core issues stem from core schemas embedded in our internal "templates," sexual scripts with the SDML&B. A detailed view of this developmental process is found in Figure #1 on the following page. In this depiction, the offender encounters a developmental event. The following initial perceptions lead to an interpretation of the event. This interpretation forms an offender's current frame of reference, leading to core issues and needs. The current frame of reference can be altered, depending upon the magnitude or intensity of the experience.

The "fusion" process refers to the incorporation of deviant information associated with specific needs or issues. Coping strategies are the methods used by the offender to manage or regulate his behavior in relation to his needs. At some point, a cycle or pathway of deviance and offending is initiated, reinforced when needs are met, and maintained. It is thought that this entire process involves the SDML& B system.

This line of thought follows McFall's (1990) informational processing model as described by Polaschek and Ward (2002) regarding serial rapists. "There has been a modest amount of research focusing on what is arguably

Figure 1
Developmental/Motivational—Offending Dynamics

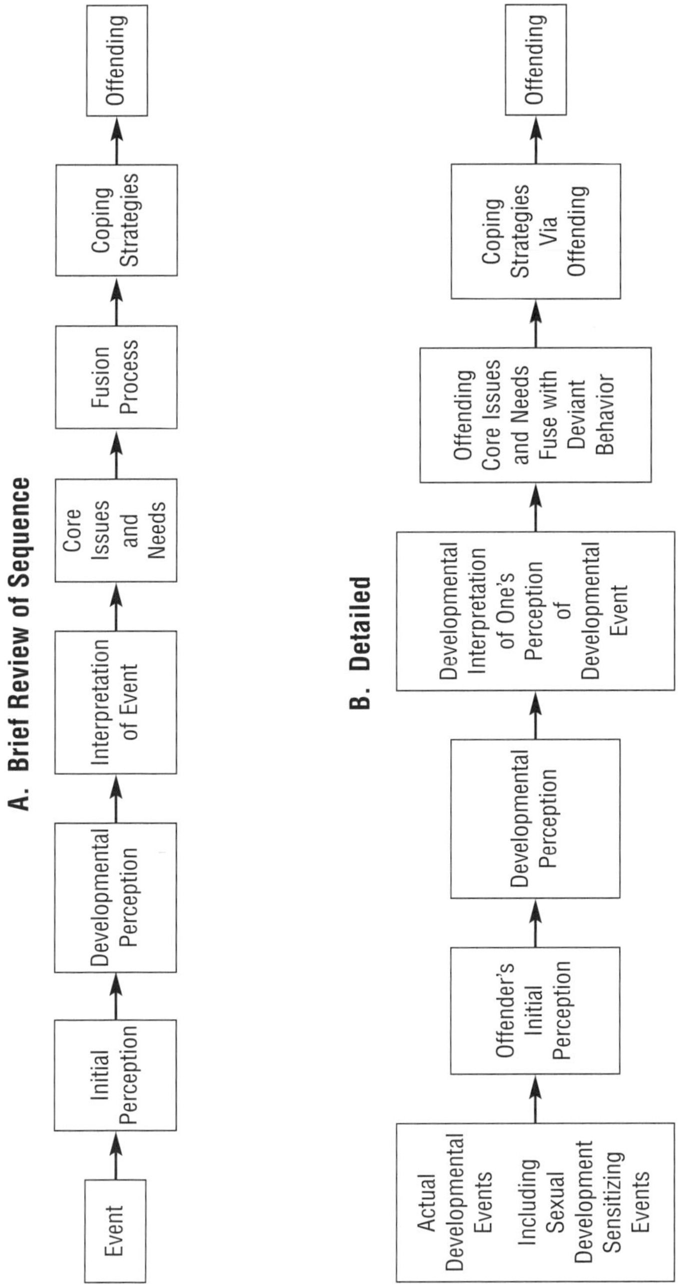

one of the most preliminary parts of an information-processing model: men's perceptions of women's heterosocial cues, or the process of receiving, perceiving and interpreting the relevant incoming sensory information in heterosocial situations (McFall 1990). Polaschek and Ward (2002) state,

> We argue that rapists' cognitive distortions emerge from underlying causal theories about the nature of their victims, themselves, and the world rather than stemming from unrelated, independent beliefs. These implicit theories function like scientific theories and are used to explain empirical regularities (e.g. other peoples' actions) and to make predictions about the world. They are relatively coherent and constituted by a number of interlocking beliefs and their component concepts and categories. We suggest that there are likely to be a number of schemas, or as we prefer to call them, implicit theories, that are causally related to individuals' sexually abusive actions toward women. We have addressed this issue recently, arguing that sexual offenders' cognitive distortions stem not from unrelated independent beliefs, but from underlying causal (implicit) theories that first develop in childhood.

In essence, Polaschek and Ward emphasize:

> Implicit theories develop in individuals from early in life as ways of organizing knowledge about their own experiences and behavior, as well as that of others. Most implicit theories are thought to be acquired in childhood, although they may develop over the life-span in response to the discovery of substantial contradictory evidence. Additionally, different cultural models and social norms can impact children's early learning environments and influence the way they understand and interpret the world.

Implicit theories define one's frame of reference and are held in unconscious levels. These theories can change, and do in fact seem to change, depending upon how rigidly an offender upholds the theory. Most serial killers appear to be locked into a particular theory. Throughout his adult life, Gary Ridgeway rigidly believed that prostitutes were "garbage" and deserved to die. Implicit theories are encoded through the mind-body connections or the SDML&B systems. In treatment, an offender's implicit theories are accessed, targeted and changed if the offender is to maintain long-term treatment effects. Implicit theories seem to include, at varying levels, the lifestyle themes mentioned earlier in this chapter.

Beech et al. (2005) explored the types of implicit theories held by sexual offenders. Polaschek and Ward (2002) identified five offense-related implicit theories that are common with both rapists and serial sexual murderers:

1. *Women are unknowable* and thus are deceptive in their communication with men.

2. *Women as sex objects.* Women exist to meet the sexual needs of men and constantly desire sex, even if it is coerced or violent.

3. *Male sex drive is uncontrollable.* By denying sex to men, women cause men's sexual drive to be beyond the offender's control.

4. *Entitlement.* Men are more powerful than women, and their needs are more important than women's.

5. *Dangerous world.* Since men live in a dangerous world, they need to control and dominate others.

More about these implicit theories is addressed in Chapter 5. The essential point made in this chapter is that implicit theories—underlying beliefs about the world—make a direct contribution to the thoughts and behaviors of sexual serial killers.

Mind-Body Developmental Encoding Process

The information processing system occurs at multiple levels of awareness through the SDML&B systems. These systems are housed in the hypothalamus limbic system of the brain (Rossi 1993, 2000, 2002). One proposal is that the sexual serial killer's deviant behavior is encoded through the SDML&B systems. A specific typology of development defining the etiology of aggressive behavior is illustrated in Table #1.

This typology includes general themes (ongoing life experiences and situations) and specific events or life experiences that can be traumatic and have

---

Table 1

TYPES OF THEMES OF DEVELOPMENTAL EXPERIENCES

1. *General Themes—ongoing situations, relationships, etc.*
2. *Specific Events—single life experiences or incidents.*
3. *Initial Sensitizing Events in the Deviancy.*
   a. Direct exposure—direct involvement, participation or observation (exposure) to the deviancy.
   b. Indirect exposure—indirect exposure and more involvement in the deviancy (participant-observer).
   c. Self-generated—deviant events that one generated or discover on one's own.

great impact. Until he was a teenager, Ted Bundy was told (and he believed) that his birth mother was his sister, and that his grandparents were his true birth parents. When Bundy discovered that his sister was in reality his mother and that he was born illegitimate, this event had a traumatic impact upon his ability to form genuine, empathetic relationships later in life. This may be viewed as the etiology of his violent behavior. Within these developmental life experiential themes, an offender becomes sensitized as he is exposed to deviancy.

This sensitization process may be due to direct exposure, observation from a distance, or random self-generated behavior. Life experiences are encoded into contextual memory states. Deviant patterns are engrained into stored memory or sexual scripts within an offender's internal template. The deep-seated core beliefs that form one's implicit theories of life support these deviant patterns. An offender accesses his implicit deviant theories and then behaves accordingly when "cycling" or committing crimes. Therefore, the serial killer accesses deviant states derived from sexual scripts and implicit theories. These killers, at an extreme level, seem to exclusively access deviant states, while other types of offenders may not.

A serial sexual killer learns to meet various needs from sexual aggression and violence. Needs or core issues stem from translating life experiences into one's own frame of reference. All people have issues and needs that stem from life experiences which, in healthy individuals, are met through socially acceptable means. Most people have life experiences that teach them to meet needs and core beliefs in non-aggressive ways. A violent offender learns to meet his needs through deviant behavior. Examples of the specific needs of such an offender include abandonment/acceptance/rejection issues, feelings of inferiority, poor self-esteem, lack of real intimacy with others, loneliness, power and control needs, desires for revenge, and a need for attention. Jeffrey Dahmer had such a poor sense of self-worth—as an alcoholic homosexual— and fears of abandonment and rejection that he killed, dismembered and ate his victims in an attempt to create love slaves that would never, ever leave him. The mere act of committing a sexual assault and/or homicide evokes a high level of adrenaline, thus reinforcing the process and false fulfillment of needs. At least, until the next time the offender's needs overwhelm him after a cooling-off period.

Mind-Body Process

Rossi (1993, 2002) proposes that the key mind-body processes occur through the hypothalamus limbic system of the brain. Information from the outside world is perceived and encoded within the brain through bio-molecular processes via the exchange of informational substances. Thus, learning occurs at all levels of awareness as information is processed and translated within one's frame of reference through Piaget and Inhelder's (1963) concept of accommodation and assimilation; thus incorporating new data into existing beliefs and changing current beliefs to include conclusions arrived at through new data. It's thought that most learning occurs within a psycho-bio-physiological state, thus creating state-dependent memory systems as information is perceived, interpreted, translated and stored into memory at multiple levels. The specific mind-body processes occur at molecular levels involving manipulation of the "housekeeping genes" (Rossi 1993). Although some researchers suggest that aggression stems from "hard-wired" structures within the brain (Hare 1993), this chapter's authors suggest that "soft-wiring" (nurture) interplays with "hard wiring" structures (nature) and this inter-relationship produces learning. Thus, the encoding process involves the interplay of both housekeeping and genetic genes to create the outcome.

Case Example: The clinical description of a pedophile child/adolescent rapist illustrates the concept of SDML&B. Rapist "Jack" had a dysfunctional childhood, complete with numerous negative life experiences including sexual molestation by his father and perceived abandonment by his family and peers. After completing a fourteen-year sentence for molesting his seven-year-old daughter, he was very proud of completing an associate degree in college. Upon returning to his parents' home one evening, he noticed there was a footprint on his degree certificate. He accessed and entered a rage state and blamed his now fourteen-year-old daughter. In fact, he intended to rape and kill her; he ripped her clothes off and trapped her in the bathroom. His daughter vomited out of fear and "grossed him out." Jack abruptly left the scene and ran down the street—the aggressive state had collapsed. Prior to the contemplated rape and murder, his apartment overlooked a playground that fed his deviant fantasies of raping children. Jack's thoughts and behavior has special relevance to the treatment of sexual offenders, including sexual serial killers.

Treatment Applications

The current treatment approach with sexual offenders is cognitive-behavioral group therapy. The authors have added the term "dynamic" to this approach, with emphasis on all experiential domains. This reflects a deeper, more intensive treatment approach that accesses and restructures the offender's implicit theories and underlying core schemas. This process typically occurs at intense emotional unconscious levels.

Amenability Issues

Many professionals view serial killers and psychopaths as untreatable, even with today's scientific technology and advances in treatment techniques. It is certainly true that some of these offenders cannot be reached due to their high level of deviant thoughts and behaviors. Clinical experience with this population indicates distinct differences between those that can be treated versus those who cannot includes the available level of internal resources incorporating inhibitions or barriers, their of motivation to change, their level of violence or psychopathy as indicated by past behavior, their victimology pattern (i.e. number of victims, types of victims, length of offending time, etc.), and their degree of psychopathology (i.e. the presence of psychosis, other personality disorders and paraphilias). To be successful in treatment and to avoid recidivism, the sexual serial killer must have the desire to stop his violent sexual homicides. Although, after apprehension and conviction, sexual serial killers are invariably confined to correctional institutions, it should not be assumed that their violent behavioral patterns will cease. They do not. If housed in general population, these offenders merely turn their sexual violence onto other prisoners whom they perceive as vulnerable, or even onto the correctional authorities who may be under-trained in how manipulative and dangerous these offenders are. Taxpayers whose dollars are spent to warehouse sexual serial killers for the rest of their lives often wonder, "Why bother to treat them? They'll never get out of prison." Thinking dispassionately, the answer is clear: although these offenders will never stalk our streets again, a maximum security correctional facility is one of the most expensive to maintain and dangerous communities in the world today. Untreated violent offenders pose a tremendous threat to other non-violent offenders who are amenable to rehabilitation, to the correctional support staff, and to the public at large when an escape is successful. On 4 November 2005, multiple murderer Charles Thompson escaped from death row in a Houston penitentiary. Thompson had only been at the facility for one week before he escaped. He managed to obtain civilian clothes and a phony ID badge, told the correctional staff that he was an attorney, and simply walked out of prison. Considering the extreme violence of his double murders, Thompson was certainly a threat to society and was captured a week after his escape (CourtTV.com 2005). Long ago we abandoned the concept of "prison colonies" such as Botany Bay (Australia), and Devil's Island in favor of more humane and civilized approaches to crime.

But this humanity comes with a price—paid by the American taxpayers—and consistently stirs up controversy about the death penalty as being "cruel and unusual punishment."

Treatment Parameters and Considerations

The authors of this chapter have direct clinical experience with the criminal justice system and with the violent offender population (adult and juvenile), including chronic/serial offenders of all sorts. In our experience, serial killers were placed into intensive sex offender treatment groups. These offenders were either civilly committed or had been sentenced by the justice system to extensive time in prison—including those who drew life sentences without parole. These treatment groups were highly charged emotionally and followed the key assumptions discussed earlier in this chapter as specific elements are targeted. These elements and methods of treatment are described by Carich and Calder (2003) and Carich and Mussack (2001).

Key Assumptions

The basic assumptions described earlier in this chapter apply to treatment methods commonly used with sexual offender rehabilitation programs (ATSA 2001; Carich and Calder 2003; Marshall and Eccles 1991; Marshall 1996, 1999, 2005; Marshall et al. 1999). Some of the key assumptions include self-determination and holistic views. Offenders are held completely accountable and responsible for their actions. There are conscious and unconscious choice points throughout the offending process, and these choices become the focus of treatment goals.

The holistic view allows the therapist to include the mind-body connection of the SDML&B systems and all other experiential domains within the treatment process. This includes accessing developmental deviant states, collapsing or restructuring existing core schemes and sexual scripts as well as implicit theories. To achieve and maintain long-term change, developmental life experiential states and related issues need to be accessed and re-coded. If successful at any level, the offender learns different interpretations of outside data (the re-coding of information) along with issue resolution. Therefore, an offender who utilizes available and newly developed resources can rebuild non-offending states. The offender's existing constructs or meanings within his life are altered into non-offending states.

This entire process directly involves accessing and changing existing SDML&B systems while developing new ones. The psycho-physiological processes are altered as old memories and experiences are de-coded and then re-coded. This is accomplished by targeting key elements or dynamic risk factors within the treatment process. A detailed treatment plan of this type was designed by Metzger and Carich (1999), Carich and Adkerson (2003), and Carich and Calder (2003). It is beyond the scope of this chapter to provide the details of treatment plans since they are unique to each offender. However, a list of necessary treatment elements includes:

1. Offense disclosure and acceptance of personal responsibility
2. Offense-specific cognitive restructuring
3. Offending process (assault cycle) and interventions
4. Victim empathy
5. Arousal control
6. Clinical core issue resolution
7. Social skills, interpersonal restructuring, and affective regulation skills
8. Lifestyle restructuring

These factors are supported in relevant literature (Calder 1999; Carich and Mussack 2001; Carich and Adkerson 1995, 2003; Carich and Calder 2003; Hanson and Harris 2001; Marshall and Eccles 1991; Marshall 1996, 1999; Marshall et. al 1999; Grossman 1985; Grossman et al. 1999; English 1998; Schwartz and Cellini 1995; Metzger and Carich 1999; Thornton 2002).

With the higher-level or "hard core" offenders (i.e. serial/chronic psychopathic personality disorders) and serial killers, the intensity of treatment it elevated in order to bring about a higher level of change in the behavior of the offender. "Change" is defined in terms of recovery based upon eight factors mapped in various treatment plans and recovery schemas (Carich 1999; Carich and Adkerson 1995, 2003; Carich and Calder 2003; Metzger and Carich 1999). To evoke change, several key points are emphasized in conjunction with the targeted elements.

Key Points

First, it's important to facilitate some level of internal motivation by the offender. "Motivation" is defined as the desire and commitment to stop offending (Carich 1999; Carich and Calder 2003). The higher the level of motivation, the more receptive the offender is to engage in the therapeutic process and make necessary changes to avoid recidivism. This process is enhanced by developing a good therapeutic relationship with the offender (Marshall 2005; Blanchard 1995).

The second key point is that the clinician needs to connect or develop rapport with the offender. There should be an acceptable level of professional bonding or attachment. The best strategies for developing timely rapport with an offender include motivational interviewing skills and approaches (Miller and Rollnick 1991, 2002) and utilizing Ericksonian approaches (Erickson et al. 1976; Lankton and Lankton 1983).

A related area to core schemas is motivating core issues and needs. The offender's vulnerabilities are further revealed, as his antisocial behavior begins to change. At the same time, the offender is held fully accountable for his behavior. Ultimately, the serial killer targets, and then changes, lifestyle behaviors while learning self-regulation and arousal control skills. He identifies his cycle and/or offending processes and develops effective interventions.

An important aspect of treatment is enhancing victim empathy and remorse. This is balanced with developing an appropriate self-concept. Within the intensive treatment process, the offender must take risks and develop adequate relationships based upon quality and true intimacy, thereby learning interpersonal and relationship skills.

The key task in treatment is "reaching" the offender, mobilizing his resources toward change, reducing deviancy while increasing appropriate behavior and teaching management skills. Treatment is a very long-term process, at best, and is viewed on a continuum, perhaps indefinitely. Again, we note that some sexual serial killers just cannot be therapeutically reached with our current practices and technologies; therefore he must be carefully managed in secure correctional centers.

Conclusion

Sexual homicide offenders are distinguished from non-sexual serial killers; for example, Jeffrey Dahmer committed sexually motivated murders, while Charles Starkweather killed, but did not sexually assault his victims during his infamous spree killings. Sexual serial killers are typically severely personality disordered and psychopathic to various degrees. These individuals are some of the most difficult to treat, and the vast majority of professionals in the forensic field will not attempt this type of treatment.

This chapter has examined the developmental process of the serial killer, and a mind-body developmental theory was outlined. Offenders journey through a developmental process just like any other person. By this process, along with soft- and hard-wiring processes, deviant behavior becomes encoded through the SDML&B system that is housed in the hypothalamic-limbic system of the brain. This creates the offender's deviant sexual scripts and implicit theories found in one's internal templates. Ward and Hudson (2000) describe templates and scripts that are consciously and unconsciously constructed of deep-seated inner belief, cognitive schemes and themes. They state "A third view construes 'scripts' as a set of rules for predicting, interpreting, responding to, and controlling a set of interpersonal meaningful scenes, for example, knowing how to respond appropriately during an argument with a partner in a restaurant. Finally, social scripts provide a template with which to structure fundamental social interactions and help individuals locate values, beliefs, and goals within a cultural context."

In terms of treatment, perhaps the most severe sexual serial killers could not benefit from treatment sufficiently to warrant their release from incarceration. However, to effect treatment, a therapeutic relationship with the offender is essential. This requires cohesive group involvement where there is a combination of support, challenges, and accountability. It is self-defeating if group members enable each other to continue deviant patterns of thought and behavior. The offender needs to be receptive to the treatment process since this opens up vulnerabilities within the offender. At this point, various necessary changes can be evoked and sustained. The underlining key point is that the offender must have internal motivation to change.

Chapter 4

Sexual Homicide, Serial Murder, and Lust Killing: Theoretical Integrations and Practical Limitations

Bruce A. Arrigo and Catherine E. Purcell

Introduction

In a recent volume titled *The Psychology of Lust Murder* we examined the role that paraphilias assume in sexual homicide and serial killing, arguing that existing theoretical typologies fail to adequately account for the significance of aberrant eroticism in the emergence of these criminal acts (Purcell and Arrigo 2006). Central to our analysis was the development of a more integrated model: one that assimilated the insights of the motivational (Burgess et al. 1986) and the trauma-control schemas (Hickey 2006b) respectively. At issue here were the explanatory and predictive properties of the synthetic paraphilic framework, as well as its capacity to deepen and extend our knowledge of lust murder and those offenders responsible for its commission. Several tables and figures were carefully constructed and the case of Jeffrey Dahmer was prominently featured, all of which demonstrated the considerable practical implications stemming from the proposed integrated typology. These implications were linked to police administration and management, criminal and clinical psychology, and law and public policy.

In this chapter, we return to the thesis of our book, providing a more summary description of its fundamental tenets. This exercise is useful in that it supplies a concise and cogent overview of the principal conceptual facets of our volume (cf. Arrigo and Purcell 2001). Moreover, this undertaking is worthwhile in that it succinctly addresses the absence of any systematic theory construction in the extant literature on the subject (e.g., Hickey 2006b). Accordingly, several observations on the phenomena of paraphilia and lust murder are delineated. Next, the essential features of the motivational and trauma-control models are specified. We then present our integrated framework: a model that incorporates the most salient components of the sexual homicide and serial murder typologies. As we demonstrate, this synthesis furthers our regard for the onset, progression, and maintenance of pathologically deviant sexuality, including its role as a motive underscoring the crime of lust murder. The chapter concludes by drawing attention to the sort of theoretical and related work that remains, noting full well the limits to the proposed integrated typology. Throughout the ensuing commentary, in-text citations are deliberately kept to a minimum. Our goal is to spotlight the summary descriptions of the theory work on lust murder. For more detailed referencing, readers are encouraged to review the texts and articles listed at the end of this chapter.

Background on Paraphilia and Lust Murder

Paraphilias are unique, bizarre, and, often, violent in nature. Moreover, they constitute an exclusive category of sexual offending. Expressions of aberrant eroticism are diverse and manifold, and many of them are criminal in nature. In his most recent research on the subject, Eric Hickey devised a classification system concerning this phenomenon (Hickey 2006b). Five such categories were noted and included the following: (1) nonviolent, physical paraphilia, (2) nonviolent, nonphysical paraphilia, (3) sadistic paraphilia, (4) masochistic paraphilia, and (5) sadomasochistic paraphilia.

Deviant sexual behavior exists on a continuum; they vary in severity from mild, to moderate, to severe. The average number of paraphilias is 4.8 per person (Holmes and Holmes 2002). Multiple paraphilias are often found in an individual; however, one expression of aberrant sexuality typically becomes dominant until it is replaced by another such manifestation. On the most extreme end of the paraphilic continuum is "erotophonophilia," commonly referred to as lust murder. This is a crime committed by males.

Erotophonophilia is the acting out of deviant behavior by means of brutally and sadistically killing the victim to achieve ultimate sexual satisfaction (e.g., Douglas et al. 1995; Simon 1996). Lust murderers are likely to repeat their offenses, thereby making them serial in disposition. Mutilation of body parts, especially the genitalia, is a standard feature of this paraphilia (Hickey 2006b).

To date, sadistic sexual homicide has typically been viewed as a perplexing phenomenon. It has defied efforts at useful explanatory and predictive models, despite being based on some theory-driven conceptualization for the behavior. However, we know thus far that fantasy is a key component to understanding and interpreting lust murder (MacCulloch et al. 1983; Schlesinger 2003). This notwithstanding, a cogent theoretical formulation regarding the role of paraphilia as a driving force or motive for explaining this form of sexual criminality has mostly eluded researchers.

Studies contributing to our conceptual understanding of sadistic sexual homicide include the work of MacCulloch and colleagues (1983), Burgess and colleagues (1986), and Hickey (2001). Earlier research by DeRiver (1949) on the sexual criminal and Brittain (1970) on the sadistic murderer are also noteworthy. In their respective ways, they established some of the important conceptual groundwork for those investigations that followed.

MacCulloch and his colleagues were instrumental in demonstrating how a pattern of sadistic fantasies propels sexual criminals into compulsive acts of behavior, first in the form of fantasy and then in the form of assaultive conduct. Their findings suggest that when erotic arousal is involved in the sadistic image, offenders are increasingly motivated to act out their violent thoughts and images understood in terms of habitual behavior. This repetitive conduct, sexual and violent in nature, is linked to conditioned responses and *cognitive* interpretations regarding the fantasies themselves.

Extending the cognitive model of MacCulloch et al. (1983), the Federal Bureau of Investigation introduced a *motivational* dimension to sexual homicide (Burgess et al. 1986; Douglas et al. 1995). They argued that fantasy was an internal driving mechanism for serial acts of sexual violence. However, they also pointed out how the interaction of critical personality traits and cognitive mapping processes were integral to generating the sexual images that produced violent behavior.

Unlike MacCulloch et al. (1983) who addressed fantasy, thoughts, and impulses and Burgess et al. (1986) who focused on sexual homicide per se, Hickey's (2001) work more squarely considered serial murder. Mindful of the previous literature on cognition and motivation, Hickey assessed how certain predispositional factors and facilitators led some individuals to engage in serial murder. His model demonstrated how psychological and/or physical *traumatic events* occurring in the formative years of a person's life could function as triggering mechanisms where increasingly violent fantasies, fueled by facilitators (e.g., alcohol, pornography, drugs), produced homicidal behavior (see also, Egger 2002; Giannangelo 1996).

Interestingly, none of the preceding models examines lust murder with any appreciable degree of specificity. This notwithstanding, we contend that the previous work on sexual homicide and serial murder is assimilable, especially for the development of an integrated model that accounts for the etiology of paraphilia and the manifestation of its extreme variant lust murder. In particular, the motivational and the trauma control schemas possess key components suggestive of a viable and useful synthesis. Clearly, both typologies discuss some aspects of the paraphilic process as a system of behavior. However, neither of them offers a detailed conceptualization of aberrant sexuality, especially when expressed through the crime of erotophonophilia.

The Motivational Model

The Federal Bureau of Investigation conducted a study looking at the motivational factors of thirty-six sexual murderers and presented a five-phase model explaining how various elements influence an offender's conduct (Burgess et al. 1986). The motivational model principally focused on psychosocial and cognitive factors. The distinct features of this typology are described in the following subsections.

Ineffective Social Environment

Burgess and his colleagues identified several factors that contributed to the social environment of an individual. Specifically, they examined the developmental aspects of one's early childhood and the quality of life found within the kin structure. They argued that perceptions of one's surroundings and the family unit were important dimensions that underscored a child's generally healthy (or unhealthy) maturation. Moreover, the nature of one's attachments to parents, parental surrogates, and intimates were pivotal to how an individual eventually related to and valued others, as well as the social order. In the Burgess et al. (1986) study, all of the subjects either failed to bond with their primary care providers as children and/or developed selective and limited attachment styles. These ineffective social bonds contributed to the child's negative appraisal of reality, as well as his cognitive distortions concerning sexuality.

Formative Events Child/Adolescent

According to Burgess et al. (1986), there are three distinguishing elements that can influence the formative events in one's childhood and adolescence. These components include trauma, developmental failure, and interpersonal breakdown. Each of these notions is briefly enumerated, consistent with the motivational model.

Traumatic events can either be "normative" or "non-normative" in orientation. Normative events consist of such things as illness, divorce, or death, and occur as a function of ongoing, routine life. Non-normative experiences involve such things as physical, psychological or sexual trauma that directly or indirectly affect the child. These encounters are not consistent with ongoing, routine life. Burgess and his colleagues argued that, in combination with an ineffective social environment, the child often felt unprotected by and confused about the non-normative events he or she experienced.

Developmental failure also contributes to the formative events of childhood or early adolescence. A collapse occurs when the quality of the relationship between the youth and the primary caregiver is negative in scope and content. Under these conditions, the child is unable to bond with the parent or parental surrogate, resulting in strained or absent social attachments. As such, the adolescent feels psychologically rejected and emotionally deprived.

Following the motivational model, interpersonal breakdown is the third factor that helps anchor the nature of one's formative childhood or young adolescence. Interpersonal breakdown refers to the inability of the primary care provider to serve as a suitable, positive, and prosocial role model for the child, particularly during the course of the youth's upbringing. Typically, this is manifested in the parent's or parental surrogate's lack of sustained and meaningful involvement in the adolescent's life. Moreover, if the child's home environment is one in which violence is experienced, "the aggressive acts may become associated with the inappropriate sexual behavior of the adult caretaker" (Burgess et al. 1986, p. 264).

Patterned Responses to Formative Events

In the motivational model, patterned responses follow the presence of formative events, and are comprised of critical personality traits and cognitive mapping processing. When these components interact, they generate fantasies or imaginative constructions of oneself, others and situations. The pattern that emerges (often ritualistic and compulsive) signifies how the person copes with or adapts to the formative events, thereby contributing to one's sense of childhood or early adolescence.

Personality traits can either be positive or negative. Positive personality traits are a result of a maturation process in which the youth engenders feelings of security with, autonomy from, and trust in others, ultimately enabling the establishment of healthy, productive relationships.

Conversely, negative personality traits emerge when the developing child is unable to establish or has difficulty maintaining prosocial emotional attachments with others. If the attenuated (or failed bonding) is unresolved, the maturing adolescent is ill equipped to approach others in a confident manner, thereby increasing the likelihood of social isolation. Propelling this social isolation are increasingly intense feelings of frustration, disappointment, rejection, and anger toward others in one's physical universe and toward the social order more generally. These negative and cynical assessments fuel one's steady withdrawal into virtual anonymity and aloneness.

Social isolation enables one to rely on fantasy. Imaginary representations (of oneself, others and situations) are a substitute for the human encounters the individual simply cannot form. Social isolation, coupled with deep-seated anger and hostility, interact in the form of fantasy and hostility. Indeed, the individual is able to relate to others only through the use of one's (elaborate) image-based system. Thus, illusory, rather than real, experience "becomes the primary source of emotional arousal, and that emotion is a confused mixture of sex and aggression" (Burgess et al. 1986, p. 265).

Cognitive mapping is the second component that informs the patterned responses stemming from formative events in a child's life. Cognitive mapping functions as a filtering system where the individual interprets new information and gives meaning to past (traumatic) events that occurred in the youth's life. This process consists of daydreams, fantasies, nightmares, and thoughts, possessing a strong visual component. Common themes located within these intensely experienced images are power, control, dominance, revenge. In the extreme, they consist of violence, mutilation, rape, torture, and death (Hickey 2006b; Simon 1996). During the period of cognitive mapping, the fantasy symbolizes the profound lack of control the individual experiences over both the intra-psychic and external dimensions of his every day reality. Thus, escaping into this pseudo-existence (i.e., images of power, revenge, and death) enables one to be erotically stimulated. Moreover, this arousal reduces the tension traceable to isolation, aloneness, and helplessness the individual might otherwise embody or exhibit.

Actions Toward Others

Behavioral patterns of children, adolescents, and adults reflect their private, inner worlds. The motivational model fully endorses this notion, demonstrating its salience in relation to sexual murderers. Specifically, as Burgess et al. (1986, p. 266) noted, the behavioral patterns of their subjects indicated that in their "internal worlds [they] were preoccupied with troublesome, joyless thoughts of dominance over others."

Troubling or adverse thoughts such as those just mentioned manifest themselves at various stages along the developmental continuum. In childhood, they are expressed through negative play, cruelty towards animals, fire-setting, property damage, and a genuine disregard for others. In adolescence, these cognitions assume the form of delinquent and criminal conduct and consist of such actions as burglary, arson, assault, rape, and non-sexual murder. In adulthood, the progression of these thoughts is more sadistic and violent both in orientation and scope. They include such behaviors as rape, murder, necrophilia, and cannibalism (Egger 2002; Holmes and Holmes 2002).

Following the motivational model, a failure to identify, intervene, and resolve early childhood expressions of violence leads to future expressions of abusive behavior that grow in severity and intensity. Burgess et al. (1986) maintained that if a child was not held accountable for his early displays of violence, the behavior would merely be reinforced. Thus, the absence of establishing consequences in the face of destructive behavior served to prolong and/or fuel the disturbing conduct. These investigators argued that children engaged in such activities experienced a more difficult time establishing meaningful and genuine friendships. Thus, as they concluded, when transitioning into adolescence (and adulthood), these individuals failed "to develop positive empathy and to control [their] impulses" (Burgess et al. 1986, p. 267).

Feedback Filter

The term feedback filter refers to the way in which an individual reacts to and evaluates his actions toward himself and others. To be clear, the context in which a person responds to and assesses the surrounding milieu does affect his future behavior. The individual justifies his actions, analyzes behavioral errors, "and makes ... mental correction[s] in order to preserve and protect the internal fantasy world, and to avoid restriction from the external environment" (Burgess et al. 1986, p. 267). As such, the person's imaginary world escalates, particularly in terms of arousal state, feelings of power, and dominance and control. An increased knowledge of how to avoid detection, apprehension, and punishment is also evident. Each of these factors is assimilated into and accommodated by the self-and-society schema of the individual.

The Trauma Control Model

Hickey (1997, 2001) proposed a trauma control framework as an explanation for the crime of serial murder. Interestingly, his research utilized several aspects identified in the motivational model on sexual homicide. In addition, though, Hickey examined certain predispositional factors and facilitators, arguing that they influenced an individual's behavior resulting in repetitive acts of killing. In what follows, the specific features of the trauma control typology are succinctly described.

Predispositional Factors

According to Hickey, some serial killers are known to have certain predispositional factors that shape or impact their conduct. Typically, these are biological, sociological, and/or psychological in nature. These factors can function independently or in some interactive, combinatory fashion. The extra Y chromosome in males is an example of a biological factor that, in some instances, can contribute to violent behavior. The presence of mental illness is an instance of a psychological factor that, if manifested in the form of a personality order (e.g., schizophrenia) can contribute to aggression, hostility, and crime. The existence of a dysfunctional home environment is an illustration of a sociological factor that, in some adolescents, can increase the likelihood of negative or destructive behavior occurring during the formative years of one's life.

Traumatic Events

Hickey (2001) asserted that predispositional factors could amount to traumatizations. Moreover, when experienced during the formative years of one's life, the disturbance was more likely to be exacerbated by social and environmental issues (e.g., family discord, marital strife). Both the trauma control and the motivational models respectively address the debilitating consequences stemming from adolescent abuse caused by an adult caretaker (e.g., neglect, abandonment, rejection). Indeed, as Hickey (1997, p. 87) noted, "the child or teen feels a deep sense of anxiety, mistrust, and confusion when psychologically or physically [harmed] by an adult."

Low Self-Esteem/Fantasies

Other expressions of trauma can include interpersonal failure, hopelessness, and helplessness, as well as ostracism in school and exclusion from social groups and/or activities. When young children encounter profoundly disappointing sentiments and experience thoroughly upsetting events early in their psychological development, feelings of inadequacy, self-doubt, low self-esteem, and worthlessness are engendered (Moorman 2003). Fantasy and daydreaming become substitutes for the social relationships adolescents have difficulty cultivating because of their poor social identity and depleted self confidence (Bader 2003). This aspect of the trauma control typology is consistent with the patterned response factor found in the motivational model.

Dissociation

When children experience psychological or physical trauma during their formative maturation and when they are unable to effectively confront and positively cope with the shock or pain that ensues, they may perceive themselves and their surroundings in a distorted way (e.g., Kennerley 2000). Serial murderers want others to believe that they maintain complete control over their thoughts, desires, impulses, and actions. Instead, they are socially restricted and morally limited. Under these circumstances, image and illusion become the only realities that sustain them. Moreover, following the trauma control schema, it is also common for the individual to suppress Real (or perceived) debilitating events to the point where one is unable to recall or remember them. This is often referred to as "splitting off," or "blocking out" the experience. In other words, the murderer carries out the homicide in an altered state of consciousness, unaware of his own actions. This, then, is the phenomenon of dissociation.

Trauma Reinforcers

Hickey (1997, p. 87) observed that "childhood trauma for serial murderers serves as a triggering mechanism or reinforcer, resulting in an individual's inability to cope with the stress of certain events, whether they are physical, psychological, or a combination of traumatizations." An example of a triggering factor is rejection, stemming, perhaps, from the unrequited displays of affections showered upon a girlfriend, or the intense and caustic work-related criticisms emanating from a boss. When the individual experiences the rejection, the person may internalize the feeling, may become immobilized, and may be unable to cope with it in a constructive manner. In these instances, the person retreats psychologically into his fantasy world, often embracing cynical and negative sentiments, until finding comfort and relief from the (sadistic and sexual) images that subsequently are conjured.

Facilitators

Throughout the course of the trauma control process, the offender immerses himself in facilitators (e.g., alcohol, drugs, pornography). Over time, they can have a desensitization effect on one's behavior. Moreover, when habitually utilizing facilitators, the individual's experience is comparable to the addiction process. This process consists of three stages. The first of these is dependency. This is similar to the phenomenon of addiction encountered by those who are compulsive substance abusers. The second phase is escalation. During this period, the person's "appetite for more deviant, bizarre, and explicit sexual material is fostered" (Hickey 1997, p. 89). The third stage is desensitization. Within this phase, the individual becomes immune to the graphically violent and degrading nature of the pornography. Thus, given its failed stimulating effect, the offender then acts upon the imagery into which he has engulfed himself.

Increasingly Violent Fantasies

Traumatic events occurring in the formative years of a child's development can adversely influence one's perception of the world, as well as the individual's developing sense of self. Fantasy and daydreaming become a refuge from the world in which one lives: a social environment fraught with painful and debilitating rejection, producing feelings of isolation, despair, and helplessness. When coupled with the experience of dissociation, stemming from one's trauma reinforcers, and the various facilitators that fuel one's (sexually sadistic) imaginary constructions, a synergistic and potentially lethal effect materializes. This synergistic outcome is the presence of increasingly violent fantasies that can grow in duration, frequency, and intensity.

Homicidal Behavior

According to Hickey (2001), the experience of killing may generate new images of injurious behavior. Each act of violence is an attempt to satisfy totally and completely the fantasy of the perpetrator. Generally speaking, when the serial murderer experiences rejection, criticism, or the lack of personal power, the act of killing in and of itself leaves the offender feeling relieved as well as in control over his life. Moreover, the rejection essentially acts as a catalyst, triggering feelings of depression and low self-esteem in which the assailant relies on his increasingly violent fantasy. These images compel the person to engage in progressive displays of aggression and hostility, including the serial act of homicide.

The Integrated Model

The elements constituting the integrated framework are presented in a way that explains the development and progression of sexually deviant behaviors and illustrates how they work as a process, sustained by several factors comprising the paraphilic system itself. Thus, the model conceptually describes both the etiology of this phenomenon, as well as its essential disposition. We note further that a feedback loop is described. This illustrates how paraphilias manifest themselves, reinforce existing fantasies, and progress and cycle back into the overall self-generating process.

Formative Development

This initial dimension of the synthetic schema functions as the foundation upon which paraphilic behaviors originate. Formative development refers specifically to childhood and early adolescent experiences. Thus, consistent with the explanations provided by Burgess et al. (1986) and Hickey (1997, 2001), one's formative development significantly impacts the manner in which one appropriately and successfully experiences psychosocial adjustment throughout the lifecourse. All three models examine sociological, environmental, interpersonal and biological risk factors. Two interdependent concepts, essential to the emergence and maintenance of the paraphiliac, further specify how the formative development component of the integrated typology operates. These include predispositional factors and traumatic events.

Predispositional Factors

Research indicates that certain biological factors influence paraphilic behavior (Schlesinger 2003). For example, Money (1990, p. 27) explained that the cause of all sexual aberrations, particularly sexual sadism, was "due to a disease in the brain which affect[ed] the centers and the pathways that [were] responsible for sexual arousal, mating behavior, and reproduction of the species." This perspective examines how that region of the brain known as the limbic system is responsible for predation and violence in defense of both one-self and the species. Moreover, Money (1990, p. 28) noted that with the disease of sexual sadism, "the brain [was] pathologically activated to transmit messages of attack simultaneously with messages of sexual arousal and mating behavior." What this suggests, then, is that paraphilias are constituted by certain predispositional factors (e.g., sociological, psychological, biological) that can, in some instances, produce erotically sadistic and serially aggressive conduct. In the extreme, these tendencies can give rise to homicidal behavior.

Traumatic Events

Studies on the phenomenon of lust murder demonstrate that the early years of psychological maturation and adjustment are crucial to establishing the personality structure of the offender (e.g., Holmes and Holmes 2002; Douglas et al. 1995). Indeed, it is unusual for this assailant to come from a nurturing family environment devoid of abuse, alcoholism, drugs, or other factors that could cause considerable childhood pain and suffering (Palermo and Farkas 2001). Thus, consistent with Burgess et al.'s (1986) and Hickey's (1997) assessment of distressing events, it follows that sexual deviance originating, in part, from inadequately addressed or inappropriately resolved traumatic life circumstances (occur during the impressionable period of one's development) can adversely effect childhood and adolescent maturation.

Low Self-Esteem

Events occurring in the formative stage of the lifecourse are critical to creating a solid basis on which a child can develop a positive self-image and learn prosocial behavior. The largely dysfunctional background of the paraphiliac mitigates this possibility. The motivational and trauma control models acknowledge the consequence of traumatic events in an adolescent's life. Additionally, they recognize how negative personality traits, self-doubt, and social isolation act as catalysts for the reproduction of violent fantasy. The integrative typology similarly endorses the emergence of low self-esteem as emanating from such troubled (psychological, sociological, and/or biological) circumstances.

The distressed child is likely to experience a deep-seated sense of personal failure and a genuine lack of regard for others and the society from which he feels rejected. Ultimately, these sentiments interfere with the child's ability to form positive and healthy attachments with others. Consequently, daydreaming and fantasy become stand-ins for the social relationships the maladjusted individual is incapable of forming.

Early Fantasy and Paraphilic Development

A cyclical conceptualization of aberrant sexuality is unique to the integrated model. Specifically, the framework focuses on the presence of several factors occurring simultaneously, essentially producing a synergistic effect. Social isolation arising concurrently with the early development of sexualized fantasy mobilizes and initiates the paraphilic system. Eventually, however, this mobilization becomes both self actualizing and self sustaining. Imaginary configurations of self, others, and situations; compulsive masturbation; and facilitators—along with sexually deviant stimuli (e.g., fetishes, unusual objects, sadistic and erotic rituals)—function to reify the paraphilic process. The fantasies progress in intensity and severity, especially when the individual fails to experience arousal and/or orgasm.

Admittedly, it is difficult to ascertain the exact trajectory under which an individual appropriates sexually deviant stimuli and engages in erotically sadistic behavior. However, fetishes have been described as symbolic links to persons of importance in the life of a sexual killer (e.g., Egger 2002; Hickey 2006a; Simon 1996). A number of theorists suggest that a fetish possesses some quality associated with an individual the offender was closely involved with during childhood (e.g., Bancroft 1985; Hensley and Tewksbury 2003). This significant other is both loved and needed; however, the individual is also responsible for the adolescent's traumatization (Holmes and Holmes 2002; Palermo 2004). The analysis implies that in the formative years of the offender's life, he made a connection between the paraphilic stimulus and a traumatic event.

Paraphilic Process

As a unique component of the integrated conceptual model, the paraphilic process illustrates how aberrant sexuality functions as a system of intensifying behaviors. Moreover, the paraphilic process is cyclical and consists of several mutually interactive elements. These elements or factors consist of: (1) paraphilic stimuli and fantasy; (2) orgasmic conditioning process; and (3) facilitators. Each of these elements is briefly explained.

*Paraphilic stimuli and fantasy.*The research undertaken by MacCulloch and colleagues (1983) found that the sadistic fantasies of their subject pool (sexual offenders) experienced difficulty in both social and intimate relationships at a young age. These difficulties affected their self-esteem. Consequently, social isolation and reliance on imaginary constructions surfaced. Over time, these images became more violent and erotic. Assorted fetishes, rituals, and/or unusual and sexually charged objects employed as stimuli were incorporated into their elaborate fantasy systems. The repetitive and routinized nature of these constructed images furnished a sense of personal relief from the internal failures the assailants experienced. The felt sexual arousal, in conjunction with the sadistic fantasy, reinforced each other by means of classical conditioning. The conditioning increases the likelihood of escalation and habituation. Thus, the conditioning model of MacCulloch and his associates explains not only the strength and permanence of sadistic fantasies in abnormal personalities, but their progression in content from non-sexual to sexual as well. We contend that this analysis substantiates the notion of a paraphilic process in which ongoing sadistic and erotic behaviors are featured.

As such, fantasy is very influential in facilitating the paraphilic process. Indeed, the hallmark of a lust murder is the association between sex and aggression (Hickey 2006b). The assailant's internal image-based system reflects themes of power, domination, exploitation, revenge, molestation, degradation, and the humiliation of others. These themes are sustained through one's reliance on the sexually deviant stimuli.

Orgasmic conditioning process. Compulsive masturbation enables the individual to experience a sexually satisfying result. The person fantasizes and rehearses the paraphilia and then masturbates to the point of orgasm. This is a conditioning process in which the sexual deviant eventually loses all sense of normality. He depends on the paraphilic fantasy for both erotic stimulation and felt pleasure. Initially, a person might experience "normal" paraphilias; however, as the nature and content of the fantasy becomes increasingly violent and erotic (in order to sustain arousal and climax), the paraphilias progress in intensity, frequency, and duration.

Facilitators. The use of drugs, alcohol, and pornography are important components to the paraphilic process. Hickey's (1997, 2001) trauma control model on serial murder examined the use of these facilitating agents in relation to serial murderers. Investigations of sexual homicide have reached similar conclusions (e.g., Douglas et al. 1995; Holmes and Holmes 2002). The paraphiliac becomes firmly entrenched in a cycle of addiction, experiencing dependency and craving more of the stimulus for erotic gratification. The reliance on these enabling agents escalates until the person becomes desensitized to the facilitator's effect. In these instances, the paraphiliac may act out his erotically charged fantasies, engaging in extreme forms of criminality, including lust murder, to experience sexual arousal or relief.

Stressors. The integrative model proposes that triggering factors (e.g., rejection, isolation, ridicule) are stressors, constraining or thwarting one's capacity to adequately cope with the strain of everyday life. These stressors are akin to Hickey's (1997, 2001) trauma reinforcers, making it impossible for the individual to deal effectively with routine conflict or strife. Burgess et al. (1986) described the manner in which the offender was motivated to respond to circumstances based on the person's cognitions. Depending on the nature and severity of the triggering mechanism, the individual might experience a momentary loss of control. Indeed, the stressor might activate childhood trauma, rekindling the negative and debilitating feelings associated with the traumatization. The triggering effect then cycles back into the paraphilic process of behavior by way of a feedback loop. The behavior is sustained by masturbation, facilitators, and fantasy. In extreme cases, the response to the stress manifests itself in erotic and sadistic conduct, including erotophonophilia.

Behavioral Manifestations

The feedback loop has the potential to escalate into behavioral manifestations, if the person is compelled to actualize his sexually sadistic images. By enacting the paraphilic fantasy and stimuli, the individual attempts to satisfy, complete, and reify his illusions. The sexual deviant experiences an exhilarating rush of bodily satisfaction, as well as an increased need for stimulation, each time the behavior is inaugurated. The behavior, whether criminal or otherwise, functions as a reinforcer, and sequences back into the fantasy system.

Both the motivational and trauma control models depict this process. The former focuses on the offender's need to evaluate his actions toward others and toward one's self by way of a feedback filter (Burgess et al. 1986). The latter specifies how the imaginary world of the individual escalates, generating new and sustaining existing illusions (Hickey 2001).

Increasingly Violent Fantasies

As the fantasies become increasingly violent in nature, the paraphilic stimuli also progress in intensity, duration, and frequency. Each time an individual carries out the erotic and sadistic fantasy and stimuli through criminal behavior, the need for increased stimulation becomes apparent. This need for continued violent arousal is a part of the paraphilic feedback loop. Thus, it cycles back into the process accordingly.

The trauma-control model specifically designates an increasingly violent fantasy component when explaining the behavior of serial killers. We contend that it essentially serves the same function as outlined in the integrated paraphilic typology. The motivational model also supports our theoretical analysis. It accounts for increasingly violent imagery by examining the actions-toward-others and feedback filter components.

Practical Limitations and Future Directions

The behavioral and social science literature remains mostly in its infancy when engaging in theory construction and model making relative to the phenomenon of lust murder. While the proposed integrated typology certainly moves this underdeveloped field appreciably forward, several shortcomings within the paraphilic synthetic framework are noted. In this final section, these deficiencies are delineated. By succinctly specifying them, the aim is to encourage researchers to undertake more systematic inquires. This sort of task is most assuredly needed, especially as society endeavors to understand the etiology of aberrant sexuality, the crime of erotophonophilia, and those responsible for such criminality.

Confusion within the Literature

First, the extant research on sadistic, sexual, and serial murder is not clearly demarcated. In fact, considerable confusion within and conflation among these offense categories is found throughout the pertinent literature. For example, theses distinct crimes are typically classified as types of murder without a systematic assessment of their unique as well as similar components (e.g., Douglas et al. 1995; Hickey 2006b; Holmes and Holmes 2002). Admittedly, while an assessment of murder stemming from and motivated by increasingly violent forms of aberrant sexuality specifies the inherent problem with this practice (especially on a theoretical level), the integrated model does not supply any further elucidation regarding these separate forms of homicide. In other words, the proposed synthetic framework does not indicate how the paraphilic process is uniquely implicated in sadistic killing, sexual murder, or serial homicide. This is a shortcoming, particularly when noting the fact that sadistic deviance, predatory aggression, violent sexuality, and serial conduct are all underlying facets regarding the psychology of lust murder.

This notwithstanding, the issue reviewed in this chapter is whether an integration of the motivational and trauma control typologies (and, where appropriate, the classical conditioning model), provides a more comprehensive theory for and better predictor of erotophonophilia. Future investigators would do well to conceptually examine the discrete personality and behavioral factors of the paraphilic process, especially in their ability to account for sadistic, serial, and sexual murder. Moreover, these respective formulations should then become the basis for ongoing theory testing and refinement in model making.

Definitional and Operational Problems

Second, many of the constructs specified in the integrative paraphilic typology are not comprehensively or discretely operationalized. Instead, a more generalized explanation for the paraphilic process as a system of increasingly aggressive and erotic behavior is described. Moreover, the terms that are specified are not standardized on the basis of race, gender, or class differences. Instead, a more homogenous depiction of erotophonophilia and those responsible for its serial commission are enumerated. Additionally, this more global explanation, as fundamentally based on the insights derived from the Burgess et al. (1986) and Hickey (1997, 2001) frameworks, is only broadly linked to the phenomenon of lust murder through the synthetic project. Subsequent efforts that account for erotophonophilia must provide greater and more precise definitional clarity, especially with respect to the etiological and interactive elements that compose the synthetic framework. This same recommendation applies to the discrete ways in which such variables as class, minority status, age, and gender figure prominently into the overall analysis. Inquiries such as these are crucial to deepening and extending our knowledge of lust murder. This undertaking is noteworthy, especially when ascertaining whether the integrated model leads to the valid and reliable identification of erotophonophilia's onset, progression, and maintenance in distinct cases.

No Sophisticated Empirical Studies

Third, the synthetic model is based on limited inquiries that explore the phenomenon of sexual killing and serial homicide. To date, much of what we know about these crimes is anecdotal, unreliable, or otherwise the result of very small samples. The lack of larger data sets impedes rigorous statistical analysis and likely results in theory construction based mostly on conjecture and speculation. This is a deficiency, especially when the aim is to construct a sensible model that can be subjected to systematic theory testing. Accordingly, future investigators would do well to consider how quantitative research designs could be constructed, lending further empirical support to the more qualitative studies that presently exist. Inquiries such as these could then become the basis for assessing the relative explanatory (and predictive) properties of the proposed integrated typology.

Conclusion

Paraphilias represent a complex system of behaviors and constitute a unique category of sexual offending. Interestingly, while much of the research to date has focused on describing the many facets of sexually aberrant behavior, little attention has been directed toward explaining its etiological underpinnings. This chapter addressed this very important and timely matter.

By summarily reviewing the essential features of the sexual homicide and trauma control typologies (and, where useful, the classical conditioning schema), the possibility for assimilating these respective frameworks became increasingly apparent. This integration was useful, especially since each model acknowledged, at least implicitly, the importance of paraphilias in the commission of violent crime. As the proposed synthetic typology made evident, its capacity to account for the onset, progression, and maintenance of sexual deviance, particularly in the context of lust murder, far exceeded its theoretical counterparts. As such, the integrated typology was identified as a useful framework whose explanatory capabilities warranted future research attention. Pursuing these sorts of inquires was considered worthwhile, particularly since hurdling the model's limitations would help decrease the conceptual confusion that presently exists in the literature, would facilitate greater definitional precision and clarity, and would enable more empirical testing, including those studies based on statistically animated research methods.

Part 2
Paraphilias and Lust Murders

Chapter 5

Sexual Homicide: A British Investigation of Motivation and Implicit Theories

Dawn Fisher, Anthony Beech, Mark S. Carich, and Margaret R. Kohut

Introduction

Sexual homicide is a complex topic in terms of why these crimes occur. There appears to be a complex set of factors that motivate an individual to commit a sexual homicide. This chapter will examine those factors both theoretically and practically—i.e., through the use of known sexual killers in the "real world." Essential research has been done on this subject in Great Britain by the chapter's first author. We will examine this research and its crucial link in helping forensic professionals understand why a sexual serial offender makes the decision to kill. This chapter also addresses treatment implications for the violent sexual killer.

Roberts and Grossman's study (1993) of sexual homicide in Canada found that between 1974 and 1986, sexual homicides accounted for four percent of all homicides recorded by law enforcement. Current estimates in the UK place the sexual murder rate at six percent (A. Carter, HM Prison Service, personal communication with first author, May 2003). Gresswell and Hollin (1994) reported that just over three percent of homicide victims in England and Wales die in incidents involving multiple homicides. However, not all of these homicides have a sexual component. Indeed, Levin and Fox (1985) estimated that seventy-two percent of multiple murders in the UK have no sexual component. In contrast, American sexual serial killers receive a twisted sort of in-famy: names like Dahmer, Bundy, Gacy, Ramirez, DeSalvo, and Ridgeway are endlessly fascinating to the public not only for their homicides, but because their murders contain that deviant sexual pattern so riveting to the American public.

Differentiating Rapists From Sexual Murderers

To begin, we need to examine the differences and similarities between adult male rapists and serial sexual killers. Sex offenses are viewed along a contin-uum ranging from such noncontact crimes as voyeurism and exhibitionism, to fondling and molestation, to actual rape, and finally, to sexual homicide. Sexual murder, the ultimate "contact offense," often involves elements of can-nibalism and necrophilia; other sexual crimes, of course, contain neither of these deviant behaviors. How, then, does a sexual offender make the decision to cross that pathological line between rape and murder?

These two groups of sexual offenders are distinguished by the frequency of their offenses and the formation of the intention to commit sexual homicide. Forensic evidence for sexual motivation in serial murder can be very difficult to discover (Grubin 1994). Thus, a number of those convicted of rape or mur-der may actually be sexual serial murderers who are undetected. There are also a number of sex offenders who employ levels of physical violence in the com-mission of their crimes but who do not ultimately kill their victims. Evidence is beginning to emerge that suggests that sexual murderers against adult women may not be qualitatively different from offenders who have raped but not killed. Proulx and colleagues (2002) reported no significant differences in the Canadian penal system between samples of sexual murderers and sexual aggressors against women who had not killed. They also found no significant differences in the personality profiles of sexual murderers and rapists as meas-ured by the Millon Clinical Multiaxial Inventory (Millon 1997). Milsom and colleagues (2003) also found that sexual killers reported more similarities than differences when compared to rapists in self-reported levels of emotional lone-liness and fear of social intimacy in adulthood. In terms of life histories, Ressler and colleagues (1988) reported a high level of physical and emotional abuse, caretaker instability, and perception of unfair treatment within the fam-ilies of sexual killers. However, these problems are not inconsistent with those reported by sexual offenders who have not murdered. Proulx makes the point that the differences between sexual killers and rapists may lie in the situation where the offense took place rather than in any underlying differences in offense-related thought process (personal communication with second author, April 2003). For example, it was quite common for serial sexual murderers like Ted Bundy, Ken Bianchi, and Angelo Buono (the Hillside Stranglers), and Wayne Williams (the Atlanta Child Killer) to snatch their victims and transport them to another location before raping and killing them. In contrast, rapists tend to commit their crimes by surreptitiously entering a victim's home or assaulting them in a nearby but isolated location. In understanding these differing types of offenders (i.e. rapists versus serial sexual killers), it is important to look at the characteristics of these two groups to determine whether they are indeed distinct groups or just one group whose members have committed one type of crime rather than another.

The only differences Proulx and colleagues (2002) reported between sexual murderers and rapists were the following situational factors: anger (fifty-five percent of sexual killers reported feeling angry prior to commission of the offense compared to thirty-three percent of the sexual aggressors); alcohol consumption (eighty-three percent of the sexual murders had consumed alcohol prior to the offense compared to fifty-two percent of rapists); and possession of a weapon (sixty-seven percent of sexual killers had a weapon in their possession prior to the offense compared to thirty-four percent of aggressive rapists). Proulx et al. also found that there was a higher level of deviant fantasies (thirty-five percent compared to twenty-three percent) and drug consumption (fifty-two percent compared to thirty-seven percent) between these two groups.

Sex Crimes and Implicit Theories: A Constructivist Position

The construct of *implicit theories (ITs)* stems from a postmodern view, which entails both constructivism and social constructivism (Hansen 2005; Rychlak 1981; Durant 1926; Neimeyer and Bridges 2003; Kelley 1955, 1963; Keeney 1983; Mahoney 2003). Postmodern views can easily be traced to the philosophies of Plato and Kant (Rychlak 1981). More contemporary views stem from Kelley (1955, 1963), Adler (1941), Erickson, Rossi and Rossi (1976) and were applied to sex offenders by Carich (2000), Carich and Calder (2003), and Polaschek and Ward (2002). The constructivist position reflects the view that a person ultimately constructs or creates his own implicit current beliefs, historical life experiences and interpretations of those experiences, and his current personal frame of reference. External reality is a mere reflection of internal reality. Hansen (2004, pp. 131-133) stated: "Human experience is extraordinarily complex, layered and multifaceted. It seems naïve to suppose that language—a simple system of symbols and vocal noises—could adequately capture and convey the nuances of subjective human experience. All human beings filter, transform, and overlay communications from their own psyches. The basic postmodern assertion is that observers create reality rather than discover it. In other words, a totally objective reality, one that stands apart from the 'knowing' subject can never be fully known."An example of how one's reality is constructed is illustrated by the life of serial killer Henry Lee Lucas. As a child, Lucas was forced to watch his mother, a prostitute, have sex with innumerable men. His mother, being disappointed that Henry was a male child, dressed him as a little girl until he started school. Lucas was severely beaten by his mother for cutting his long, feminine-appearing hair. Based upon these life experiences, Lucas constructed a reality where women were bad and not to be trusted; his first murder was that of his mother. Again, based upon his life experiences, Lucas constructed a bi-sexual orientation; at one point he had a young female girlfriend, whom he ultimately murdered, yet he also had a sexual relationship with his sometime-partner, Ottis Toole. Hansen (2005, p. 133) described social constructivism as indicating "things, events, and behaviors having no inherent meanings. Observers can never transcend their perceptual sets."

Implicit theories, then, are underlying constructed beliefs that determine the decisions that are ultimately used by an individual to interpret reality. ITs set up an individual's frame of reference and how that person will view and incorporate reality. This is true of sex offenders, including sexual serial killers as discussed by Polaschek and Ward (2002) who wrote "Implicit theories develop in individuals from early in life as ways of organizing knowledge about their own experiences and behavior, as well as that of others. Most implicit theories are thought to be acquired in childhood, although they may develop over the life-span in response to the discovery of substantial contradictory evidence. Additionally, different cultural models and social norms can impact children's early learning environments and influence the way they understand and interpret the world."

To further the explanation of constructivism, Neimeyer and Bridges (2003, p. 274) define postmodern perspectives: "Proponents of postmodernism argue that people live in an interpreted world, one organized as much by their individual and collective categories of meaning as by the structure of an objective world of external stimuli. People actively construct experience rather than simply registering environmental stimuli." This viewpoint is particularly relevant to offenders who commit sex crimes, including homicide as it very well may provide an explanation of why sexual murderers rape and then kill their victims; their "constructed reality" involves the belief that their victims deserve what happens to them. Neimeyer and Bridges (2003, p. 276) further stated that "constructivists typically emphasize the role of personal meanings in shaping people's responses to life events and regard human beings as capable of at least an agency in determining the course of their lives. In this view we *are* our constructs. Personality can be seen as the composite of our myriad ways of interpreting, anticipating and responding to the social world." Mahoney (2003, p. 6) makes the quintessential point: "In constructivism, the individual is an active agent in the process of experiencing. We need order; we organize our world, we develop patterns and create meanings. We are creatures of habit."

Studies of sexual aggressors and sexual murderers have looked at different types of motivations, different offense processes and the role that sadistic fantasies play in the commission of sexual crimes. One approach which has recently been applied (Beech et al. 2005) is that of investigating the presence and type of the implicit theories held by the offenders. Ward (2000) argued that sex offenders' cognitive distortions emerge from underlying causal theories rather than stemming from unrelated, independent beliefs. In effect, these underlying beliefs generate the offense-supportive attitudes/cognitive distortions that are measured at the surface level (Ward et al. 1997). Ward goes on to suggest that these beliefs are ITs that the offender has about the world. These theories are similar to scientific theories in that they are used to explain, predict and interpret interpersonal phenomena.

Polaschek and Ward (2002) identified five offense-supportive ITs in rapists. They are:

1. *Women are unknowable.* With this IT, rapists, because of biology or socialization, see women as inherently different from men and believe that these differences cannot be readily understood by men. One variant of this theory is that women are unable or unwilling to communicate honestly with men; women are portrayed as inherently deceptive (Malamuth and Brown 1994). Rapists with this type of IT are likely to see women as knowing that their own desires and needs are incompatible with those of men. Hence, they do not communicate these desires and needs directly, but instead present them in a disguised manner. More recently Polaschek and Gannon (submitted) have suggested that this IT would be better titled "women are dangerous" to more explicitly acknowledge the combination of these two elements in this IT.

2. *Women as sex objects.* Here rapists see women as existing in a constant state of sexual reception and believe that they have been created to meet the sexual needs of men. In this IT women's most significant needs and desires center around the sexual domain. Therefore, it is anticipated that women will constantly desire sex, even if it is coerced or violent and women are primarily

sexual entities with no other purpose. Offenders with this type of IT believe that women should always be receptive and available to meet men's sexual needs whenever they arise. One implication of this theory is that there is often a discrepancy between what women *say* and what they actually *want*. This inconsistency surfaces because women's sexual needs may be unknown to them. An example of this IT in operation is the age-old rationalization "she said no, but she meant yes." This aspect is different from the first theory in that in this IT the argument is that women don't deliberately deceive men; instead, they simply don't know that they are fundamentally sex objects. They are unaware of the unconscious messages their bodies are emitting.

3. *Male sex drive is uncontrollable.* This IT states that men's sexual energy is difficult to control and that women have a key role in its loss of control. Like child molesters, men who rape adult women attribute the causes of their offenses to external factors (i.e. external to themselves and beyond their personal responsibility). These external factors stem directly from the victim or in other features of the environment such as the widespread availability of alcohol and other intoxicants. Offenders with this IT cite serious involuntary sexual depravation due to insufficient access to consensual sexual conduct with adult women.

4. *Entitlement.* This is one of two ITs that overlap with those that have been identified in child abusers by Ward and Keenan (1999). This IT is based on the core belief that some people are superior to and more important than others. Because of their superior status, offenders with this IT have the right to assert their needs above others, and to expect that this will be acknowledged and agreed to by those who are judged to be less important. The source of legitimacy for this narcissistic sense of entitlement might be based upon gender, class, or some other factor. For example, men might be viewed as more powerful and important than women, and therefore have the right to have their sexual needs met when they want and with whom they want. In this IT the desires and beliefs of the offender are paramount and those of the victim are ignored or viewed as only of secondary importance.

5. *Dangerous world.* This is the second IT that overlaps with those identified in child abusers. The offender sees the world as a dangerous place and believes that other people are likely to behave in an abusive and rejecting manner in order to promote their own interests. Therefore, it is necessary for them to fight back and achieve dominance and control over other people. This involves punishing individuals who appear to inflict harm on the offender. If women are perceived as threats, they may become victims of sexual crimes. The beliefs and desires of other people are a focus of this IT, particularly those signifying malevolent intentions. The content of this theory refers to the de-

sires of other people to dominate or hurt the offender, and the beliefs associated with his mental state. In addition, the offender views himself as capable of retaliation and asserting his dominance over others.

Implicit Theories and Sexual Homicide

With this crucial preamble of the ITs of serial rapists, it's now possible to extend this theoretical framework to sexual murderers. Beech et al. (2005) investigated the presence of these ITs in a group of twenty-eight sexual killers. They hypothesized that an examination of sexual murderers' offense descriptions would result in the uncovering of the same types of ITs and schemas reported in rapists. Additionally, they wanted to examine how any identified ITs would relate to each other and whether the presence of a particular IT would help to provide understanding of the motivations of the homicidal sexual offender.

All of the subjects were serving a mandatory life sentence for murder. The murder was judged to contain a sexual element to the extent that they were offered treatment and had all completed a treatment program. Twenty-four subjects had committed their offense(s) against adult women (mean age of the victim = 39.78, SD= 22.02, range 17–86), three against girls (mean age of the victim = 11.67, SD 2.0, range 9–14), and one against a nine-year-old boy. Thirteen men (forty-six percent) had committed offenses against a stranger; two (seven percent) against an ex-wife or ex-partner; three (eleven percent) against a family member; nine (thirty-two percent) against a friend/acquaintance; and one against a prostitute.

The average age of the sample at the time of interview was 38.39 (SD 9.75). Their average age when they had committed the offense for which they were incarcerated was 23.82 (SD 7.29). The average IQ of the sample was 102.17 (SD 13.17). Twenty-four men (eighty-six percent) in the sample were white; four (fourteen percent) were African-Caribbean. Eight of the sample (twenty-nine percent) had previous convictions for sexual offenses, nine (thirty-two percent) had previous convictions for violent offenses, eighteen (sixty-four percent) had previous convictions for non-sexual/non-violent offenses. Two of the offenders committed the homicide with a co-defendant (seven percent). Nine of the men (thirty-two percent) were in a relationship at the time of the offense, four (fourteen percent) were in a casual relationship, four (fourteen percent) had been in a relationship at the time of the offense. Eleven men reported that they had received some form of psychiatric treatment prior to the commission of the murder; three for depression, four for personality disorder, and four unspecified.

Subjects participated in a semi-structured interview which focused on their account of the offense and their motivations for committing the crime. Care was taken to use open-ended questions and avoid leading or closed questions. Typically, questions in the first part of the interview would consist of inquiries about whom they had committed the offense against, whether they knew the victim prior to the offense(s) they had committed, and what had led up to the offense. Here, prompt questions were asked about the offender's motivation, to find out whether the offense was related to sex or anger. Other areas covered in the interview were regarding their feelings at the time of the offense towards the victim (if known), and others in their lives; distal and proximal antecedents of their offending including fantasies about sex and violence; sexual behaviors they had committed in the offense(s); and the *modus operandi* of the killing. Where appropriate, questions were also asked about their previous offenses. Other prompt questions were asked of the offender on the basis of their answers to these questions.

Interviews were recorded and transcribed, and then coded for the presence of ITs by two independent raters. Any additional offense-supportive beliefs that did not fit into one of the five categories were put into a miscellaneous category. Once the coding was completed, this category was examined to see if there were any other ITs of significance. Both of the raters looked at the context of the whole offense chain before identifying whether an IT was present or not, and there were some borderline cases which required that a third rater make the decision as to whether an IT, identified by one of the raters, was or was not present. The inter-rater reliability of whether an IT was present was high (Spearman's rho = .77, p<.001).

An analysis of the interview protocols using the five rapist ITs supported the research hypothesis, that the way sexual murderers viewed themselves, the world and their victims could be coded into the five established rapist ITs. In other words, there were no appreciable differences in the kinds of ITs exhibited by rapists and individuals who had committed a sexual murder. Examples of each of the ITs and how they were represented in the sexual murderers are described below:

1. *Dangerous world.* The form this IT took in the sexual murderers' description of their offending behavior was that of generalized malevolence. The offender viewed other people as being unreliable and having treated them abusively and unjustly. This view resulted in entrenched feelings of resentment and anger, and the adoption of retaliation interpersonal strategies. That is, many of the sexual murderers decided to retaliate against the individual(s) whom they believed had wronged them or else simply selected someone they could vent

their frustrations upon. This IT was the most common, and typically was related to extreme episodes of violence and anger. It was present in twenty-two (seventy-nine percent) of the twenty-eight cases. No disagreements were found between the two initial raters in terms of identifying the presence or absence of this IT suggesting that the content of this theory (i.e. reporting that other people are out to dominate or hurt the offender) and that the offender views himself as capable of asserting his dominance over others and retaliating for any perceived hurts are fairly readily identifiable. Serial killers with this IT have an "I'll get them before they get me" core belief. It could be argued that the most infamous serial killer of all time, Jack the Ripper, held this particular IT. However, since Jack's true identity is forever unknown, a forensic specialist would have to adopt the oft-posed, but never substantiated, view that Jack's true identity was none other than Prince Edward Albert, grandson of Queen Victoria. According to legend, "Prince Eddie" was suffering from syphilis, which ultimately caused his death at age twenty-eight. The Prince, allegedly, acquired this disease from the prostitutes he often visited in the notorious Whitechapel slum of London's East End. Legend has it that the Prince killed five prostitutes in angry retaliation for having been inflicted with syphilis. The post-mortem sexual mutilation of his victims was particularly vicious. Considering the infestation of disease found in 1888's Whitechapel district of London, it was indeed a dangerous world.

In their study, Beech et al. provide examples of how this IT was found to be present among the twenty-eight killers they interviewed. Responses to the question, "what do you think the motivation for your offense was?" included:

a. "I committed the offense because I was not thinking of anybody but myself, I was taking my anger, bitterness, my hatred and my frustration out."

b. "The pain I was feeling I wanted to transfer it onto someone else and all that … because its stuff that's happened in the past and also stuff that was going on around at the time. It meant quite a lot, too, everything just boiling up, boiling it all up, and then it all came out at the same time. I was abused as a child by my foster father…. I think it was kind of like, the humiliation part was from then, the abuse was, it was all inside of me and I just wanted it out, I wanted it out."

c. "We went to a night club, started to have sex and she refused to have sex with me and because of all the anger and the emotions of the previous events. A break-up previous to that, an assault charge previous to that all got on top of me that night and I took all my frustrations and anger out on [the victim]. "Speaking of what he did to the victim, the offender said "OK now you've been hurt as much as I've been hurt, you won't mess with me, or anybody else, about again."

2. *Male sex drive is uncontrollable.* There were three strands to this IT. First, the participants would often report feeling powerless in their lives and unable to control their actions, including their sexual behavior. Second, the aggressive emotions that resulted in the murder were often described as external to the offender; they simply overwhelmed him. Third, individuals described feeling overwhelmed by their sexual fantasies and the associated sexual urges. The sexual element in their offending was viewed as particularly compelling and compulsive in nature. It was as if the sexual fantasies took on a life of their own and it was inevitable that sooner or later they would rape and/or murder a victim. In some instances, the fantasies contained explicitly sadistic components that revolved around the infliction of pain and suffering (and death) upon the victim. Albert DeSalvo, the Boston Strangler, was a married man with an active sex life with his spouse, although DeSalvo stated that he and his wife did not have sex as often as he would have liked. He confessed that he felt compelled to rape and murder women because he could not control his sexual urges.

Beech et al. provided examples of how the twenty-eight study subjects related to this IT:

a. "All sorts. Rapes, murders … all kinds of fantasies. Anything that made me feeling good as, I would fantasize about. The majority of them were about, I suppose, rape, yeah, because sex became involved then.… It was mostly about having someone within my power so I could, because I felt powerless at the time."

b. "I lost it. I lost my temper and I lost it altogether. I tried to dominate physically, by using physical force and then she went for me, that's where it was.… I've got to get the upper hand here and that's where I lost it and the physical violence started."

c. "Things have built up for a long time which allowed me in a way to choose a deviant set of behaviors as a sexual outlet, peeping and exposing and stuff like that if I liked someone I'd expose myself to them.… On the night I killed (the victim) if that had been someone else I would have chosen that person (to rape). I recognized her so I assumed that she'd recognize me and I panicked."

3. *Entitlement.* In this IT, there was a sense that offenders were entitled to take sex if they wanted it because they were males, more physically powerful, or simply deserved it because the woman victim had sexually aroused them or was in an existing (or previous) relationship with them. This IT was found in twelve (forty-three percent) of the offenders. An extremely prolific sexual serial killer, Ted Bundy was aroused by young women with long hair parted in the middle. He knew none of his victims, and had a narcissistic view of

himself as somehow superior to those he killed. Bundy knew that he was smart and good-looking—much more so than his victims in his own eyes. He was entitled to do whatever he wanted, and the rules of society did not apply to him. He was certainly lacking in victim empathy.

Beech et al. provide a chilling example of this IT among the twenty-eight offenders in their study:

a. "I was strung along by a prostitute, I got angry because she was stringing me along, playing games, if you know what I mean. She wanted more money.... I thought well, I'm going to have sex with her for whatever.... I thought she's a prostitute and she's holding out for more money. I got her round there (the victim's home) and I was talking to her and during the course of the evening, it was pretty late, say about half an hour into the conversation. I was telling her about my problems … and I made a pass at her. Which was I kissed her for a couple of seconds. She pushed me away so because of not being able to handle the rejection, I took my frustrations and anger out of her which I regret and after that I killed her which was, how should I say very over the top, but I'm used to getting everything my own way y' know."

4. *Women as sex objects.* In this IT the participants reported viewing women as sexual objects, existing merely as recipients of males' sexual attention. They were regarded as conduits of male sexual interest and not viewed as autonomous beings with preferences and interests of their own. This IT functioned as a background and frequently led to situations where the offenders simply expected sex and if it was not forthcoming, they would become aggressive. It was coded as only being present in nine (thirty-two percent) of the twenty-eight cases. Gary Ridgeway, the Green River Killer that eluded law enforcement for more than twenty years, saw women as "human garbage," especially prostitutes. He never knew their names nor anything about them as people. He viewed them as existing to satisfy his sexual needs, nothing more. Ridgeway used them sexually and then discarded them as if they were less than human.

Beech et al. provided examples of this IT:

a. "I took on so much y'know, proving myself to be top dog at work, living a life of a lie, with having two girlfriends, lying to them, seeing women as sex objects, having bets with work colleagues over how many you could bed, things like that."

b. "I had a tendency to sexualize, I still have a tendency to sexualize women, is that a trait of a sex offender or is that just me being … a Neanderthal type man? A bit of both I suppose, I think what I learnt it's not so much a problem per se, initially it's where you go, that's the problem that's where the problem starts to arise. Personally if I saw women with a great ass, I personally do not consider that to be a problem. If I pursue it and it starts leading into thoughts of offending, or I start to properly sexualize women, then there would be a problem."

5. *Women are unknowable/women are dangerous* (Polaschek and Gannon 2004). This IT was relatively rare and only apparent in a few cases; five (eighteen percent) of the twenty-eight cases. In these cases, women were viewed as deliberately misleading men and causing them to feel inadequate and rejected. The participants expressed frustration and confusion and tended to behave in a sexually aggressive way to teach women a lesson. Thus the key ideas seem to be that women are believed to be responsible for failed relationships and intentionally set out to make life difficult for men. This is the more malevolent version of the women of this IT, stressing their perceived wish to create problems for the males they encountered. Florida serial sexual killer Danny Rolling believed himself completely unable of having normal sexual encounters with consenting partners. His abysmal interpersonal skills caused him to be constantly rejected by women whom he found attractive. Rolling, however, blamed his victims for his failure to develop and/or maintain a meaningful sexual and emotionally intimate relationship with women. So Rolling "got even." He raped and mutilated his victims, inflicting as much damage upon them as possible.

Examples of this IT from the subjects of Beech et al:

a. "She went into a verbal assault on me which I couldn't handle so I said to myself the only way I can get you back for hurting me is to rape you. So I dragged her upstairs."

b. "I used to think it was a case of just rape and it being a sex thing but it wasn't, it was much deeper than that, and I realize I was carrying a lot of bad attitude about women, and the way I've not dealt with rejection at all, it was my fault. I was the one carrying all the crap if you were, because I never coped with it and dealt with it and it all came out on my victim that day."

6. *Miscellaneous.* There were very few cognitions that could not be coded into the five ITs and those, on closer inspection, were found to be closely related to one of these primary categories. A number of the participants stated that they committed the offense because they were expressing displaced anger toward a parent or caregiver because of the abuse they had inflicted upon them as children. This is actually a similarity with the *dangerous world* IT. Other men described feeling sexually attracted to women or to the prospect of violent sex. On reflection, it was felt that these were instances of *women as sex objects, uncontrollable male sex drive,* or *dangerous world* ITs.

An emerging challenge for forensic behavioralists is same-sex homicide such as that found in the crimes of Jeffrey Dahmer, Wayne Williams, and John Gacy. It is enticing to ponder whether homosexual murderers have ITs similar to those of heterosexual killers. This chapter's third author speculates that homosexual killers do at least have the narcissistic entitlement and the uncontrollable sex drive ITs. Examination of their crimes appears to indicate that all three murderers viewed their victims as objects who existed solely to provide them with sexual gratification, and that their needs were more important that the needs or rights of their victims. Before his murder in prison, Dahmer told forensic interviewers that he could not control his sexual urges, and that he kept body parts in his apartment because he could not bear to be alone, abandoned—even if it meant the victim had to die. The presence of a dead victim in the freezer was preferable to being alone (Kohut 2004b). Although Williams continues to proclaim his innocence, a forensic analysis of the crimes for which he was convicted, and the many more that he was suspected of committing, it seems plausible to the third author that the *dangerous world and the entitlement* IT figured prominently in his murders. Williams fancied himself as "special"; he had ideas and plans that would make him rich and famous (e.g. as a music producer although he lacked both the experience and talent to succeed in this endeavor). He was angry that the rest of the world did not recognize his special abilities and brilliant future. Williams was clearly an angry young man who acted out his rage at society through his murders (Kohut 2004b). Gacy also seems to have had a significant amount of feelings of entitlement; he cared nothing for the torture and pain he inflicted upon his victims. In the commission of his thirty-three murders of young men, it was not uncommon for him to strangle a victim into unconsciousness, "bring him back," and then strangle him again, this time until death. In his daily life, Gacy appeared to be a social and financial success; in reality, he was merely a chameleon who lived for the times when he would torture and kill young men whom he thought would "never be missed" and who were society's "undesirables" (Kohut 2004b).

Considering the rising number of infamous same-sex homicides, it would serve our society well to more closely examine the implicit theories and the mind-body development of the homosexual killer. They aren't going away.

Beech et al. went on to examine the pattern of occurrence of the ITs in sexual murderers. By a process of sorting the most common ITs (*dangerous world*), present in seventy-nine percent of the cases and *male sex drive is uncontrollable* (seventy-one percent), it was found that there appeared to be three main groups by IT in the data. When these groups were compared on a number of offense demographics, clear differences were found between the groups:

Group 1 offenders were motivated by a prior intention to kill, and had violent, sadistic thoughts and fantasies. Some men in this group also reported specific thoughts around control and domination. These thought patterns co-existed with *male sex drive is uncontrollable,* and in half of the group—*entitlement* (where the offender holds that his desires and beliefs are paramount) —led men in this sample to commit brutal sex crimes. Their victims tended to be unknown to them, targeted strangers, or those who were known and targeted for sexual assault. A high level of sexual violence was committed in these men's offenses and post-mortem sexual mutilation was prevalent, as was sexual interference with the body after death (e.g. necrophilic acts). Dahmer, Lucas, and Bundy had sex with their victims' bodies, sometimes days after their deaths. In fact, Bundy returned to the isolated location where he had dumped his victim, applied cosmetics to her face and posed her in sexual position prior to having intercourse with the decomposing body. Mutilation and interference included acts such as exposure of, and bites to, the breasts (a favorite modus operandi of Rolling and Bundy), partial severance of the breasts, and vaginal mutilation. Albert DeSalvo was known to have inserted objects such as broomstick handles into the vaginas of some of his victims. The last of Jack the Ripper's five known victims, Mary Kelly, had her breasts entirely removed and placed on a table beside her bed. Ed Kemper's final murder was that of his own mother; after killing her, he cut off her arms, legs and head; he placed the head on the mantelpiece and threw darts at it. He also removed her vocal cords—a sure tip-off of Kemper's feelings about his mother. He then had sex with his mother's torso. After these atrocities, Kemper called the police and waited quietly until they came to arrest him at his mother's home (CourtTV.com 2005). This behavior can be considered ritualistic in nature. One of Beech et al.'s twenty-eight participants admitted to necrophilic acts with the body of his victim. Strangulation was often used as a method of murder in this group, which was rarely found in the two other groups. Strangulation is considered as a method of killing where the perpetrator has complete control over the life of the victim at all times until death occurs. Members of this group were found to be the most dangerous serial sexual offenders; half of this group was rated as high or very high risk of re-offending.

Group 2 sexual murderers were found to be driven by grievance towards women. Most men in this group reported that their motivation to offend was primarily driven by anger and resentment towards women. The *dangerous world* IT appears to be the primary underlying IT in terms of how men viewed the world where thoughts about punishing and controlling his victims were primary motivations. The sexual murder itself was characterized by a high level of expressive violence with multiple attacks on the victim, using different weapons (knives, blunt instruments, hands), clearly indicating an "overkill" of the victim that included gouging the victims eyes out, attempted scalping, numerous stabbings or repeated blows such that body parts were partially severed. For example, one victim received over 140 different wounds to her body. The four assassins (Susan Atkins, Patricia Krenwinkle, Leslie Van Houten and Charles "Tex" Watson) that were sent forth on murderous errands over a two-night period by Charles Manson in August, 1969, inflicted more than thirty stab wounds upon most of their seven victims. Atkins stated in a jailhouse confession to another inmate that she wanted to cut Sharon Tate's full-term child from her womb. When Sharon Tate begged her killers not to harm her because of her pregnancy, Atkins told her "Bitch, I don't care about you or your baby." After stabbing Leno LaBianca to death on the second night of Manson's planned serial homicides, Krenwinkle stuck a large fork into his abdomen and "just watched it wobble back and forth" (Bugliosi and Gentry 1974). However, in this group sexual mutilation of the victim's body was low, although a third of the group had sexually interfered with the body after death. This behavior took the form of further humiliating acts upon the victim such as inserting knives or other objects into the victim's vagina. This group was the most likely to have known their victim prior to the offense.

Group 3 sexual murderers were found to have committed their crimes in order to keep the victim quiet during the offense, or in order to avoid detection by making sure that the victim was not available to subsequently identify the perpetrator. Some men in this group admitted that they were prepared to murder their victim before they committed their sexual offense. Here, the primary IT was *male sex drive is uncontrollable,* hence there was generally little evidence of a history of overt hostility towards women or overkill in this group compared to Group 2. There was also little evidence of ritualized elements in the murder itself; there was a low level of sexual mutilation and sexual interference after death, as might be predicted given the lack of synergism between the *dangerous world and male drive is uncontrollable* control schemas. But the *male sex drive is uncontrollable* IT acts as a motivator to commit a sexual offense whatever the cost to the victim. In his riveting novel *Native Son,* Richard Wright (1940) tells the story of a young black man named Bigger Thomas who was employed as a chauffeur to a wealthy white family. After driving the family's daughter for a night of drinking about town, Bigger carries the passed-out girl up to her room. He becomes uncontrollably sexually aroused by her and forms the intent to rape her. However, the girl's blind mother enters the room; although Bigger knows she cannot see him, he fears the girl will awaken and cry out in alarm. Bigger smothers her to keep her quiet so the blind mother will not detect him. After burning the girl's body in the furnace, Bigger flees to the home of his girlfriend, Bessie. He confides to Bessie that he has killed a white girl— certain death for a black man in that era. He and Bessie flee to avoid Bigger's arrest. Hiding in an old tenement building, Bigger and Bessie have sexual intercourse—after which Bigger strangles her and throws her body down an airshaft; he fears that Bessie will somehow accidentally reveal the murder of the wealthy white girl to the police. Wright clearly (though unintentionally) describes the thoughts and behaviors of sexual murderers in this group.

Discussion

These groupings seem to relate to motivations that have been described in the profiling literature concerning sexual murder. Group 1 contains what might be considered the prototypical, usually serial, sexual killer where the murder is the primary sexual motive. Myers and colleagues (1999) described such an offense as a fusion of sexual assault and murder where an overt (penile penetration), or symbolic sexual assault (e.g. insertion of a foreign object into a victim's orifice) is present. Ressler and colleagues (1988) note that in such a sexual homicide, exposure of sexual parts of the victim's body, insertion of objects, sexually positioning the body, as well as evidence of necrophilia indicate a sexual element of the murder has occurred. Hazelwood and Douglas (1980) note that murder may play an *instrumental* role in the commission of a sexual assault to keep the victim quiet and avoid detection, also ensuring that the victim will not be alive to identify him to the police. This type of sexual murderer appears to have been identified in Group 3. While Revitch (1980) noted that murder with a sexual component may be *motivated* by an angry outburst or in response to a perceived rejection of a proposed or actual sexual advance. This type of sexual killing appears to be identified in Group 2.

The groups identified by Beech et al., purely on the basis of identified ITs, also seem to relate to clinical descriptions of sexual murderers who received treatment as reported by Clarke and Carter (2000). They identified three main types of sexual murderers. Although there are a number of differences in the offense demographics of the men identified in their study, there are a number of commonalities to warrant mentioning in this chapter. In Clarke and Carter's clinical descriptions, the *sexually motivated murderer* is characterized by a primary sexual motivation to kill, in which there are sophisticated and detailed masturbatory fantasies about killing where the victim is usually unknown and has been specifically targeted through stalking behavior by the offender. The method of killing is sexually stimulating. This description is similar to the profile of Group 1 men. The *sexually triggered/aggressive control* sexual murderer is characterized by Clarke and Carter as having a primary motivation to sexually offend, and where the killing is instrumental but intentional. This categorization is strikingly similar with Group 3 in research by Beech et al. The *sexually triggered/aggressive dyscontrol* sexual killer in the Clarke an d Carter system is described as having no prior intention to kill or sexually offend. The offender explains the killing as having resulted from something the victim said or did in a sexual context, triggering a substantial sense of grievance held for some time against an intimate partner. Extreme violence or humiliation against the victim occurs in the offense suggesting loss of control and perspective. Sexual intercourse may or may not take place, but violence against the victim has sexual characteristics (e.g. mutilation of the genital area). This type of sexual offender according to Clarke and Carter is quite similar to Group 2 in the Beech et al. research.

Treatment Applications

The Beech et al. study has implications for treatment as it suggests that sexual murderers are not qualitatively different from rapists in terms of the underlying schemas they have about the world. Therefore, it appears that schema-focused treatment, such as that employed by the U.K. Prison System in England and Wales, would be just as beneficial with this type of sexual offender as it has been with other high-risk sexual offenders as reported by Thornton and Shingler (2001). Specific treatment should be guided by the particular type of IT present in each individual.

Group 1, where the offenders have both *dangerous world* and *male sex drive is uncontrollable* ITs running at the same time, are very dangerous offenders. They need a high level of treatment intervention in order to reduce the possibility of committing further serious sadistic sexual crimes. In such initiatives there clearly needs to be behavioral work to modify deviant sexual arousal to their violent/sadistic fantasies. However, the identified synergism of the two specific strands of how the offender views the world should be addressed and disentangled through targeted schema-focused therapy.

For Group 2, where the *dangerous world* IT is operating *without male sex drive is uncontrollable,* problems appear to manifest grievance and hostile thoughts about women rather than any deviant thoughts/fantasies that are specifically sexual in nature. Here, the data suggests that offense-focused work may be better targeted towards anger and hostility problems, as well as schema-focused work around these men's long-standing grievance schemas about women.

In Group 3, where the *male sex drive is uncontrollable* IT is operating, there is a willingness to undertake sexual assaults to satisfy their sexual urges and a general failure to control such deviant sexual thoughts and behaviors. These men could be considered as individuals driven by urges to commit sexual offenses. Therefore, cognitive-behavioral techniques typically employed with sexual offenders (Beech and Fisher 2002; Marshall et al. 1999) may be useful with this group. Here, any offense/schema-focused work should be clearly related to getting the offender to control his actions so that he does not regard any sexual or offense-related thoughts as being unstoppable and resulting in a sexual assault.

The findings in the Beech et al. research clearly indicates that it is possible to identify an offender's underlying motivations, even though the sexual murderer may not acknowledge these motivations. This study also demonstrates that the identification of ITs prior to the implementation of treatment could clearly define the focus of such treatment for offenders who are less than honest and open about their reasons for the commission of their crimes.

Additionally, sex offender treatment has been fully described by Carich and Mussack (2001), Carich and Calder (2003), Marshall (1996, 1999) and Marshall et al. (1999). These authors note that essential cognitive restructuring is necessary for effective treatment and involves cognitive restructuring, including the shift of core schemas or ITs.

Conclusion

Sexual homicide is a complex and difficult area to explore. Fortunately for society, the numbers of sexual homicides and, therefore, the sample sizes of research participants are small within the group of over-all sexual offenders. However, there are a few enlightening and ground-breaking research projects dedicated to the study of motivational factors in sexual homicide. One such investigation was conducted by Beech and colleagues (2005) in England. This project centered on accessing belief systems or underlying implicit theories of sexual murderers. The investigators used semi-structured interviews to detect the offender's underlying implicit theories. These ITs were categorized for rapists by Polaschek and Ward (2002) into five offense-supported ITs: (1) *Women are unknowable and can't be understood.* (2) *Women are viewed as sex objects.* (3) *Male sex drive is uncontrollable.* (4) *Entitlement* ideation where the victim's needs are secondary to the rapist's needs. And (5) *dangerous world* in which people in general behave in an abusive and rejecting manner.

This study involved twenty-eight sexual murderers who were serving life sentences and had completed a treatment program. The 28 offenders were placed into three groups and then defined by specific percentages. These groups were: (1) Group #1—those who were motivated by the *dangerous world* IT with a prior intent to kill, and with sexually violent and sadistic fantasies, along with the *male sex drive is uncontrollable* and the *entitlement* ITs. (2) Group #2—those who were driven by a grievance towards women and a desire to punish them; this group had significant anger and resentment issues. And (3) Group #3—those whose motives in murdering were primarily to avoid detection and uncontrollable sexual arousal. Groups #1 and #2 reflect traditional definitions of serial killers while Group #3 does not necessarily represent the "classic" definition of sexual murderers.

The authors suggested specific treatment targets for each group. The focus of treatment for Group #1 is to address the IT of *dangerous world* and their uncontrollable deviant sexual arousal patterns that need to be modified along with shifting their IT beliefs about the world. The treatment of Group #2 offenders should focus on the ITs of *male sex drive is uncontrollable* and underlying anger and resentments towards women. Group #3 offenders can benefit from contemporary cognitive-behavioral group sex offender treatment.

In closing, students and practitioners of the forensic arts and sciences should keep in mind that there is not one simple, all-encompassing profile of a serial killer. These offenders do, however, have some common characteristics, dynamics and behaviors on one level and yet they vary at other levels. The term "serial killer" was first coined by FBI agent Robert Ressler in 1972. Since that time, forensic behavioral experts have constantly sought to unravel the mystery of why serial homicides occur, and what might be the personal dynamics of an individual who commits this crime. The terms "psychopath" and "antisocial personality" are often used simultaneously to describe these killers. In 1990, Egger provided a working definition of a serial killer:

> A serial murder occurs when one or more individuals commit a second murder and/or subsequent murders. There is no prior relationship between the killer(s) and the victim. The murders occur at different times and have no apparent connection to the initial murder and are usually committed in different geographical locations. Further, the motive is not material gain and is believed to result from the killer's desire to have absolute power over the victim(s). Victims may have symbolic values and are perceived to be prestigeless, powerless and/or lower socio-economic groups.

Our own definition of serial homicide as stated earlier in this chapter emphasizes the point that sexual offenses occur on a continuum ranging from voyeurism and/or exposing themselves, all the way to sexual homicide.

Whoever they are, wherever they are, serial killers pose a dangerous and very real threat to any society. They remain undetected for long periods of time. They are elusive and chameleon-like in their ability to blend in to the world around them. When they are eventually caught (*if* they're caught at all), they become instant celebrities to the news media and the public in general. We never tire of hearing about their horrific crimes, most likely because either they are so very different from us, or they *are* us—us without boundaries. They are a dangerous enigma that may never be truly solved.

Chapter 6

Piquerism: The Investigative Challenge of Serial Murder

DeVere D. Woods, Jr.

Introduction

Interpreting crime-scene artifacts and wounds to the victim can be one of the more onerous tasks in the investigation of serial murder. The bodies of some victims appear excessively and senselessly mutilated. Understanding the psychological motivation for mutilating wounds can assist investigators to better understand the perpetrators of these crimes. Misinterpreting the motivation for mutilating wounds may hinder efforts to identify perpetrators. A thorough understanding of the concepts of MO, signature, overkill, and piquerism will help investigators to better interpret crime-scene evidence.

MO versus Signature

Many police investigators are ill prepared to investigate serial murder. In part this results from the rarity of serial murder and also the manner in which police investigators develop their skills. With a few notable exceptions (Rand, PERF), there have been few comprehensive studies of the police investigative process. Much of what investigators rely upon emanates from occupational norms but remains untested by research. Occasional seminars only provide piecemeal supplements to the traditions and folklore investigators learn during their apprenticeship in policing.

A tool frequently used by investigators is *modus operandi* or MO. The MO is the perpetrator's method of operation (Brandl 2004; Horgan 1974; O'Hara

1973). It is considered an essential tool of criminal investigation (Gilbert 2004). It includes the offender's choice of crimes to commit and the means to accomplish them (Weston and Lushbaugh 2006). The MO can reflect many factors and experiences, but it is simply the manner or the characteristic way in which the perpetrator commits the crime (Bennett and Hess 2004).

Though each perpetrator has his own MO, an MO tends to fall within a normal range of behaviors for that specific crime. MOs for a category of crime are similar overall but vary in detail. Investigators rely upon the MO to link crimes to suspects and to link crimes together (Brandl 2004). A perpetrator's level of craftsmanship or style may help investigators identify the perpetrator's work.

The MO is, in part, established by the past success of the perpetrator (Swanson et al. 1996). Some have argued that a perpetrator's MO tends to remain relatively stable. O'Hara (1973) attributes this to superstition, lack of imagination, and inertia. Others see it as the propensity for human behavior to repeat itself (Gilbert 2004; Horgan 1974). In other words, an offender does what works for him[1]. What the criminal incorporates into future crimes is what has been successful in the past (Peña 2000).

A perpetrator's MO can change and develop over time as he learns from his experience and becomes more efficient (Brandl 2004; Douglas and Olshaker 1999; Horgan 1974; Keppel and Birnes 1997, 2003). Past experience, trial and error, or necessity shape his methods. The MO evolves as the perpetrator learns (Douglas and Olshaker 2000; Hickey 2006a) or may be changed to fool the police or to be more emotionally satisfying (Brandl 2004; Keppel and Birnes 2003).

The evolution of MO continues throughout the perpetrator's criminal career in response to changing circumstances and needs: "whenever any of the factors (opportunity, need, desire, motive, or intent) are dissimilar from those of the criminal's last crime, the result of the present combination of factors will be different from the past" (Horgan 1974, p. 42). Most investigators never deal with serial homicides, so it may be difficult for them to identify the MO and other identifying characteristics of serial killers. Unless there are compelling indicators pointing to a series, investigators are likely to view crimes in the context of their normal experience and treat them as unique incidents.

While the MO reflects the perpetrator's creativity and experience, a signature reflects his personality. A signature is something the perpetrator does to

---

1. Males commit most of the crimes discussed here, and much of the research on these topics is focused on male offenders. Because of this, throughout this discussion the perpetrator will be assumed to be male.

make the crime meaningful to him. It gives him emotional satisfaction (Douglas and Olshaker 1999). "Signatures include verbal, sexual, and physical acts" (Hickey 2006a, p. 336). They are not the crimes a perpetrator commits or the means he uses to commit them. A signature is the perpetrator's personal marker (Hickey 2006a) or a calling card he is psychologically compelled to leave (Keppel and Birnes 1997). The signature is not necessary to complete the crime (Hickey 2006a) but is essential to the satisfaction the perpetrator derives from the crime (Wrightsman 2001).

Signature killers are a subcategory of serial killers who leave unusual evidence of their psychological makeup at the crime scene. Signatures are helpful in profiling criminal behaviors and can be used to link offenders to their crimes. The concept emerged from the efforts of former FBI agents John Douglas and Robert Ressler to predict characteristics of the offender from crime-scene evidence. Douglas and Ressler conducted prison interviews of convicted sexually motivated killers to assess their methods and personality traits (Ressler et al.1992). From their interviews and case studies of thirty-six incarcerated murderers, they constructed a framework for profiling offenders using crime scene artifacts. They argue that the perpetrator's personality is reflected in the crime scene evidence. "Signatures also can help determine the level of progression and sophistication of the predator" (Hickey 2006a, p. 338).

A signature reveals valuable insight into the perpetrator's motive and personality (Douglas and Olshaker 1999). Unlike the MO, a killer's signature is fairly constant or static (Brandl 2004; Keppel and Birnes 2003). The signature is based in the predator's fantasies so it is much more difficult for the predator to change his signature than his MO (Hickey 2006; Wrightsman 2001). The psychological core of the signature does not change, but it may evolve over time (Brandl 2004; Douglas and Olshaker 2000; Keppel and Birnes 1997).

Part of a killer's signature may involve posing the body or inserting foreign objects into the body. Signature killers often take mementos or souvenirs from their victims (Keppel and Birnes 1997): "the amount and level of sexual activity the killer has with his dead victim are very specific indicators of his signature" (Keppel and Birnes 1997, p. 191). These activities may have some symbolic meaning for the killer and are rare, occurring in less that one percent of murders (Keppel and Birnes 1997).

Recognizing the signature can greatly aid the investigator. "Homicide detectives who know how to find a killer's signature and understand what a signature means are usually more successful in solving serial crimes than their counterparts who proceed, sometimes unthinkingly, along traditional paths" (Keppel and Birnes 1997, p. xxi).

Isolating a signature from other aspects of the crime can be challenging. Some authors, such as Weston and Lushbaugh (2006), make no distinction between MO and signature using the terms synonymously. Others recognize that discerning a killer's signature from his MO is not always possible (Brandl 2004).

Piquerism As a Signature

Sometimes the novice killer is surprised at how easily a blade can separate living flesh, and how quickly the burning blade melts away its victim's life. Before the perpetrator fully comprehends, his adrenaline-laced act is finished. Actions may more rapidly outpace the killer's understanding when alcohol or drugs are added. Other times, the killer is stunned by the ineffectiveness of the knife's thrust into the victim. Multiple strikes are required as the victim stubbornly clings to survival. In either case the wounds are utilitarian. Each wound is struck to extinguish life but no more. Death brings completion to the task. The killer's mission is over. Such is the character of the traditional murder.

Some murders, though, appear exceptionally vicious. Wounds are inflicted in numbers far greater than necessary to cause death. A victim can be stabbed to death without physically taxing the perpetrator. Stabbing the victim twenty, thirty or even a 100 times, however, expends significant energy. This type of overkill is physically demanding and indicates the killer is experiencing more than the urge to murder.

Overkill has been described as "[t]he repeated infliction of injuries ... so intense that murder was incidental to the actual wounds" (Keppel and Birnes 1997, p. 13). It goes beyond the normal defense wounds and cutting associated with stabbing deaths (Spitz and Fisher 1980). The perpetrator inflicts many more injuries than are necessary to kill (Ressler et al. 1992). Consequently, overkill often involves multiple causes of death (Keppel and Birnes 1997).

Such a killer does not stop with the death of the victim. He may not be able to stop his assault upon the victim until he reassures himself of his own potency (Keppel and Birnes 2003). Excessive injuries to the face often indicate the killer knew the victim and was overcome by extreme rage (Geberth 1983). Attacking the victim's face in this manner dehumanizes the victim for the perpetrator (Ressler et al. 1992). The killer does not just take the victim's life, he obliterates the victim's existence. This may indicate the victim knew the killer or the victim symbolizes someone the killer knew.

Ressler and colleagues (1992) found evidence of mutilation and overkill in many sexual homicides. The sexually motivated killer needs to accomplish more than cause the victim's death. "[A]cts of mutilation and overkill give him a sense of control and domination over his sexually degraded victim" (Keppel and Birnes 1997, p. xxi). Mutilation is often accompanied by strangulation, which feeds the killer's ego by giving him the power of life and death (Keppel and Birnes 1997). The killer is not satisfied by a victim's quick death. He wants to fully experience the process of taking life from the victim.

Piquerism is a concept emerging from efforts to profile serial murder crime scenes. It is the cutting and stabbing for sexual pleasure, a counterintuitive concept beyond normal comprehension. How can such a grotesque and brutal act provide sexual gratification? How can a normal human need be fulfilled by such repulsive behavior? This is a bizarre linkage of violence and sexual gratification. It is a mystery to most people how someone obtains sexual excitement from mutilating another.

Sexual homicides are usually committed by predators who become sexually aroused by inflicting pain on their victims (Geberth 1983). Piquerism is a subcategory of signature murder. This deviant sexual behavior is termed a paraphilia. Sexual paraphilias involve arousal through the use of nonhuman objects, suffering or humiliation, or non-consenting persons (Meadows and Kuehnel 2005).

The piquerist achieves sexual orgasm by stabbing his victim (Hickey 2006a; Holmes and DeBurger 1998). Piquerism includes jabbing, stabbing, cutting, and gouging with a knife or sharpened instrument to instill terror and achieve sexual gratification (Keppel and Birnes 1997). Sadistic predators commonly mutilate their victims by excessive stabbing or slashing their breasts and genitals (Geberth 1983). Keppel and Birnes (1997) incorporate a very broad definition of piquerism that includes cutting, stabbing, slicing, biting, and sniper activity. Most definitions are limited to cutting and stabbing.

These behaviors are acts to achieve satisfaction not to cause death (Keppel and Birnes 1997). Sexual release occurs through the acting out of anger and cutting the victim (Keppel and Birnes 1997). The phallic nature of edged weapons (Freud 1970) comes to fruition in the hands of the piquerist. Penile satisfaction is transferred to the cutting instrument. Mutilation becomes foreplay to the killer's sexual gratification. For some of these killers, it no longer matters if life remains in the victim's body. Sexuality can be expressed in postmortem mutilation and exploration (Keppel and Birnes 1997). Some killers even return to their crime scene to derive satisfaction by inflicting more cutting on their victim's bodies in an attempt to make the victim feel the killer's pain (Ressler et al. 1992).

Overkill and piquerism both involve cutting and mutilating the victim's body. Both acts appear senseless. How are investigators to distinguish the mutilation of piquerism from the mutilation of overkill? If the investigator cannot identify the motivation behind the victim's wounds, then the presence of these wounds do little to further the investigation. Distinguishing between overkill and piquerism can be guided by examining the basic concepts.

Overkill is a product of extreme frustration and not sexual in nature. It is an eruption of frustration. A flurry of violence focused at dehumanizing the victim as the killer releases his repressed pain. The attack is vicious, and the killer may use more than one weapon (Keppel and Birnes 1997). The killer seeks to not only kill but to eradicate his victim.

Piquerism is a more controlled act. Rather than an explosion of repressed pain, it is a transfer of pain. The killer may cover a body part in wounds or create a pattern of wounds (Keppel and Birnes 1997). Wounds may be inflicted either antemortem or postmortem. Sexual organs are often the focus of the attack.

Evidence of obvious sexual activity may not be present. Piquerism is necessary for some killer to achieve sexual gratification, but the acts of mutilation and gratification may be separated by time and place. Frequently, the mutilation is necessary so the killer can achieve gratification later. These killers flee to safety away from the crime scene to visualize their actions and masturbate (Keppel and Birnes 1997).

Investigating Serial Murder

Investigators face many challenges when trying to solve serial murders.[2] These brutal crimes reveal rare and unusual behavior that is not easily recon-

---

2. A ringing telephone breaks the tranquility of a Saturday morning. Such unexpected calls can knot the stomach of an investigator too frequently summoned to the tragedy of others. This would be one such day that would not end until physical and mental exhaustion demanded submission.

The telephone call was a summons to the scene of a double homicide. Earlier, a young man found the body of his great aunt lying in the living room of her home. There was blood everywhere. The home was an old farmhouse once considered to be located safely away from the brutality of urban life.

After fleeing from this horrible scene, the terror-filled young man notified police. Officers responded and quickly surrounded the house. They sealed off potential escape routes and plotted their strategy to search the house for the killer. Inside the home, veteran officers found an eighty-year-old female enveloped in blood. Her death was brutal. She had been bludgeoned until her skull was fractured. Her throat was slashed to open a large wound to her neck. Her slacks and panties were pulled down to her ankles exposing her blood-smeared vagina. A few feet away, a shirtless seventy-five-year-old man lay in the

ciled with perceptions of normal criminal activity. The skills detectives develop and hone investigating common murder may be of little aid in interpreting serial murder. Many aspects of serial murder make sense to the killer but not to anyone else (Holmes and Holmes 1998). The more bizarre or unusual the murder, the less likely it is that the investigators will recognize or understand. How does one rationalize a serial murder? How do you make sense of mutilation and evisceration? Traditional police training and staffing practices offer little help.

Training for police investigators has improved greatly in recent years but a substantial amount of skill development is still learned on the job. The experience of policing enables veteran police officers to understand violence more

---

blood that drained from a gaping slash wound to his neck. He was very muscular for his age, and in life was probably more fit than many men half his age. A bloody chainsaw sat on the kitchen table, but officers found no suspects in the house. They quickly returned to the front yard for fresh air and a chance to comprehend what they had witnessed.

When the investigator arrived, he was greeted by the stunned silence and sickened looks of those who had viewed the bodies. Even these veteran officers found it difficult to deal with the mutilation of two elderly people. What kind of monster would do this to such harmless people? A savage killer was on the loose. Officers knew their next task was to devise a strategy to apprehend the murderer.

Officers conveyed to the investigator a disturbing description of what they had found. Now it was time for the investigator to enter the house to conduct a preliminary survey for the forensic crime scene team. After ten minutes in the house, the investigator emerged with his assessment. He informed the officers that there was no murderer for them to find. This was not a double murder but a murder and a suicide. The faces of sickened officers now showed disbelief. Heads lowered, eyes refused to make contact. That was ridiculous! Did he see those bodies? Even the medical examiner, who later came to view the bodies, was skeptical of the investigator's theory. Senior citizens do not murder and mutilate one another! Murder suicide—impossible!

The forensic evidence was clear. The blood spatters convincing. The nature of this crime was obvious once one examined the physical evidence. To accept it, though, one had to abandon preconceived notions of normal rationality and human behavior. It was not until after the autopsies and a forensic pathologist confirmed the events that officers accepted what happened.

The elderly man bludgeoned his victim with a 30-inch long, two-inch thick wooden rod before using it to sexually assault her. Next he cut her throat with a single-edged razor blade. He then tried to cut his own throat with the chainsaw. He started the saw and placed it on the kitchen table. Then he and leaned into the spinning blades. The cutting chain, though, derailed from its guide bar before it caused serious injury. Faced with disassembling the saw to restore the chain to its track, he went into the bathroom and cut his throat with a razor blade. He then stumbled back into the living room to collapse and die next to his victim. The previous account was not a serial crime, but it illustrates the challenge investigators face when trying to solve serial murders.

thoroughly than their civilian counterparts. Most people are shielded from the intensity and levels of violence that is commonly encountered by police officers. Officers learn that most murderers and rapists commit their crimes within certain parameters. Experienced officers see so many of these crimes that they can predict how these abnormal acts are normally accomplished. Officers develop and sharpen their investigative expertise through training and familiarity with the violent methods of perpetrators. This can be both a strength and weakness as the boundaries of experience shape investigators' judgment and investigative strategies. They become proficient in dealing with recurring crimes but are ill prepared to understand crimes outside their experience.

Most police investigators come to their positions through promotion or transfer from the patrol division. Their years as uniformed police officers serve as an apprenticeship to developing skills in investigating crimes. In part, this practice ensures that investigators are well schooled in how crimes are committed. By taking reports and investigating hundreds of crimes, investigators recognize how perpetrators normally behave. It is not that every crime is the same, but norms are established. When expected parameters are breached, suspicion is raised. Investigators then need to explain or resolve the discrepancy.

This method of skill development encourages investigators to look more deeply into unexpected circumstances. This may uncover an unusual method or a false claim of a crime. Behaviors falling far outside the normal rationality for a specific category of crime, however, may mystify or misdirect investigators. In these cases, the experience of investigators may foster incorrect interpretations. Through misinterpretation or failure to recognize the significance of these indicators, investigators may misinterpret rare and unusual crimes. Investigators may attempt to rationalize what they have encountered into a more common perspective. That is, their expectations may compel them to disregard important investigative artifacts.

Conclusion

Understanding serial murder can be difficult even under the most favorable circumstances. Investigators are hampered not by lack of talent but by lack of experience. Serial murders are not common or intuitive crimes. Investigators are often confronted with evidence of bizarre and seemingly contradictory behavior. Crime scenes can be chaotic and confusing leaving investigators to struggle for a place to begin their search for the perpetrators.

Crimes of mutilation are not common, and because of their rarity they may provide unusual challenges for investigators. The grisly remains may confound even experienced investigators. Such wounds, though, may provide important clues to solving these crimes. These acts of mutilation may be very symbolic to the perpetrator and offer useful insights about him. Investigators sorting through a maze of unusual crime scene artifacts can further their investigations by correctly interpreting these symbols.

Signature evidence provides some insight into the killer's personality. Interpreting the wounds to the victim's body may reveal not only how the crime was committed but also the motivation of the perpetrator. Overkill represents the pent-up rage of the killer. Piquerism stems from the union of sexual satisfaction and violence. Correctly interpreting the victim's wounds may provide clues to identifying the killer.

Chapter 7

A Synthesis and Reinterpretation of Necrophilia in the Context of Lust Murders: The Role of Fate

Deanna Cahill, Rachel Dickey, and Phillip C. Shon

Introduction

A cursory review of the literature reveals that necrophilia has been a topic of interest for clinicians and academics for some time; while that interest has been brought to the foreground as a result of the behaviors of highly publicized cases of sexual serial killers, the literature indicates that necrophilia has been a pivotal topic of concern in the development of certain cultural practices.

While necrophilia is defined as engaging in sexual intercourse with a corpse, recent work has included other behaviors, such as "touching or stroking a corpse, masturbating on or in the vicinity of a corpse, rubbing body parts including genitalia on the corpse" (Heasman and Jones 2006, p. 274). This chapter explores the etiology of necrophilia, briefly reviews the literature on the subject, and explains its theoretical and behavioral link to lust murders. The chapter also conceptualizes necrophilia as a point in a constellation of other paraphilias and violence, a cognitively and behaviorally anticipatable extension of anteceding sex crimes.

The chapter does so by presenting a critical rereading of the cases that have been presented in the previous works, and attempts to provide a cogent synthesis and integration of the extant works to reconfigure the internal and situational dynamics of necrophilia. Consequently, rather than assuming the etiology of necrophilia in the intrapsychic pathology and dysfunctional infantile sexuality of offenders, this chapter reassesses the role of chance and situational factors behind necrophilia, along with the possible adaptive functions it may serve.

Necrophilia in Context

That notorious serial killers such as Jeffrey Dahmer and Ted Bundy engaged in acts perverse to the imagination, established social and legal codes, as well as sacred taboos, has thoroughly seeped into the popular consciousness of our time; hence, sexually deviant acts, such as voyeurism, bestiality, sadism, necrophilia, and cannibalism, while unpalatable, have become the parlance of ordinary discourse and understanding of serial sexual murder in America. A cursory review of the literature reveals that necrophilia has been a topic of interest for clinicians and academics for some time (Brill 1941a, b; Bierman 1962; Burg 1982; Foraker 1976; Heasman and Jones 2006); and while the practice of necrophilia straddles the borders of the absurd, its tentacles have reached into the cultural habits of some civilizations in practices such as funerary and burial customs (Burg 1982). For instance, it has been well noted that King Herod continued to engage in sex acts with his wife Marianne for seven years after her death. Herodotus, the ancient Greek historian, notes that the wives of high-ranking men, along with beautiful women in general, were forbidden to be directly delivered to the embalmers; they were allowed a three-to-four-day decomposition period to disincline any sexual interest that may have arisen on the part of embalmers (Nobus 2002). Such practices came to be adopted after one zealous embalmer had been caught "mounted" on a fresh female corpse, and was exposed by a colleague.

Magic and cult worship have also been linked to death, and noted to contain elements of necrophilia. For example, the modern day Asmats of Irian Jaya were said to have placed a human skull against the genitals for up to three days in order to absorb the sexual power of the skull's owner (Huber 1962). The alchemist, Thomas Vaughn, hints at having sex with his wife on the day of her death, claiming that he couldn't live without her. Disciples of Indian Tantra have had sex with the dead in their rituals. In some cultures, sex with the dead has been used for healing the sick; for instance, some believed that hermaphrodites could be cured by sexual intercourse with a deceased virgin (Burg 1982; Rosman and Resnick 1989). This practice, while unemployed at times, was often incorporated as a dogmatic practice of the occult (cult worship). It has also been hypothesized that the funeral pyres of India may have been motivated by a desire to deter necrophiliacs from defiling the bodies. A preliminary observation of the literature shows that necrophilia has been a topic of concern for some civilizations throughout time.

The most comprehensive review of necrophilia was undertaken by Rosman and Resnick (1989, p. 154). They classified necrophiles into two principal categories: (1) genuine necrophile and (2) pseudo-necrophile. The latter was defined as those who only have a "transient attraction to a corpse"; that is, those for whom corpses are not the objects of recurring fantasies. As an illustration, Rosman and Resnick proffer the example of a thirty-seven-year-old man who "accidentally" shot his girlfriend after a heavy bout of drinking; while in the process of hiding her body, he became sexually excited and had sex with the corpse. The authors implicitly suggest curio as the motivating factor since they note that the subject had read about necrophilia in pornographic magazines; they mention no subsequent cases of this type.

The genuine necrophile's interest in corpses is not transitory but a persistent recurrence. Rosman and Resnick classify these subjects into three categories: (1) necrophilic homicide, (2) regular necrophilia (3) necrophilic fantasy. The homicidal necrophile kills precisely for the purposes of acquiring a corpse for sexual purposes, and represents the most serious type of offender. Consider the following example: "A 25-year-old, single, white male college senior engaged in conventional sexual relations with his girlfriend. He had a high sex drive and masturbated approximately seven times a day. He had a large collection of pornography and had committed acts of bestiality, urophilia, and coprophilia. He had engaged in necrophilia with animals he had killed and with bodies in the morgue of the hospital where he worked as an orderly. He had a longstanding fantasy of having 'all kinds of sex' with a dead body.... He murdered an eight-year-old girl to carry out his fantasy" (Rosman and Resnick 1989, p. 155).

Regular necrophiles, on the other hand, do not go out and commit murder for the sake of acquiring a body for their deviant sexual desires; instead, they commonly situate themselves in professions where they have periodic contact with corpses; hence, embalmers, mortuary attendants, morticians, pathologists, grave diggers, and hospital orderlies and others whose occupation might place them in the vicinity of corpses have been suspected of necrophilia. The third category in the Rosman and Resnick study is delimited to those who merely fantasize about necrophilia, and for the time being, contain their sexual activities to role playing and fantasies. In this type, fantasies are scripted in advance and scenarios of bondage, mutilation, and other acts are played out on a cooperative partner who assumes the position of a corpse. That is, necrophilic fantasies are confined to mere substitutes, but no contact with the actual corpse takes place.

More recently, necrophilia committed in the context of lust murder has been classified into three distinct categories (Keppel and Birnes 1997). The first type of necrophile commits the offense driven by themes of unification. Offenders in this category have sexual intercourse with the corpses and eviscerate the victims, sometimes, wearing their skin. These types of necrophiliacs sometimes consume the flesh of the victim; these postmortem behaviors represent a necrophile's way of preserving and achieving harmony with the dead. Keppel and Birnes (1997) refer to the second type as the "jackal," a person who chooses corpses because they are available, accessible, open to the limitless, depraved sex acts that can be conjured up by the necrophiliac. Keppel and Birnes (1997, p. 270) write, "this process is extremely seductive to the necrophile, who, because he is in complete control, craves for an increasingly intense gratification from each encounter." The third type of necrophile chooses corpses because they are safe—safe from potential rejection from a live partner who might find their sexual advances and proclivities undesirable (see Segal 1951). Keppel and Birnes maintain that these types of necrophiles essentially fear their victims, fear the rejection they might face, and seek to contain that fear by controlling, mutilating, and having sex with them, even eating them. According to Keppel and Birnes (1997), hatred is the fuel that drives this emotional engine, and its primary aim is control and domination.

Despite variance in the levels of nefariousness in necrophiles, certain characteristics common to them have emerged. Over ninety percent of the necrophiles tend to be men, homicidal ones almost exclusively so; there is a wide range of ages, from teens to the elderly, and a predominant number of them tend to identify themselves as heterosexual (see Burg 1982; Rosman and Resnick 1989). Consequently, they choose corpses of the opposite sex. One particularly noteworthy aspect of necrophiles is their prior history of sadistic acts and paraphilia. There is overwhelming consensus that necrophilia is but one sexual deviance in the lives of necrophiles, that they have a history of sexually deviant behaviors such as bestiality, voyeurism, frotteurism, sadism, etc. (Baker 1984; Calef and Weinshel 1972; Hickey 2006b; Hucker and Stermac 1992; Kenworthy and Litton 2006; Lancaster 1978; Peven 1993).

Etiology of Necrophilia

If there was a hall of distinction for those who have been discovered kissing, fondling, touching, masturbating on or near a corpse, and engaging in vaginal, oral, anal intercourse with the dead, then there would be two inductees into such a place, Sergeant Francois Bertrand and Victor Ardisson.

These two figures have been the subject of Richard von Kraft-Ebing's seminal work on the topic, and continue to be cited and widely regarded as the paragon of sexuality gone awry (see Burg 1982).

Sergeant Bertrand's induction began when he walked into the Val-de-Grace hospital with a gunshot wound and came to the attention of a grave digger from Montparnasse, who happened to overhear soldiers from Sgt. Bertrand's unit talking about his wounds and deduced the true identity of the grave defiler since he had been wounded by the trap the grave digger and his colleagues had set for the defiler (Nobus 2002). Based on this chance encounter, Sergeant Bertrand confessed to a laundry list of crimes against the dead across the country; Sergeant Bertrand related that he acquired his cadavers from cemeteries, and in addition to having had sexual intercourse with the corpses, he was known to have mutilated and eviscerated them to much of his delight; similarly, his partner in the halls of necrophilia was known to have a distinct preference for "oral contact": "I recall having sucked the nipples of that woman like a child does his mother" (Klaf and Brown 1966, p. 646). While both individuals were convicted of violating corpses, each displayed a unique style— signature—to their methods. Despite the time between the reported cases and today, there is much to be learned and analyzed from the two celebrated cases that can serve as the guidepost to understanding necrophilia.

Sexual contact with the dead illustrates two principal points that mark this inquiry's genesis. First, it is a highly anti-normative act that deviates from the mainstream standards and practices of sexuality, in almost every culture. Second, that non-consenting partners are selected as the outlets of the necrophile's sexuality justifies its conceptualization as a sexual paraphilia (see Heasman and Jones 2006; Hickey 2006c). Consequently, it behooves us to situate necrophilia not as a discrete activity but as a point at the far end of the continuum in a constellation of other paraphilias and violence in general (Keppel and Birnes 1997). In that vein, then, before a necrophile can be classified as thus, certain conditions have to be met.

First, there are temporal demarcations that are imperative to classifying paraphilias as such; a minimum of six months of "recurrent, intense, sexually arousing fantasies, sexual urges, or behaviors involving the use of non-living objects" must exist (see Healy 2006, p. 57; APA 1994). That is to say that the second necessary condition for the diagnosis of paraphilia entails the substitution of the representation for the real, and this preference causes "clinically significant distress or impairment in social, occupational, or other areas of functioning" (see Healy 2006, p. 57; APA, 1994). Third, there is the infliction of humiliation and suffering on the self or other; fourth, the use of children or other non-consenting adults as objects of sexual gratification. The last criterion in particular is relevant to this paper since it intersects with the nexus of sexuality and intimacy.

Normative sex is a consensual and cooperative activity, and as scholars have observed, deviations from this pattern result in the production of behavior that is cosmetically sexual but non-sexual in motive (Peven 1993). It is argued that the aim and behavior of paraphilias are a misguided one in that they substitute the object for the real (Kline 1987); such an embodiment has been ascribed to the grossly inadequate sense of security and self-esteem (Dimock and Smith 1997; Pam and Rivera 1995). Hence, necrophiles protect themselves and their egos by securing a "sure thing," a guarantee in the embrace of a corpse rather than facing the humiliation of a rejection (Moses 1991); they "hesitate" to establish a meaningful human bond and find the most expedient route to intimacy, falsely preserving their egos, security, and status (Peven 1993).

There is agreement that such behaviors occur because individuals (mostly men) are unable to see the cooperative and mutually exchanging character of sexuality and intimacy; they burden themselves unnecessarily with the "onus of performance" upon themselves, turning an intersubjective relation into an intrasubjective one. Such sexual dysfunctions occur because individuals are "self absorbed, fearful of making a mistake, cower before 'normal' interpersonal activities, afraid that others will find out what they are really like. Sexual gratification with a loving partner requires cooperation and self-revelation, a risk of exposure to the eyes of another" (Peven 1993, p. 443). Consequently, sexual paraphilias are conceptualized and seen as manifestations of 'distance keeping behavior'—behavior that is programmatically designed to delimit the exposure of the self to the judgment of another, thus facing the possibility of rejection, behavior that is designed to preserve the fragile status of one's ego. This intrasubjective thrust of paraphilias has two divergent origins with convergent outcomes.

As well noted, neglect, or perceived feelings of neglect, in children produce feelings of insecurity and inadequacy (Arrigo and Purcell 2001). That is to say that since they have never been the object of affection and love from their primary caretakers, they do not have the capacity to reciprocate such emotions; concurrently, they are not able to develop and cultivate a sense of the other since they have never occupied such a position in their developmental history (Keppel and Birnes 1997). The converse of this view is pampering; in this view, those who are pampered acquire everything with ease, hence, as adults, they are poorly equipped to deal with rejection. By being conditioned to receive with minimum amount of effort, pampered individuals also are not capable of reciprocating since they see themselves as the center of attention. As Peven

(1993) insightfully summarizes, these two conditions are two of the most important etiological factors in the history of persons with psychosexual disorders and paraphilias.

Extant research on the personality characteristics of paraphiliacs and necrophiles supports a view consistent with the aforementioned, despite the divergence on one of the factors. For instance, Rosman and Resnick (1989, pp. 158-159) posit that necrophiles are not psychotic, that they are principally motivated by a desire to "possess an unresisting partner." This assertion is consistent with personality assessments of paraphiliacs and fetishists in general: "the typical fetishist is usually described as someone who has not developed appropriate social skills and is emotionally estranged ... they are 'insecure, passive', dependent and inadequate" (Kenworthy and Litton 2006, p. 157). These common features of paraphiliacs lead to the conclusion that paraphilia (including necrophilia) may serve an adaptive function since it is an attempt to overcome the impotent self, regardless of its ontology.

In a frequently cited and highly regarded paper on necrophilia, Brill (1941a, b) examines its etiology by discussing two of his patients, D and H. He uses these two clinical cases to illustrate that necrophilia is not an abrupt and sudden deviation in sexual progression, but a logical extension of a cognitive and behavioral pattern. While Brill (1941b, p. 69) concludes that perversions (including necrophilia) are "nothing but a magnified component of the infantile sexuality," he also strongly suggests that "necrophilia, like the other perversions, depends on many cases, but is not perhaps as deeply determined psychologically as the others." These two sentences are brimming with tension and require further exegesis, for the former and the latter entail diametrically opposed assumptions about the phenomenon.

By conceptualizing necrophilia as "magnified components of infantile sexuality," Brill admits the normalcy of paraphilic behaviors such as desiring to inflict pain for sexual gratification, espying on others without their knowledge while in a state of undress, but states that perversions become bona-fide cases when these types of behaviors become ends rather than means to an end. Hence, for Brill (1941b, p. 65), as well as Freud in general, "a certain amount of aggression, looking, touching, and tasting normally participate as fore-pleasures in the sexual act," but seeking sexual release solely through these means represents a deviation and perversion since they do not coincide with the aim of genital sex (Kline 1987). Brill attributes the behavior of paraphiliacs by what he refers to as a "constitutional disposition," meaning that there is something latent in the paraphiliacs that draws them toward the deviant practices; but such a strong psychoanalytic bite is mitigated by the last word of his two-part article: "the perversion, as shown above, is nothing else but a magnified component of the infantile sexuality brought about by constitution and fate" (Brill 1941b, p. 73). This last word works hard to undermine the psychic—constitutional—and genetic factors that may have played in the etiology of paraphilia, and opens the door to variables extraneous to intrapsychic forces. This kismet-like character of paraphilias is buttressed in the two clinical cases he uses as examples.

Brill's (1941a) first patient is only identified as D, a thirty-year-old clerk who had been referred to him because of his attempt at fellatio of a corpse. The reader is told that D is feminine in thought and appearance, that he experimented with homosexuality beginning at the age of four. In his younger years, he had attempted to fellate a sleeping farmhand on his father's farm, only to be thoroughly embarrassed, rejected, and ostracized from the community; it is at that point that his first spark of interest in an "un-rejecting" partner is planted. D, having always had a fear of the dark, when told that his fears could be conquered by touching a dead person, bravely does so, magically curing his fear of the dead, but also bringing to life another morbid attraction: D discovers that he has been sexually excited by the handling of a corpse, and is consumed by thoughts of reproducing that initial thrill. Consequently, he procures a job as an undertaker's assistant and repeatedly attempts to abuse the corpses he encounters at work.

Brill's (1941b) second patient, H, is described as a single male (thirty-two) who is blind nearly from birth, and has sought counseling for his recurring desire to kill in order to procure a dead body for the purposes of mutilation, cannibalism, and general "wallowing in." In his second article, Brill traces the incremental disposition of H's fascination with the perverse: H is obsessed with "kissing and hugging" girls who are taller and bigger than him, but finds no reciprocation from the girls, only rejection. It is from there that his preoccupation with the acquisition of corpses of girls takes hold. Also during this period, he develops an interest in drinking blood, after he gets a bloody nose and accidentally tastes it. He acquires a taste for other body fluids as well, sweat, particularly licking his own and the sweat of others; he then graduates to eating the manure of animals as well as that of humans, and when that is no longer sufficient, he attempts to move toward animals, for mutilating and eating.

These two cases, while possibly illuminating the psychoanalytic origins of paraphilia, also strengthen the *serendipitous hypothesis of necrophilia*, as well as paraphilia in general. While D's undue and abnormal fear of the dark may be constitutive of an underlying psychopathology, his introduction to and interest in corpses is entirely incidental—fate (see McGuire et al. 1965). That is, had D found another way to alleviate his fear of the dark besides touching a corpse, the condition would either have manifested in a different form, or not altogether. And once this incipient interest is ignited, notice how his entire life is structured to accommodate that new passion: he immediately acquires a new profession that will give him unfettered access to corpses (i.e., regular necrophile). H's case, although a bit unusual because of his near-blindness, follows the contours of sexually deviant behavior in a paradigmatic way. His paraphilia begins with vampirism (drinking of blood), then to salirophilia (desire to lick sweat); from fluids, he graduates into solid matter (feces) or coprophagia; he reaches the end of the continuum when he expresses the desire to consume human flesh (cannibalism). But notice again that H's foray into the world of paraphilia is ignited by the serendipitous dripping of blood from his nose and into his mouth and incidentally discovering that he liked it. The only common ground amongst D, H, and other necrophiles who have come to the attention of the law and the clinical community is that they have an enduring need to be accepted without rejection; after having experienced traumatic rejection at one point in their lives, both D and H seek partners who are safe—those who will not pass judgment, leave them or reject them.

D and H illustrate the progressive unfolding of paraphilias, and support the co-morbidity thesis—the view that paraphiliacs often have two to three other paraphilias in addition to the one they are being treated (and often arrested) for. Furthermore, both D and H's involvement in their necrophilic fantasies illustrate the contingent character of paraphilias in general ("fate"). Consider the following account from a foot fetishist: "at six or seven I had my feet worshiped by a thirty-year-old uncle. He would massage my feet and either masturbate on them or sodomize me. I began finding men in their stocking feet sexually exciting, my primary fantasy that permeates all my sexual activities is a male with socks on" (Weinberg et. al. 1995 in Kenworthy and Litton 2006, p. 158). That this fetishist later turned out to develop a foot fetish of his own is entirely contingent upon chance factors (i.e., his own victimization).

Necrophilia in Relation to Other Paraphilias

While the foot fetish cited above exemplifies the harmless attraction to various body parts, there are times when this attraction to body parts takes on a more ominous tone. Take the case of "Whitney Post" that Pincus (2001) discusses: "Post" was convicted of killing six prostitutes, and amputating the feet of his victims. After interviewing "Post," Pincus discovers that Post's partialism is related to the family environment of his upbringing. For instance, Pincus (2001) writes that Post was punished by being struck with a belt on his back and thighs and the soles of his feet—all while prostrate on his bed, hands bound behind his back, and his pants pulled down to his ankles so as to be immobilized. Furthermore, Pincus (2001, p. 147) writes that Post's mother would "lie on her stomach in her bedroom, wearing only her slip, and ask him to rub her feet ... she would gasp softly as he rubbed her feet." Post related to Pincus (2001, p. 147) that his mother's foot was "very soft, like a breast or my penis ... touching it had an effect on me. It was an unpleasant effect, not exactly like a woman's fear of touching a snake, but odd." Later in his life, Post would recreate the images of his childhood punishment and sexualized chore with the prostitutes he would pick up: he would have them lay naked on their stomachs while inserting his penis between their feet.

These foot fetishes poignantly illustrate the serendipitous nature of paraphilias which can be retained in the latter processes of an offender's criminal repertoire. Similar to D and H, what appears to be constitutional is merely situational—shaped by forces extraneous to the psyche in origin, a coincidental byproduct of childhood experience, sexual abuse, and physical punishment—and attributable to chance factors. In extreme cases of sexual perversions, there is no one factor that predisposes a subject to those acts; instead, they are gradually and incrementally brought about and evolve into existence. This culminating pattern of deviant sexual behavior can be illustrated in one of the most prolific lust killers in U.S. history.

In 2001 Gary Ridgeway (a.k.a., Green River Killer), was arrested by the police for the series of murders dating back thirty years; during that time, Ridgeway had killed over fifty women, mostly prostitutes, and had dumped them in the Green River. The victims were bound, raped, and strangled; after killing his victims, he would dump their bodies in secluded areas, and repeatedly return to rape the corpses. Reichart (2004) notes that Ridgeway's upbringing is a textbook example of the beginnings of a sexual killer: he is raised by an overly authoritarian, strong-willed mother while his meek father's presence is minimal; he is the victim of "covert" sexual abuse from his mother, planting in Ridgeway puerile thoughts about sexuality while simultaneously sexualizing her encounters with him; he is a bed-wetter, a fire-setter, and an animal abuser from adolescence. But Ridgeway's interest in necrophilia begins at the dinner table where his father often related his brief stint as a mortuary attendant; Ridgeway tells that his father told stories of witnessing a coworker having sex with a corpse. Reichert (2004, p. 274) writes that "this scene became a subject for his son's teenage sexual fantasies," that Ridgeway liked the idea of having sex with someone that is dead because "you wouldn't get caught ... she wouldn't feel it."

Rather than conceptualizing necrophilia as an aberrant activity brought on by intrapsychic deficiencies inherent in the offender, an alternative theory might reconfigure the dynamics of necrophilia by examining the allure that a corpse might offer, and the situations that cultivate its genesis. As it has been argued, paraphilias in general seem to have an "accidental" quality to them; rather than illuminating any constitutional defects, paraphilias strongly suggest chance factors at work. Even necrophilia cannot be divorced from this contingent face.

Notice that Ridgeway's first exposure to necrophilia is a story that is overheard at the family dinner table; and from that alone, his thought patterns and behaviors escalate into a predictable one. Consider some of the other cases that have been discussed in the literature. Rapoport's (1942) well-cited case of "W.R." is such an example. W.R. is brought to the attention of the law and clinical community when he is arrested by the police for "kissing and touching the breast of a female corpse" at a funeral parlor. The subject attends his aunt's funeral and sees her laid out in a casket; according to Rapoport, W.R. becomes stimulated at the sight of his aunt, and immediately retreats to a nearby bathroom to bring relief to hand. From that moment, the subject takes proactive steps toward fulfilling his sexual fantasy by scouring the obituary columns and begins visiting them, arriving early so as to not arouse any suspicion; he then retreats to the bathroom to masturbate, thereby undergoing a conditioning response after each subsequent event (Arrigo and Purcell 2001).

Or consider the case of D.P. whose necrophilia begins when during one of his sexual encounters with his wife: he chokes her with his legs while she is performing oral-genital sex (Smith and Braun 1978). He then begins to fantasize about her completely under his control; he demands that his wife "play dead" during sex, and when she refuses, he chokes her until she loses consciousness, then performs sex acts upon her body. And much like W.R. he begins to pore through obituary columns in newspapers seeking access to corpses, as well as frequenting graveyards; when that is insufficient, he procures a job as a hospital orderly because of his newfound fascination with death; his compulsion with death, dying, and necrophilia culminates when the anteceding behaviors no longer satisfy his appetite: he begins assaulting and strangling women in the streets rather than defiling bodies in the morgues, hospitals, and cemeteries.

Finally, consider the case of a thirteen-year-old boy and a forty-year-old man whose link to necrophilia can be traced to their exposure to a funeral home during their childhood. John, a thirteen-year-old-boy, begins his interest in death, dying, and necrophilia after the mortician who handled his older sister's death asks him to tend the funeral home for a few hours while he is away (Bierman 1962). Klaf and Brown's (1966) forty-year-old patient demonstrates his interest in death at the age of nine when he helps around

with chores at a local funeral parlor. These discussed cases are not too distant from Ridgeway's interest in the funereal and necrophilia—one happens
to overhear a story about a man who has sex with a corpse; one happens to
stumble onto the sight of his deceased aunt; another happens to be asked to
tend a funeral home; another asked to work in it. The mere presence of a
disruptive and dysfunctional upbringing is not enough to "produce"
necrophilia per se, as much as it co-occurs with events during offenders'
formative years that provide fantasy stimulation; and once that initial connection is made, the steps that unfold seem to do so in a linear and logical
manner. Necrophilia can be conceptualized as an anticipatable and logical
extension of the sexual deviance because it is not a discrete occurrence as
much as it is an evolution and a graduation from a preceding set of cognitive and behavioral patterns. Conceptualizing violence in this continuous
way rather than a discrete set of offenses provides a theoretically expansive,
yet cogent, way of accounting for the often inter-related and incremental nature of violence, not only in sexual murders, but in other predatory crimes
as well.

Discussion and Conclusion

From a critical rereading and reinterpretation of the cases that have been
presented in the previous works, it is evident that the role of chance factors
can not be overlooked. Even according to one of the eminent theorists in this
area, "necrophilia, like the other perversions, depends on many cases, but is
not perhaps as deeply determined psychologically as the others" (Brill 1941b,
p. 69). The reason necrophilia is not as deeply determined as others might be
is that it is situated at such a far end of the violence continuum that harbin-
gers are ineluctably bound to surface. This chapter has sought to illuminate
such pre-offense behaviors that have not been thematically examined in the
previous works in relation to lust murders (but see Hickey 2006b).

That sexual serial killers have a well-documented history of predictors such
as enuresis, fire-setting, and cruelty to animals is, by now, criminological
gospel. Recent works have identified criminal offenses and paraphilias that precede lust murders as well, such as voyeurism, stalking, trespassing, breaking
and entering, retaliation-free offenses, and verbal and physical assault prior to
their involvement in murder (see Keppel and Birnes 1997), as well as other ec-
centric behaviors such as vampirism, salirophilia, coprophagia, telephone scat-
ologia, and zoophilia (see Hickey 2006d). What has been neglected with regard
to necrophilia is the behaviors that portend much serious offenses to follow.

The case of D.P. is again instructive here (Smith and Braun 1978). Recall that his interest in necrophilia begins "accidentally" when he chokes his wife into unconsciousness during oral-genital sex. He begins to fantasize her completely under his control and demands that she simulate a corpse; when uncooperative, he uses coercion to render her unconscious before sexually assaulting her. There are two dangerous paraphilias that resemble the escalating character of D.P.'s behaviors: asphyxia and somnophilia. The former involves choking or strangling a partner into unconsciousness before the sexual assault while the latter involves sexually assaulting those who are asleep. As Peck (2006) notes, these types of behaviors are logically related to necrophilia in that they simulate the more dangerous behaviors to come; for example, D.P. "practices" his necrophilia in such a manner before his actual run; with the prevalence and availability of drugs that can render victims unconscious with ease, these types of paraphiliacs represent a snapshot of a potential sexual killer and serial rapist in evolution. Furthermore, notice that there are behavioral features that occur with predictability: the desire to be near corpses necessitates the perusal of obituary columns, and habitual visits to funeral homes, morgues, and hospitals.

What is particularly disturbing is that necrophilia does not represent the end point in the continuum of human violence. Behaviors such as vampirism, necrophilia, and cannibalism represent the far end of the continuum, as but Keppel and Birnes (1997) argue, there is little intrinsic allure to those types of aberrations as much as they are embodiments of a much expansive acquisitive drive toward "compulsion for control." To illustrate signature theory and the continuum of violence, they discuss two of the most prolific and "evolved" sexual serial killers in the history of the United States, Ted Bundy and Jeffrey Dahmer. Bundy was a necrophiliac lust killer of the anger-retaliation type while Dahmer combined necrophilia with cannibalism into his repertoire, constructing a pseudo-alter/temple in his apartment, accessorizing it with "body parts, skeletons, and skulls of his victims. He had even drawn a crude diagram of this temple from which he hoped to receive special powers that would help him financially and spiritually" (Keppel and Birnes 1997, p. 289).

If necrophilia and cannibalism reflect the depraved acts that lie at the far end of the violence continuum, then the next logical question that warrants further investigation and exegesis is what the next level of violence might entail. Keppel and Birnes (1997) note the eerie resemblance of the behaviors exhibited by the prolific serial sexual killers (e.g., Gacy, Bundy, Dahmer) to the ritualistic aspects of religious worship; and that the murders become a ceremonial and formalized set of expressions and fantasies enacted and performed in a context of sacredness, involving objects of fetish laden with power, localized in a space imbued with the majestic awe in the psyche of the doer, connote a justifiable incursion into the theological realm to elucidate and inter-link the profane with the sacred. This nebulous distinction between the holy and the profane, along with the rites of religious worship, seem to be recognizable as such in the boundaries set by the killers themselves. For example, when Ridgeway was arrested and interrogated by the police, he confessed to placing the corpses farther and farther away from his residence to avert his necrophilic desires. He then intimated that he thought of cannibalizing the corpses; but just as shocking, he confessed to his deepest fantasy, that of impaling a woman on a pole, watching her suffer before choking her to death (see Reichart 2004). While this fantasy never materialized, it points to the uncanny similarities to the final behaviors of other notable sexual killers. Notice again the ritualistic and totemic flavor to his fantasy that is not dissimilar to the power and magic that religious symbols evoke from the worshippers. Furthermore, building a shrine in remembrance of the dead, keeping symbolic tokens of the victims' possessions as a way of reliving the crime and possessing the victims, and surrounding oneself with the bodies of those killed or re-visiting the scene of the crime in a reflective yet frenzied sexual trance parallels the practice of worshippers gripped by the throes of religious fervor. An implicit and yet unexamined part of the theorizing about serial sexual killers ought to provide a cogent and sound account as to why the strange and bizarre move toward religion is seen in the terminal behavior of the offenders.

Part 3
Media Influence and Edgework

Chapter 8

The Portrayal of Extreme Crime by the Media: Reflecting or Creating Fear?

John Randolph Fuller

Introduction

The taking of a human life is an awesome act that society roundly condemns. Homicide is one of the few crimes for which capital punishment is sometimes prescribed. Yet, all homicides are not created equal. Murders that the public finds to be especially heinous attain an iconic status. The Ted Bundy murders, the Columbine school shootings, and the O.J. Simpson case found their way from being mere news to the public's popular imagination. This essay explores the prevalence and effect of extreme crime and attempts to discover the reasons it causes so much fear and fascination. In short, this essay argues that extreme crime, while being a real concern for many individuals, has been elevated to celebrity status by media looking for sensational stories and by a public with an insatiable appetite for the lurid, grotesque, and bloody.

To the violent crime victim, all acts that cause physical harm or death appear extreme. Without negating or minimizing the trauma those victims experienced, this essay focuses on three types of crime that are particularly interesting because they garner so much attention in the media and the public's imagination. These three types of crimes are often confused, but they are distinctly different. For definitional purposes, we will delineate these crimes as follows:

- · Serial murder. Serial murder comprises a series of crimes in which individuals are killed at different times and in different locations. Each murder is a separate crime and punishable by itself. However, something usually links the murders, making it more likely that law enforcement officials will eventually catch the perpetrator(s). The link is often the type of victim. Many serial murderers seem to be obsessed with children or young women, or some other specific type of person. Ted Bundy consistently picked slender women with dark hair, as if he were killing the same woman repeatedly. Serial murderers often meticulously plan their crimes and torture their victims.

· Mass murder. Mass murder refers to incidents in which many people are killed at once. As opposed to serial murders, mass murders are more likely to be spontaneous events in which the killer reacts to real or imagined insults and just "snaps." Perhaps the most infamous such murders occur at U.S. post offices where an employee kills supervisors and co-workers. Mass murders are of short duration and often result in the suicide of the perpetrator(s).

· Lust murder. Lust murder usually involves the collapse of an intimate relationship or the final chapter in an unrequited love affair. The killer is usually male and the victim female. Often, it involves a painful divorce or other such rejection. Lust murders often involve bizarre dynamics based on sexual fetishes and psychological instabilities.

Although these types of extreme crimes (i.e. murder) reflect different features in terms of numbers of victims, motivations of offenders, and prevalence, they are not mutually exclusive. A serial murderer may have a sexual fixation that results in what appears to be a lust murder of each of the victims. While recognizing this degree of overlap in the types of murder, it is useful to maintain the distinction for the purposes of this essay so that the way the public and the press react can be more fully appreciated.

If It Bleeds, It Leads

These three types of extreme murders share an important feature. Despite their relative infrequency, they are considered to be the center of a major social problem involving extreme violence. Many people are fascinated by extreme killing, and the media—particularly the docudrama type of television program that mixes fact with conjecture—cannot get its fill of gory crime. Once a case has had its run in the news cycle (which can last for months), it gets a new life with a made-for-television movie or a book. Additionally, the myriad of investigative reporting programs will explore every aspect of the case and infuse discussions of evidence not directly linked to the crime, conspiracy theories, or suggestions that the case has paranormal features.

Unfortunately, the more gruesome the case and the more sympathetic the victim, the more appealing it is to the media and the public. For example, the murder of Lacy Peterson had some features that made it particularly attractive to those who are fascinated by extreme killing:

- Pretty white girl. The disappearance of attractive young women always seems to make the headlines. While friends, family members, and authorities plead for information and conduct searches, the media has ample opportunity to milk the story every day the victim remains missing. Pictures of the victim are displayed nationally to the point that she reaches celebrity status. The attention is so pervasive and so positive that some women have faked their own kidnappings because they believe such a case can change their lives. Although numerous individuals fall victim to foul play every day, those who generate the most publicity are attractive young women, usually white.
- Christmas. Lacy Peterson's disappearance on Christmas Eve was a particularly newsworthy detail that had the press salivating.
- Pregnant. The killing of someone about to give birth is considered to be a singularly heinous crime. The press played up this aspect of the case and went to great lengths to see that the fetus's anticipated name, Connor, was prominently mentioned in every report. American society is undergoing an emotional examination as to the possibility of a fetus having the legal standing of a non-fetal human and for whom killing would constitute murder.
- Pretty girlfriend. A girlfriend of Scott Peterson came forward as soon as she learned of the connection between the case and the fact that her allegedly single boyfriend was in fact the Scott Peterson who was suspected of killing his wife. The girlfriend came across as someone who was victimized by a pathological liar. Her story was so marketable that it produced a made-for-television movie and a book.

This is an example of a case that received far more media attention than a routine abduction and murder. It had all the elements of a Greek tragedy, complete with a heartbreaking pathos that was able to transcend the public's normal emotional distancing.

News stories about murders are unfortunately so numerous that the public has become somewhat jaded. It takes a murder with special properties to make it into the national news and turn it from a local story into a national story. These special properties revolve around the tantalizing interaction of sex and violence. Especially cold and calculating murders are contrasted with those at the other extreme that are hot-blooded and impulsive.

In what ways do these rare and scattered events drive people's fear of crime and influence their behavior? Are we in any real danger of falling victim to the types of extreme, highly publicized crime? In order to address these questions, we will examine detailed examples of each of these types of extreme killings. Famous examples are chosen because most readers will already be partially familiar with these cases and because there is plenty of publicly available material for those who wish to examine the cases in further detail. The three cases discussed are the Ted Bundy serial murders; the Columbine school shooting, and the O.J. Simpson lust-murder case. Although it is probable that more ideal cases could have been selected that would give greater clarity to the definitions of these terms, these remain part of the national conversation about violence in the United States.

The Serial Murder Poster Boy: Ted Bundy

The Ted Bundy case represents one of the more famous and less typical cases of serial murder that has found its way into the folklore of American homicide. The case is famous because it has a number of features that set it apart from other serial murder cases.

The first distinguishing feature of the Bundy case is the appearance and background of the defendant. Unlike many other serial murderers, such as John Gacy and Jeffrey Dahmer, Ted Bundy was a clean-cut, handsome young man who gave the appearance of being "the boy next door." Bundy had graduated from college and had been a law student before he began his criminal career. In 1972, he was a volunteer on the campaign for former Washington governor Dan Evans. During his trial he defended himself and apparently did fairly well for having been in law school only a year-and-a-half (Egger 1998, p. 162).

In addition to being physically attractive himself, Bundy chose young attractive women as his victims. There was a pattern to his choice of victim. The women typically had long, dark hair parted down the middle; many of his victims were students, and he was particularly good at winning their trust as he manipulated them into places where he could kill them. This pattern of killing only young, pretty females made the case extremely attractive to the media. Just as the leading lady in a movie is usually beautiful, so were Bundy's victims. A third interesting feature of the Bundy case was the number and geographic locations of the crimes. Bundy killed women in at least five states: Washington, Oregon, Utah, Colorado, and Florida. This gave the case a national foundation and made parents fear for their children wherever they lived. It meant that no one was safe. The Bundy case also proved that local news could easily become national news.

The Bundy case is especially interesting to the media because there were additional aspects that made it easy to blur the line between news and entertainment. The lurid sexual details of many of Bundy's murders have been published because the public has an appetite for them. One profile of Bundy portrays his method of killing this way:

> He raped most, if not all, of his victims; several were subjected to sodomy and sexual mutilations. Some of the victims had vaginal lacerations caused by foreign objects. In the Chi Omega sorority house killings in Tallahassee, Florida, Bundy left teeth marks on the breast and buttocks of at least one victim. In some cases Bundy would keep the body for days and is believed by some investigators to have shampooed the hair of and applied makeup to more than one victim (Hickey 2006a, p. 174).

It is this sort of scintillating detail that nurtures interest in Ted Bundy. People are tempted to try to psychoanalyze Bundy and speculate on his motivations for engaging in such unusual behavior. Why would a young man with such a normal appearance and background abuse and kill so many young women? The answer has never been adequately determined, but a look at what investigators, family members, former girlfriends, and criminologists have suggested is worth noting. For instance, many people have noted that Bundy always wanted to be in control. After one woman ended an engagement, Bundy remained in contact with her and re-established the relationship to the point that the woman believed they were engaged again. Bundy then ended the relationship again and refused to contact her anymore. He told one investigator that he simply wanted to prove that he could have married her if he had wanted to (Egger 1998, p. 149).

Bundy prided himself on his charm. He could talk to people easily and win their trust. Some have suggested that his training and experience from working at a Seattle crisis clinic was instrumental in developing a persona that allowed young women to trust him. For example, one technique that he used was to have his arm in a fake cast in order to appear helpless and non-threatening.[1] He then asked a young woman if she could go with him to help him

---

1. A demonstration of this technique can be seen in the film *The Silence of the Lambs* when a serial murderer uses it to lure a young woman into a van. Author Thomas Harris based this character partly on Ted Bundy.

secure his sailboat to his car. She refused because she had a funny feeling about getting into a car with a stranger, even a nice, clean-cut young man. That day, two other young women disappeared at the same lake, and police speculate that they fell victim to Bundy's broken-arm ruse.

The way the press presented the Bundy case was almost romantic. Some might mistake him for a misunderstood young man who, but for finding the right woman who could share his pain, was a heroic figure who battled unseen demons. By all accounts he had an engaging personality, and the photos of him taken during his trial, where he wore a turtleneck sweater and sports coat, made him look studious and scholarly, like a young lawyer or professor. Given the horrific nature of his crimes, why did the press treat Bundy as a celebrity? One reason is that he courted the press. When imprisoned, he often communicated with reporters to try to present a favorable image. In his Florida trial, the judge forbade such communication, much to Bundy's distress.

The Ted Bundy case is atypical of serial murder cases because of the reasons already mentioned, especially the attractiveness of both perpetrator and victims. More importantly, however, is the relatively favorable light in which Bundy has become to be viewed. In a made-for-television movie Bundy was played by actor Mark Harmon, a classic, leading-man actor. By having such an actor play this part, Bundy came across to the public in a much more sympathetic manner. It can be suggested then that there is an interesting dynamic between the character of the killer and the way that character is portrayed in the media. Whereas the image of Ted Bundy certainly benefited from this dynamic, someone like John Wayne Gacy, who is not considered to be handsome, has been portrayed in a much less sympathetic light.

Mass Murder

Another type of extreme crime that is subject to media sensationalism is mass murder. Unlike serial murder, all the victims are killed in one incident. The reasons for mass murder vary, but it is fair to say that revenge for humiliation is a common theme. Here, we will examine one such case in detail, the school shooting at Columbine High School, and describe how it captivated the media.

Columbine High School is situated in the town of Littleton, Colorado, near Denver. On the morning of April 20, 1999, two students, Eric Harris, eighteen, and Dylan Klebold, seventeen, brought to school guns, two twenty-lb. propane bombs, and assorted smaller bombs and ammunition in duffel bags, backpacks, and pouches. The pair's original plan, authorities say, was to detonate bombs inside the school, then shoot anyone who escaped. However, the propane bombs, which Harris and Klebold set up in the cafeteria, failed to explode. At this point, authorities believe, they changed their plans, which they had worked on over the course of a year, and began shooting victims throughout the school. The shooting began at 11:19 a.m. and ended in the school's library at 11:35 a.m., when Klebold and Harris committed suicide. In the end, the two killed thirteen people and injured twenty-one. If the propane bombs set in the cafeteria had detonated, experts say nearly 500 people might have perished (the school had nearly 2,000 students total at this time). Harris and Klebold also planted bombs inside their cars with the intention of killing responding emergency personnel. In examining Klebold's and Harris's writings and other records, investigators found a list of sixty-seven people that the teens disliked. However, only one of those people was injured in the attack, and he did not appear to be a specific target (CNN).

The list of reasons for the Columbine murders is long and includes just about every explanation one can imagine. Helen Brown (2005) of the *London Daily Telegraph* wrote, "The media ... threw a tantrum, hurling blame as indiscriminately as toys from a pram: computer games, heavy metal music, trenchcoats, America, guns. Nothing wrapped it up". Klebold and Harris were tired of being bullied (Fox and Levin 2005, p. 214). The school gave too much attention and leeway to athletes (Adams and Russakoff 1999). Klebold was a typically depressed, suicidal adolescent who happened to meet up with Harris, a classic psychopath (Cullen 2004). It was the 110th anniversary of Adolf Hitler's birth (Sprengelmeyer and Ames 2000). In 2002, a survivor of the attack sued Solvay Pharmaceuticals, claiming it was the company's anti-depressant drug Luvox that made Harris homicidal (Mulkern 2004). Some critics said entertainment media were to blame for the teens' behavior, including video games and popular music, specifically the music of pop star Marilyn Manson.

Although investigators say it appears that although no one knew of the teens' exact plans, the two had exhibited disturbing behavior. Harris and Klebold made a video for a class project advertising a service that would kill school bullies and showed the two in the school with guns. In February 1999, Klebold wrote a class essay about a man who kills a group of students and then detonates a bomb to divert police. Harris told a coworker at a pizza restaurant he was collecting propane tanks in order to blow up the school (Sprengelmeyer and Ames 2000). Harris and Klebold had recently completed a juvenile diversion course for burglarizing a van in January 1998. In February 1999, they were released from the program early, three months before the attack (CBS News 2002).

Media Coverage

The name "Marilyn Manson" has never celebrated the sad fact that America puts killers on the cover of *Time* magazine, giving them as much notoriety as our favorite movie stars. From Jesse James to Charles Manson, the media, since their inception, have turned criminals into folk heroes. They just created two new ones when they plastered those dipshits Dylan Klebold and Eric Harris' pictures on the front of every newspaper. Don't be surprised if every kid who gets pushed around has two new idols (Manson 1999, pp. 23-26).

The media coverage of the Columbine shootings was frenetic. In an April 2000 "Media Overdose Alert," Rocky Mountain Media Watch reported that between May and October 1999, the three Denver television stations mentioned Columbine in 1,199 separate broadcasts (Rocky Mountain Media Watch, 2000). A quick-and-dirty article search of the *New York Times* website turns up at least 128 stories between April 20, 1999, and March 23, 2005, with at least twelve stories as late as 2004. The paper of record has produced articles about the event every year since it happened.

In March 2005, a story by Eric Black of the (Minneapolis) *Star Tribune* drew unfavorable comparisons between the coverage of the Red Lake High School shootings and Columbine (Wilgoren 2005).[2] It can be argued that the shock of the Columbine shootings, fifteen people dead in sixteen minutes, would merit such coverage. In terms of body count, it remains the worst school shooting in U.S. history. Also, the victims' parents, as well as some of the victims themselves, continue with lawsuits and public allegations, each one earning a few more inches of copy or minutes of airtime. It was not until early 2004 that the parents of Dylan Klebold gave their first interview about their son and the attack (AP/MSNBC 2004). Columbine coverage continues because Columbine, in a sense, will never end.

However, the *Tribune*'s Eric Black pointed out, "When two students shot up Columbine High School in 1999, all three network anchors traveled to the Denver suburb to lead live coverage. No network anchors went to Red Lake. In the four days after Columbine, the *New York Times* published eight stories about the shooting on its front page. This week, the *Times* had three front-

---

2. On March 21, 2005, 16-year-old Jeff Weise shot and killed five students, a security guard, a teacher, and himself at Red Lake High School on Red Lake Indian reservation in Minnesota. Before the school shooting, he shot and killed his grandfather and his grandfather's girlfriend.

page stories about Red Lake" (Black 2005). It is true the Red Lake shootings did not garner nearly as much coverage as Columbine. This could be because the public has become accustomed to such mass murders. There have been several since Columbine, and they do not generate the press that they once did. Every shooting becomes a little less shocking; the public has heard it all before. In his article, Black points out that, "Compared with Columbine, Red Lake took longer to reach, granted less access to reporters, produced weaker video images, suffered fewer casualties and occurred after the horror of school shootings has become more common" (Black 2005). However, he also points out that factors such as poverty, cultural differences (the Red Lake shootings took place on an Indian reservation), and general racism were probably also at play. However, Black quotes news executives saying that the major difference was indeed access. The Denver suburb was so easy to get to that news crews arrived during the crisis and got footage of survivors fleeing the school. By contrast, the Red Lake reservation is five hours from Minnesota, and by the time the cameras arrived, the violence was over. Also, tribal authorities restricted access to interviewees. Black quoted Gary Hill, a manager at KSTP, as saying, "Television needs images. We need people on camera talking" (Black 2005). A Columbine that had been restricted to news copy and a few photos might have largely faded from memory today.

It is interesting that New York University professor Jay Rosen called Columbine a "media frenzy" and "overdone," adding that Red Lake was but a slightly smaller media frenzy (Black 2005). On the one-year anniversary of the tragedy, Rocky Mountain Media Watch (2000) advised citizens to do the following:

· Limit your media dose of this story. Turn the TV and radio off as appropriate.
· Resist being seduced by the emotional aspects of this story.
· Ask yourself—is this reporting really relevant to my life?
· Call your local station or newspaper and complain about excess coverage.
· Talk about the quality of news with family and friends.
· Seek alternative sources of news and information, like community radio and on-line sites.

The coverage of Columbine has not stopped with the news media. Well over a hundred books about the shooting or that reference it have been published, and as of 2004 at least four films have been produced: *Elephant*, *Zero Day*, *Home Room*, and the tangentially related *Bowling for Columbine*. *Elephant* creator, Gus Van Sant, said he had difficulty getting the film made (it eventually won the Palme d'Or at Cannes), and that he originally wanted to make it for television. Ironically, however, much of the blame for the Columbine attack had been placed on entertainment media, specifically television, movies, and video games. In a (London) *Sunday Times* article, Van Sant said, "People tend to consider any movie that's not a documentary an entertainment." Presumably, entertainment executives did not want to be seen as cashing in on a tragedy that they were considered to partly have caused (Applebaum 2004).

Lust-Murder

Lust-murder is a relatively new term in criminology that is used to label homicides in which a love/hate element is operating. Many cases of domestic violence can be considered lust-murders when one partner who is rejected decides that if they cannot have their partner then nobody can. Most often, lust-murder involves a male killing a female, but the reverse also occurs. Sometimes the lust-murder will spill over into the category of mass murder when several other victims are killed as the perpetrator kills the intended victim. This type of incident is commonly seen when a husband enters his wife's workplace and kills her along with her co-workers and anyone else who happens to be there.

The best-known case of lust-murder is probably the O.J. Simpson case. This case is used here to illustrate the dynamics of lust-murder, but with a caveat. Simpson was acquitted in his criminal trial. The jury did not find sufficient evidence to convict him. However, in the civil trial, in which Simpson was sued by the victims' relatives, he was found culpable and a large monetary judgment was levied against him. The level and quality of evidence is different for these two types of legal proceedings. In the criminal trial, the burden of proof must rise to the level of "beyond a reasonable doubt," while in the civil trial it need be only at the "preponderance of evidence" level. This chapter takes no stance on whether Simpson was guilty of the crime, but rather, we will speak about the crime as if he actually committed it because, in the public's imagination, he did. Admittedly, this posture is unfair to Simpson, but the goal here is not to attempt justice, but rather to explicate the concept of lust-murder, which the popular conception of the case illustrates so well. Because the case is so well known, the description here is brief. However, what is more important to the purpose of this essay is the media's reaction to the crime.

On June 12, 1994, Nicole Brown Simpson and Ron Goldman were found dead outside her Los Angeles home. They had both been stabbed repeatedly, and Simpson's neck was lacerated to such an extent that she was almost decapitated. The murder weapon was never found, and the police charged O.J. Simpson with the crime based on forensic evidence and his inability to provide a convincing alibi. While the state was not able to adequately prove the case against Simpson, they did portray him as a jealous ex-husband who was capable of violence against his wife. There had been previous physical violence in the relationship, and the state produced pictures of a beaten and bruised Nicole Simpson that she claimed was the result of abuse by O.J. The case has all the markings of a typical lust-murder, but it was elevated to a media sensation because of the Simpsons' celebrity status. Particularly titillating to the media and the public was the gruesome accounts of the murders that indicated a deep rage and an out-of-control murderer.

Although the murders were gruesome and O.J. Simpson was a celebrity, the case became a major public spectacle largely because of the trial's television coverage. The Simpson defense team, nicknamed the "dream team," included F. Lee Bailey, Allan Dershowitz, Johnnie Cochran, and Barry Neufeld. Millions of people watched on television and celebrity talk-show hosts made the case a nightly subject. Some of them, such as Geraldo Rivera, took extreme positions on Simpson's guilt well before the trial. Polls showed that race was a factor in whether the public believed Simpson guilty or innocent.

Conclusion

The media plays a large role in determining the public's perception of the level and dangerousness of crime. Some extreme crimes capture the attention of the media in a disproportional manner, so the public receives a distorted and overly pessimistic picture of crime. Serial murders, mass murders, and lust-murder make good copy for newspapers and draw viewers for television but are statistically rare.

It is tempting to blame the media for this situation, and they might even deserve a little criticism. However, we are faced with the old chicken-and-egg dilemma. Do the media simply give the public what it demands, or do the media play a major role in shaping that demand? The answer is probably a little of both. The media are large and fragmented, so it is not surprising that those who seek the blood and gore of extreme crime can find it in newspapers, magazines, the Internet, true-crime novels, or television. When it becomes problematic is when a story captures attention for an extended period of time based on its shock factor rather than actual newsworthiness.

Chapter 9

High Profile Serial Killers and Capital Punishment 1977–1994

Christopher Kudlac

Introduction

Gerald Stano, who was in the cell next to Ted Bundy on Florida's death row, admitted killing forty-one young women, mostly hitchhikers and prostitutes, between 1969 and 1980. He was convicted of ten murders and, like Bundy, sentenced to death three times between 1983 and 1986. But his trial and sentence received little national newspaper attention. Stano was executed March 23, 1998, also without much media attention. Why was Gerald Stano not a media sensation like Bundy, John Wayne Gacy, Richard Ramirez, or Aileen Wuornos? This chapter examines the Bundy, Gacy, Ramirez, and Wuornos cases for answers.

There is no doubt that serial murder and mass murder are newsworthy topics. This was particularly true starting in the late 1970s and early 1980s as the notion of serial killing entered into the popular culture. One needs only to note the number of movies and books and the amount of media coverage focusing on the issue. Legitimate concerns over crime were meshed with separate issues of missing and exploited children, organized pedophilia, and ill-defined concerns about the prevalence of homosexuality to create an aura of "moral panic" (Jenkins 1994, pp. 51-55). The number of victims and the gruesome details of the murder scenes were all attractive elements for a story. Media coverage of serial killing proliferated from 1977 onward with intense reporting on several cases that had attracted immense public interest, which helped shape public perceptions of the emerging problem. The media also popularized the label "serial murderer" in the 1980s. This concept distinguishes between types of multiple homicide, depending on the time intervals that separate the individual attacks: murders committed in a brief period in one place are mass murders; those carried out over a few days or a week are characterized as spree-killings; serial murder implies that the killings are spread over months or years, with a cooling off period intervening (Jenkins 1994, p. 21).

The media's interest in serial killing took off once the number of killers and victims that were allegedly present in the country was reported by the FBI on January 21, 1984. The press played upon the idea that serial killing was a new and particularly American problem. *The New York Times* published a front-page story about the "rise in killers who roam the U.S. for victims":

> history offers nothing to compare with the spate of such murders that has occurred in the United States since the beginning of the 1970s. That as many as four thousand Americans a year, at least half of them under the age of eighteen, are murdered in this way. He (Heck) said he believes that at least 35 such killers are now roaming the country (Lindsey 1984, p. A1).

Time and *Newsweek* followed up with articles dealing with the psychology of "mass killers" and "random killers," while HBO aired the television documentary, *Murder: No Apparent Motive*. There now emerged an influential stereotype of the serial killer: a white male in his thirties or forties, a sexually motivated murderer who preyed on either men or women, depending on his sexual orientation. This stereotype of the serial killer would be an important factor in the coverage of high-profile cases.

In the early 1980s, the extent of serial killing was being exaggerated across the country. The media and law-enforcement authorities reported that there were four or five thousand victims, some twenty to twenty-five percent of the total homicide victims. This figure is compared with one or two percent of homicide victims decades earlier (Jenkins 1994, p. 22). The FBI, in a 1984 press conference, indicated that the number of victims was closer to 540 than the 4,000 given earlier (Jenkins 1994, p. 69). Later challenges would further reduce the number of suspected victims.

Part of the increase in media coverage of serial killers can be explained by looking at changes in the reporting of news. Large metropolitan newspapers like the *New York Times* and *Los Angeles Times* did not expand their regional news coverage until after the 1950s. Regional and local newspapers increasingly became part of larger networks, which resulted in sensational stories being extended outside of their local market and picked up by national newspapers. Also, a growing trend in sensationalistic news practices exploded during the 1980s (Jenkins 1994, pp. 30-31). This made it possible for crimes and killers, who would have gone unnoticed earlier, to become national stories. This was especially true for serial killers, whose stories are ripe for sensationalism.

Additionally, the topic was highly visible in popular fiction, where true-crime books, novels, and films fueled the public's imagination. Considerably more fiction and true-crime books were published in the three years from 1991 through 1993 than in the 1960s and 1970s combined. Multiple murder was the theme of more American films in 1980 and 1981 than in the previous two decades together (Jenkins 1994, pp. 51-52). Even comedy movies such as *Serial Mom* and *So I Married an Axe Murderer* illustrate how the serial killer image has been integrated into the fabric of everyday life ("Serial Killer Movies" 1984, p. 7).

This point is well articulated during an interview with David Von Drehle, a national staff writer for the *Washington Post*:

> Serial killers were the zeitgeist of that time. You had family break ups, sexual liberation, end of the home town, families not living all together, suburbanization of America, postwar '60s and early '70s, people don't know their neighbor. Look at fiction, movies and journalism, you start to see archetypal figure of a drifter, lure of open road, and the anti-hero, who is turned off by American values and rebels against. You have Truman Capote making a hero out of Perry Smith and then Bundy comes along in the '70s and fits right into that. He looks like your next door neighbor, you wouldn't be nervous if you saw him on your street but secretly driving his V.W. and raping and killing somebody at night. This information in the hands of good storytellers resonates with all different fears, still talking about it 13 years later (Interview with David Von Drehle, reporter *The Washington Post* on March 28, 2002).

Serial killers became symbolic of the rising crime rates, the breakdown of the community, the need for tougher law enforcement policies and individualistic crime explanations that were being promoted.

Many people were found guilty of capital charges and executed between 1977 and 1994, but four cases received more media attention than any other: Ted Bundy, John Wayne Gacy, Richard Ramirez, and Aileen Wuornos. These cases are closely examined to demonstrate why they were the most newsworthy cases in the twenty-year period examined. Analysis of the newspaper coverage and interviews with the reporters who covered the cases was done, with specific focus on the differences between the local and national coverage, the evolution of the coverage over time, connections that were made with larger political or social issues including serial killing.

Case Studies

The Newspaper Coverage of Ted Bundy

Ted Bundy may be the most well-known serial murderer ever rivaling only Jack the Ripper for notoriety. The Bundy case retained the public interest for more than a decade. The affair first came to light in 1974 with a series of unsolved murders in Washington; murders continued to occur in Utah and Colorado over the next two years, but it was not until Bundy's arrest in Colorado in January 1977 that his name was publicly attached to the incidents. National attention continued after he was placed on the FBI's Ten Most Wanted list. On February 11, 1978, *The New York Times* described Bundy as being "the most prolific mass murderer in American history, surpassing Juan v. Corona, who was convicted of killing twenty-six migrant farm workers in California." From here on, the newspaper coverage consistently focused on the number of victims (i.e. "36 sexual slayings") ("Mass Murder Suspect on F.B.I Fugitive List," 1978).

The national news did not take additional interest in the case until he was arrested for what has become known as the "Chi Omega Murders"(in which Bundy entered a sorority house at night beating five women and raping and strangling two to death) and the death of a twelve-year-old girl, Kimberly Leach, in Florida in February of 1978. It is interesting to note that in the early coverage of Bundy, the media never refers to him as a serial killer. The notion and label would not enter the public arena until the mid-1980s.

Bundy's Trials

Bundy was now the confirmed suspect in thirty-six murders from 1974 to 1978 that stretched across five states. He was charged with only the three murders that took place in Florida. Between his arrest in Florida and the start of the trial for the Chi Omega murders, the Bundy story began to take shape in the papers. Mixed perceptions of Bundy still persisted at this point demonstrated by the *Los Angeles Times* headline on May 3, 1978 "Experts Differ on Suspected Mass Killer: Some See Ted Bundy as Scapegoat in 40 Sex Slayings." A March 12, 1978, article in *The New York Times* articulates the debate on Bundy:

> For several weeks now the police in this southern capital have held in armor-plated jail cells a man who either is a victim of unusual circumstances or—as the police in several states suspect—the killer of at least 36 women (Nordheimer 1978, p. A1).

The Bundy trial, which started in 1978, was covered in great detail by the press. Bundy's second trial in 1980, for the murder of twelve-year-old Kimberly Leach, was covered locally as closely as the first trial, but nationally was not covered as extensively as the first.

Bundy's Execution

As Bundy's execution approached, the reporters wrote about every aspect of the case. Stories about the victims and their families and the appeals that were taking place were enough to provide daily coverage regarding the Bundy case for more than a week prior to the execution. Bundy helped the newspapers' desire for something to write about by confessing to a number of additional murders.

The execution itself was covered in great detail by local and national newspapers. The sentiments surrounding Bundy's execution can be seen in the descriptions of the scene outside of the execution site:

> Crowds of death penalty supporters outside the Florida State Prison cheered and applauded his death as a white hearse left the prison with Bundy's body. Many wore T-shirts and carried sparklers and banners with "Fry Bundy" slogans. Some carried effigies of Bundy strapped in a chair (Morgan and Nickens 1989, p. A1).

Both the local and national news mentioned the lack of death penalty opponents outside of the prison. The reporters who were there compared the scene to nothing they have ever been part of before or since:

> The Bundy execution was different; it had huge crowds. It was like a festival, people were selling electrocution lapels that had Old Sparky on it and t-shirts with the electric chair. Pick up trucks were driving around with stuffed Teds sitting in electric chairs. There were signs and posters, people selling champagne and doughnuts. Don't know of any sight like this before or since. Local deejays were promoting "Fryday" on the radio. People came from all over the country and almost everybody was in favor of the death penalty (Interview with Lucy Morgan, *St. Petersburg Times* on June 22, 2001).

The Newsworthiness of Ted Bundy

Many newsworthy elements attracted journalists to the Bundy case. First and foremost, he came to be associated with a large number of murder victims. By the time he was arrested in Florida, there were few articles that did not mention that he was assumed responsible for thirty-six victims. However, it is not just the number of victims but their characteristics that must be seen as important. All of his victims were young women that are described as pretty and coming from good backgrounds, mostly college students. The two college students in Florida are frequently referred to as "two Chi-omega sorority sisters" or described as "coed". Additionally, the victims were all white with brown hair parted down the middle.

Another important element in the coverage of the Bundy case was his characteristics. Reporters frequently noted that Bundy did not fit the mold of your typical murderer:

> Bundy was different than your normal killer, he was a reasonably good looking, nice, educated person who was able to pass himself off to people, pick up victims with his personality. He had virtues that people could identify with, looks and charm (Interview with Lucy Morgan, reporter for *St. Petersburg Times* on June 22, 2001).

This focus can be seen when the *New York Times* dedicated fourteen pages to him in their *Sunday Magazine* (Nordheimer 1978, p. 46) titled "All-American Boy on Trial." The article begins:

> Here was a young man who represented the best in America, not its worst. Here was this terrific looking man with light brown hair and blue eyes, looking rather Kennedyesque, dressed in a beige turtleneck and dark blue blazer, a smile turning the corners of his lean all-American face, walking jauntily before the judge, but free of any extravagant motion that could lead one to think a swaggering—even dangerous—-personality existed beneath that casual, cool exterior.

Journalists consistently spoke of Bundy as smart, handsome and a law student. "The suspect, Theodore Robert Bundy, is handsome, articulate, and college educated. He has a flair and charm that makes him 'the kind of guy you'd want your daughter to bring home' as one investigator put it" (Nordheimer 1978, p. A1). These descriptions are offered almost to suggest that someone college educated and smart could not be capable of these crimes. Mark I. Pinskey, a *Los Angeles Times* reporter, argues: "An issue I raised, from the beginning, was that if you are white, good-looking and appear middle class you can become a successful predator because you do not fit the traditional 'criminal' profile" (Interview with Mark I. Pinskey, *Los Angeles Times* reporter on January 6, 2002).

The nature of Bundy's offenses also added to newsworthiness of the story. Newspapers consistently gave the details of his crimes including the sexual elements of the cases. He is said to have raped all of the women that he murdered. One of the key elements of the prosecution's case was the presentation of teeth marks found on one of the victims of the Chi Omega murders buttocks and breast, which only added to the sexual tones of the coverage.

Additionally, his trials were particularly attractive for the news media because of many novel elements that played out during it. Bundy acted as his own attorney and television cameras filmed the trial, which was novel at the time ("Key testimony to be allowed in murder trial," 1979). Then he asked a witness to marry him during questioning, the day that he was sentenced to die for the third time. The right mix of circumstances also came together with the newspaper coverage of John Wayne Gacy.

The Newspaper Coverage of John Wayne Gacy

John Wayne Gacy's story became the focal point of the local newspapers starting in December of 1978 when the police searched his house in suburban Chicago and discovered the remains of nearly thirty people. Gacy, a local contractor, attracted young males to his home and sexually abused and killed them, disposing of most of them under his home. The Gacy story dominated the local media for years on end. The Gacy body count would grow steadily until finally, in April 1979, the remains of Robert Piest were discovered in the Illinois River, making him the 33rd victim. Gacy told police that the reason he disposed of the bodies in the river was because he ran out of room in the crawl space under his house. Along with the number of bodies, pictures, and maps of Gacy's house showing where the bodies were discovered were featured (Mount and Kozol 1978, p. A1). The national newspapers became interested in the story once the body count began to rise, however, their coverage was much briefer.

Similar to Bundy, reporters' description of Gacy compared him to a preconceived notion of what a killer was supposed to look like. This is evident in the headline of a *Chicago Tribune* article: "Danger Cited: Killers Don't Always Look the Part" (Sneed and Kozol 1978, p. A1). The descriptions of Gacy talked about the two sides of his personality. They focused on the fact that he was a Democratic Precinct Captain, leader of the Polish Day Parade and friendly business owner. Gacy also entertained children at parties dressed as a clown. There was a cover picture of Gacy dressed as "Pogo" the clown on the front page of the *Tribune* on December 27, 1978, which was subsequently shown nationwide. An equally famous picture shows him with then first lady Rosalind Carter at a Democratic fund raiser in Chicago. All of this weighed against the fact that he killed thirty-three people. Conversely, like the stereotype being established of serial killers, Gacy was consistently referred to as evil: "If the devil's alive, he lived here" (Kozol and Sneed 1978, p. A1). Like Bundy, the label serial killer was not attached to Gacy until much later.

Trial Coverage

On February 6, 1980, John Wayne Gacy's murder trial began in the Cook County Criminal Courts Building in Chicago, Illinois. The local paper had daily stories on the lawyers, judges and witnesses that would be called. The trial coverage focused on the duality of Gacy's personality as shown by the headlines of the articles discussing the trial: "Witnesses at Sex Murder Trial: 2 Faces of Gacy: 'Beast', 'Nice Man'" (*Los Angeles Times*, 2/22/80) and "John Wayne Gacy, Jr.: A Model Citizen and a Mass Murderer" (*Los Angeles Times*, 3/16/80). Gacy's lawyer also played upon this idea, reading from Robert Louis Stevenson's *The Strange Case of Dr. Jekyll and Mr. Hyde*. The jury was presented with testimony of over a hundred witnesses over a period of five weeks. They deliberated for only two hours before rendering a guilty verdict. He was found guilty of murdering thirty-three people, more than any other person in U.S. history at the time.

The Execution Coverage

In the week before the execution, multiple stories appeared daily discussing everything and everybody involved with the case. The newspapers also, ironically, wrote articles about all the attention the case was generating (Feder 1994 p. 47; Byrne 1994, p. 37). The day before the execution, articles covered every step that Gacy would take over the next 24 hours, "after dinner, Gacy plans to confess his sins to a Roman Catholic priest, then attend a 9 p.m. mass in the prison" (Drell and Long 1994, p. 1). This is consistent with the Bundy coverage.

On the day of the execution, May 10, 1994, the *Chicago Sun-Times* had eleven articles about John Wayne Gacy. Some of the headlines were: "Death Draws Crowd But Little Sympathy," "Forget Gacy, Victims Worth Remembering," and "Justice, Not Revenge, Is Concern Of Victim's Sister." Much like Bundy, reporters detailed the scene outside the execution where many gathered both for and against the death penalty. The stories discussed everything from people selling t-shirts that read "no tears for the clown" (Cotliar 1994,

p. 7), people chanting "put the clown in the ground" (Fornek 1994, p. 6), and those speaking out against the death penalty (Cotliar 1994, p. 7). Much greater weight was given to the anti-death penalty voices in the Gacy coverage than to Bundy's execution some five years earlier, but still an overwhelming amount of attention was placed on the pro-death penalty supporters.

The Newsworthiness of the John Wayne Gacy Story

Like Bundy, the media were fascinated with the number of victims for which Gacy was responsible. Along with the daily coverage of the body count, journalists immediately picked up on the sexual elements of the case. Gacy was a convicted sex offender, due to an arrest in 1968, and this is consistently mentioned both locally and nationally along with the sexual details of the murders. The typical description of Gacy in the early accounts read like this:

> Gacy, a convicted sex offender, reportedly told investigators he had sexual relations with 32 young men, then strangled them, buried 27 under his home and threw five into the Des Plaines River ("Slaying Suspect in Restraints" p. 78).

Reporters also frequently described how the victims were killed; detailing the sexual abuse and intricate self-strangulating chair to which Gacy tied them. Steven Braun, a reporter for the *Los Angles Times*, believes that the media was attracted to this story because of:

> The magnitude of the crimes, Gacy's lack of repentance and euphoric nostalgia for the act of murder. There was also a weird symmetry of a former clown and former Democratic party apparatchik who had managed to get along so well in society while he blithely went about butchering 33 young men (Interview with Steven Braun, *Los Angeles Times* reporter on January 25, 2002).

Another important element was the Chicago location, which is home to one of the country's largest media. Competition over interviews with victims who had survived their contact with Gacy, victims' families and law enforcement officials fueled the story in the Chicago papers.

Additionally, many stories focused on the characteristics of the victims and the tragedy now facing their families. Since many of the boys were runaways, a quick linkage was also made with the Gacy story and runaways. This connection with other social problems was one of the keys, which contributed to the concern of serial killing during the 1980s. A *New York Times* article subtly shows the class and gender biases that the newspapers held when speaking of Gacy's victims: "Some were male prostitutes, but many were high school-age youths who came to his home expecting work with his construction firm" (Kifner 1994, p. A12).

The statement makes it seem like it is okay to kill male prostitutes but it was wrong when he killed high school youths. These types of biases help explain differential amounts of newspaper coverage of particular murders and murderers. If Bundy had not killed "pretty girls from good homes" would he have received the same amount of attention? If Gacy had only killed male prostitutes would the media have cared? The importance of the victims' characteristics in newsworthiness can also be seen clearly with the newspaper's coverage of Richard Ramirez.

The Newspaper Coverage of Richard Ramirez

A wave of murders swept across California in the summer of 1985 that caused widespread fear and panic. The murders were eventually connected to one man, initially called the Valley Intruder but then labeled the Night Stalker by the press (first attributed to the *Los Angeles Herald-Examiner*). His first murder occurred in June of 1984 when he broke into a house and killed a seventy-nine-year-old woman. He did not strike again until February of 1985 when he kidnapped and sexually abused a six year-old girl. His attacks became more frequent with sixteen between March and August of 1985. Yet it wasn't until August 8, 1985 that the police announced that they were after a serial killer, who was responsible for killings from Los Angeles to San Francisco. Then on August 28, the police revealed the name of the wanted killer. The Night Stalker's identity, Richard Ramirez, was not known until the LAPD was able to lift a print from his abandoned car.

The newspaper coverage consistently focused on the fact that he was a serial killer. Articles talked about his distinctive signature or "trademark" ("2 Attacks Attributed To Killer in California," 1985) that was left at each of the crime scenes and frequently discussed the stereotypes that were associated with serial killers.

> At his press conference Tuesday, during which he stressed public awareness, Gates called the Stalker—also known as the Valley Intruder—'an unorthodox serial killer' and pointed out that 'due to the Night Stalker's ... random selection process, we do not know where he will strike next.' But he said the serial killer generally 'strikes in the

early morning hours ... near freeways' and advised citizens to take several precautions to 'decrease the chance of a second incident' (*Los Angeles Times*, 8/28/85).

Early articles frequently talked about the "profile" of serial killers and differences in criminal work when one is looking for a serial killer, as can be seen by the August 29, 1985, *Los Angeles Times* article titled "Psychological Profile: Probing Killer's Mind," which discusses "Mind Hunters," the FBI's computer profiling operations in connection with the Ramirez case. The profilers "handle 300 referrals a year from local law enforcement agencies who are looking for serial killers or rapists—including the case of the Night Stalker" (Baker 1985, p. B1).

With daily features on the Night Stalker widespread fear gripped California. Reporters discussed how residents were staying up at night looking for the serial killer and that many residents "mobilized by fear, who have joined the Police Department's Operation Night Watch" (Avery 1985, p. B1). Also, articles discussed the rise in gun sales and the need for gun safety.

The case took a new turn on August 31, 1985 when residents in a ... California suburb caught Ramirez. The *Los Angeles Times* describes the scene:

> Desperate and near exhaustion, Night Stalker Richard Ramirez made a wrong turn when he dashed onto Hubbard Street—unknowingly he had stumbled into a neighborhood of heroes. Four citizens grabbed and subdued the suspected murderer after a 20-second footrace, one of them pounding at him with a steel rod (Belcher and Skeleton 1985, p. A1).

The *New York Times* detailed the capture and noted: "after Mr. Ramirez's arrest, hundreds of residents crowded outside the police station where he was being held and chanted, 'Kill him, kill him" (Lindsey 1985, p. A20).

Trial Coverage

On September 4, 1985, Ramirez appeared in court for the first of many times to hear the initial charges against him. On September 27, Ramirez was arraigned on sixty-eight felony charges including fourteen murders; the prosecutor said that the death penalty would be sought in each of the murder charges. Ramirez's trial would be delayed repeatedly. It was not until October 24, 1985, that Ramirez entered his plea of innocent to the court. This moment made for the first of many, where reporters would concentrate on Ramirez's courtroom antics. As he was led from the courtroom he displayed a pentagram with his hands and shouted "Hail Satan!"

The trial began on January 29, 1989, after a three-year delay, with television cameras allowed to shoot parts of the trial. This was a disputed topic as the judge originally banned cameras from the courtroom during the preliminary hearing ("Camera Ban At Ramirez Hearing To Face Challenge," 1985). The local newspaper provided daily coverage of the trial; the national newspapers did not follow the trial in detail. After thirty-one days, 137 witnesses and 521 exhibits, the prosecution rested on April 13, 1989. Ramirez once again struck out at the media in the courtroom yelling, "Media: Sensation-seeking parasites" ("Night Stalker Suspect Yells At Press," 1989).

The deliberations took until September 20, 1989, when the jury found Ramirez guilty on thirteen murder counts and thirty other felony counts. They recommended the death penalty. Ramirez once again addressed the court stating "You maggots make me sick—one and all. I am beyond your experience, I am beyond good and evil ..." (Chen 1989, p. A1).

The jury returned with their recommendation for the gas chamber on October 3, 1989. Ramirez was then in and out of the news occasionally when the reward money was finally handed out to his captors and whenever there were appeals of his convictions. He was also in the news briefly when in 1996 he got married to Doreen Lioy at San Quentin where he has been awaiting his execution.

The Newsworthiness of the Richard Ramirez Story

The number and details of the attacks, the Los Angeles setting, his connection with Satanism and the characteristics of victims led to immediate interest in the case. Reporters who covered the case indicated that the number of crimes and victims was the driving force behind the coverage:

> Why the Ramirez case? That case became as big as it did, I think, because of the utter randomness, brutality and frequency of the crimes. Ramirez held Los Angeles in terror like no one else in the past 20 years, killing young and old in the middle of the night for no particular reason. He didn't even limit his killings to Los Angeles going up to San Francisco for a brief period of time and killing a man there (Interview with Paul Feldman, reporter for the *Los Angeles Times* on February 25, 2002).

Reporters also focused on the graphic and sexual elements of the attacks as they noted "gouged eyeballs," "slit throats," (Feldman 1986, p. B1) and graphic descriptions of sexual abuse.

An understanding of journalist's interest in Ramirez cannot overlook the characteristics of the victims. Describing the Night Stalker's victims, an article notes that he preyed:

> upon businessmen, Asian immigrants, grandmothers, and retired couples. He kidnapped children off streets and sexually assaulted them; he dragged one woman from her car and shot her repeatedly. Most often, he crept into tidy tract homes through unlocked windows and doors before dawn, cut telephone wires and attacked victims while they slept (Holley 1985, p. 1).

It also points out that this took place "in serene middle-class neighborhoods." The importance of Ramirez's victims to the newspaper coverage can be seen in an Op-Ed piece by Frank del Olmo in the *Los Angeles Times*, which read, in part:

> What made the crimes especially fearsome was the fact that they occurred not on Skid Row, where a serial killer called The Slasher was caught several years ago, but in quiet suburbs. And the victims were not prostitutes, as were many in the Hillside Strangler case, but middle-class men and women asleep in bed. The Night Stalker captured our imagination as no other serial killer ever had. He was not killing 'them' in a faraway, dingy place. He was killing people like 'us' in comfortable, ordinary homes (del Olmo 1985, p. B5).

The newspaper coverage of Ramirez shows that his crimes were seen as especially disturbing because of the social class of the victims.

Additionally, his connection with Satanism became one of Ramirez's more well-known attributes. Journalists frequently refer to him as a "Satan-worshiper" and discussed his fondness of the rock band AC/DC, which articles state "some believe is meant to be an acronym for 'Anti-Christ, Devil's Child' (Freed and McGraw 1985, p. A1). Ramirez left satanic messages and symbols at a few of the murder scenes. The newspapers discussed how Satanism had also been linked with other killings recently, "Richard Ramirez, suspected by police in the 16 Night Stalker slayings, is the latest in a small group of American murder suspects whose crimes have been associated with Satanism" ("Satanic Symbolism Reported In Homes Of 'Stalker' Victims," 1985). The article noted that public awareness of Satanism had increased due to Christian groups' complaints about rock music lyrics and their role in recent crimes, also referring to the McMartin Pre-School case. The interest in serial killing, more generally, was linked in the media with the moral panic concerning satanic ritual abuse and killings at this time (Jenkins 1994); Ramirez became a symbol of this connection.

The Newspaper Coverage of Aileen Wuornos

Between December of 1989 and November of 1990, six bodies were found in desolate areas along Florida's highways. The victims' cars were taken and many were naked or partially clothed. By this time, journalists had noted a pattern in the killings but the police had not revealed them to the public. The media exposure forced authorities to go public with their sketches of two women suspects believed responsible for the string of murders. Then on January 9, 1991, Aileen Wuornos was arrested at a bar for outstanding warrants under the name Lori Grody (one of Wuornos' aliases). In the meantime, the police continued to collect evidence against her for the string of murders. On January 16, 1991, Wuornos summoned detectives and confessed to six killings, all allegedly performed in self-defense.

Wuornos' trial for the murder of Richard Mallory opened on January 13, 1992, with jury selection. Newspapers noted that jurors were quizzed on their views on the death penalty, whether they could administer it to a woman and if they believe a prostitute can be raped ("Potential jurors are quizzed in highway killings," 1992). The local journalists covered the trial on a daily basis and frequently noted that she could face the death penalty.

On January 24, 1992, Wuornos took the stand as the only defense witness. She detailed her killing of Richard Mallory. She insisted that she shot him dead in self-defense, using her pistol only after he raped her and threatened her life. Three days later, the jury rejected Wuornos' story, deliberating a mere ninety minutes before they convicted her of first-degree murder. Reporters took note of Wuornos' comments after the verdict was read:

> Wuornos couldn't control her rage as the jury left the courtroom. As her attorneys tried to calm her, she yelled at the jurors: 'I was raped. I hope you get raped—scumbags of America'("Woman Guilty In First Of Seven Road Slayings," 1992).

The jury recommended death on January 30, 1992, and the following day she was formally sentenced to die. The *St. Petersburg Times* describes the courtroom scene as the sentence was announced:

> The object of their debate sat sobbing like an injured child. Aileen Carol Wuornos, the woman who killed a Clearwater businessman and perhaps six other men, sat slumped in her chair, looking small. This was not the Damsel of Death, the female Ted Bundy, the Highway Hooker ("Death Sentence In Serial Murder Case," 1992).

The article exemplified the two different points of views that were established throughout the case:

> She is a remorseless, diabolical killer, State Attorney John Tanner argued, and a candidate for the electric chair if ever there was one. She is a terribly deprived victim, defense attorney Tricia Jenkins would counter, and 'a damaged, primitive child,' a case for mercy if ever there was one.

The debate surrounding Wuornos' motivation would continue long after this first trial.

In April, she pled no contest to the murders of three more victims; it is noted "a significant factor was that Wuornos, a self-described born-again Christian, wanted to 'get right with God'" ("Prostitute Waives Trial In 3 Killings," 1992). Over the next couple of weeks articles continued to focus on Wuornos' no contest plea and desire to be executed quickly. Then she requested to not be present at her own sentencing hearing in May 1992. The jury voted in favor of death. The reporter remarked, "Wuornos' absence was just one oddity in what turned out to be a bizarre trip through the criminal-justice system" ("Jury Recommends Death For Wuornos," 1992). On May 15 the judge upheld the jury's recommendation, Wuornos once again added some interest to the proceedings.

> 'I'll be up in heaven while you all are rotting in hell,' Wuornos, a self-proclaimed Christian told the court. She turned to the state attorney's table and glared. 'May your wife and kids get raped,' she told the two men. Walking out of the courtroom, Wuornos offered her final salute: an upraised middle finger and an obscene comment to the judge (Ross 1992, p. B1).

The unique thing about the Wuornos case is that much of the attention, especially nationally, came to her after she was already sentenced to die. This was in part motivated by the numerous movie and the book deals that attracted national interest in the case. Wuornos and her attorney sold the movie rights to it within a couple weeks of her arrest (she would subsequently back out of the deal). At the same time, three sheriff's investigators on her case and Tyria Moore (the other woman originally suspected in the murders) retained their own lawyer to look for offers for a Hollywood movie deal. The investigators noted, in their defense, that any money they received would go to the victims' assistance fund.

The Wuornos case took an ironic twist on November 10, 1992, with revelations on the NBC news program *Dateline*. Wuornos had always claimed that she acted in self-defense but neither her supporters, the media nor Florida prosecutors were able to find any criminal record for Richard Mallory that would substantiate her claim of rape and assault. However, *Dateline* found out that Mallory had served ten years for a violent rape in another state, information obtained by checking his name through the FBI's database. She argued that everyone was rushing to make money off, and a movie about, her—and in reality that came true. The first TV movie about her aired one-week after the *Dateline* report.

Wuornos was executed on October 9, 2002. There was both local and national coverage of the execution and the tone had changed since Gacy and Bundy. No talk of celebrations outside the prison or any of the black humor that was common in the 1980s and early 1990s were found in the newspaper accounts. The newspaper descriptions are a marked change from the early execution scenes and show the changes in public sentiment regarding the death penalty since the 1980s and early 1990s.

The Newsworthiness of the Aileen Wuornos Story

Journalists continuing search for a fresh take on an existing story was met with Aileen Wuornos, who was reported as the first woman serial killer. The initial newspaper reports about the case appeared on January 18, 1991 in the *St. Petersburg Times* and set the tone for the coverage that would follow:

> As details of the life of Aileen Carol Wuornos emerged Thursday, so did a picture of a woman whose escalating private troubles and public crimes may win her a unique position in American criminal history: The first woman to commit classic serial killing (Lavin 1991, p. A1).

Reporters continued to focus on this unique serial killing angle by noting, "Wuornos may prove to be, as one expert put it, the first 'female Ted Bundy.'" The newspaper reports frequently discussed the differences between Wuornos and other female murderers:

> While other women have been involved in multiple murders, none until Wuornos had killed in ways normally associated with male murder. Wuornos worked alone and used a gun to kill strangers, notes Boston serial-murder expert Jack Levin. For the most part, other female murderers used poisons to kill victims they knew. Levin and other experts have watched the Wuornos case closely because it appeared to offer a new wrinkle in the serial-murder phenomenon: a woman who killed like a man and seemed to enjoy it ("Death Sentence In Serial Murder Case," 1992).

The stereotypes surrounding serial killers were continually challenged and rethought throughout the newspaper coverage of the case.

In addition to her unique place among serial killers, women are also seen as novel on death row. The day the judge formalized the death sentence, newspaper accounts pointed out that she would join "a small but notorious group of female killers on Florida's death row" and "women are seldom sentenced to death in Florida, and when they are, it is usually for a particularly shocking crime" ("Death Sentence In Serial Murder Case," 1992). Other newsworthy elements were also found with the Wuornos story. While in prison, Wuornos found religion and became friends with Arlene Pralle, a religious woman. Pralle began corresponding with her in jail and started giving interviews about her and Wuornos's relationship to the media. Pralle would eventually adopt her. Much like Ramirez, Wuornos was also known for her outrageous courtroom behavior. She once stated to judge and jury: "I hope you scumbags get raped" and "I will seek to be electrocuted as soon as possible.… I want to get off this crooked, evil planet" (Lavin and Ross 1992, p. B1). This is after she fired her attorney and hired an ex-rock musician and truck driver, whose telephone number spelled out "Dr. Legal." Like Bundy, Gacy, and Ramirez before her, there were many newsworthy elements to the Aileen Wuornos story that distinguished her from other serial killers.

The Unattractive Serial Killers: Gerald Stano, Randy Kraft, and Ronald Simmons

Between 1977-1994, reporters only chose serial killers to become high profile capital punishment cases. During the same years, Americans' support for the death penalty and their generally punitive sentiments were also explicitly on the rise. Serial killers were the right stories at the right time. Yet not every serial killer during 1980s and early 1990s received large amounts of newspaper attention. After analyzing the newsworthy elements of the high profile serial killers, it is also valuable to look at serial killers who did not garner large amounts to newspaper attention. The idea that the number of victims and crimes will lead directly to the front page is mistaken. There were other serial killers during this time frame like Gerald Stano, who reportedly killed forty-nine people, Randy Kraft who was responsible for sixteen victims and Ronald Simmons, who killed fourteen people. Why were some killers chosen over others? A beginning answer to this question can be obtained by looking at the social context of the Stano, Kraft, and Simmons murders.

Gerald Stano admitted killing forty-one young women, mostly hitchhikers and prostitutes, between 1969 and 1980. He was convicted of ten murders and sentenced to death three times. But his trial, sentence and execution received little newspaper attention outside of some local Florida coverage. Why was Gerald Stano not a media sensation like Bundy? Jan Glidwell, a reporter for the *St. Petersburg Times* asks the same question:

> When people start recalling serial murderers, they talk about John Wayne Gacy and Aileen Wuornos and Charlie Starkweather, each of whom killed far fewer persons than Stano. They talk about Charlie Manson, Juan Corona, Jack the Ripper, and Ted Bundy. But they almost never mention Gerald Stano. Why? (Glidwell 1998, p. A1).

To answer this, it is essential to look at the characteristics of Stano victims. His victims were hitchhikers and prostitutes found along the Florida highway, who were not seen as newsworthy as college students or middle-class families. For example, Richard Ramirez received considerably more newspaper attention in part, because he killed men and women as they slept in their middle-class homes. In one particular newspaper article (del Olmo 1985, p. B5), the reporter asks: "would we have even noticed Ramirez if he had killed 15 people on skid row? The answer is a resounding 'no.'"

So it is not only the number of victims but also the characteristics (i.e. race, class and gender) of the victims that are important for the media. Stano's execution received very little attention and the attention he did receive can be explained, in part, because he was the first person electrocuted in Florida after the controversy over Pedro Medina (who caught fire during the execution). Simply killing forty-one people does not guarantee a spot on the front page of the newspaper.

Likewise, Randy Kraft was arrested in 1983 and convicted of sixteen murders in 1989. His victims were male hitchhikers and marines found along the California highways. He was known as the "Scorecard killer" because of the list found by police in his car that referenced over sixty different killings. The Kraft trial attracted media attention in Los Angeles because it was the longest and most expensive trial in the city's history at the time. However, nationally, Kraft did not become as high profile as some of his fellow serial killers like Richard Ramirez, who was responsible for fewer victims in the same city. Once again to understand this it is necessary to look at the characteristics of the victims. Ramirez's victims were middle class couples and families, whereas many of Kraft's victims were hitchhikers who are not deemed newsworthy by the reporters or the public.

Another killer not covered extensively by newspapers was Randall Simmons. On December 28, 1987, Simmons went on the attack in Russellville, Ark., randomly shooting and killing two people and wounding three others. When police searched his home, they found 14 members of his family, all murdered. He was convicted and sentenced to death for the crimes. Simmons did not fit the stereotype of the serial killer that had been established by the media. His case barely even made a splash on the national newspapers.

Conclusion

The death row cases that generated the most newspaper attention between 1977 and 1994 were those of serial killers. All of the cases included discussion of the profile, methods and stereotypes that came to be associated with this newly coined phenomenon. None of the cases raised too many questions about the fairness and justness of capital punishment. While each newspaper cited one source or mentioned a small group of protesters outside the execution of Gacy and Bundy, no widespread discussion against their executions was found in the newspaper accounts. The newspaper coverage of the Wuornos and Ramirez trials also displayed no questioning of the capital sentence. This is not surprising; support for and the number of executions rose throughout this time period. Society's sentiments were very much in favor of the death penalty and the types of cases reporters chose to cover corresponded to that. Reporters made the choice of cases seem self-evident: commit a series of crimes, receive large amounts of media attention. This fails to account for the criminals who commit a series of crimes and do not attract large amounts of media attention. The journalists fail to acknowledge the importance of the social context of the event in determining the newsworthiness of the story. The times began to change in the early 1990s; support for capital punishment began to waiver, and with this, the types of cases reporters chose to cover would also change. No longer would serial killers and executions with celebrations dominate the headlines.

Chapter 10

Crime, Subjectivity, and Edgework: The Case of Lust Homicide

Phillip C. Shon and Dragan Milovanovic

Introduction

Mainstream criminology seeks to explain the causal variables behind crime, with the ultimate aim of prediction and control. As a result, this stance largely misses the phenomenological and existential function of crime. While crime may be a direct assault on the cohesive and peaceful state of social life, the criminal events themselves constitute a unique and idiosyncratic way for offenders to adjust to their real and perceived strains. In this chapter, we examine how certain homicides function as adaptive mechanisms, a creative—albeit destructive—force in the human subject's (offender's) mode of being.[1]

Also in this chapter, we are more interested in foregrounding the theoretical and conceptual nexus between lust murder and other analytically relevant phenomena, such as edgework and religious worship, than in explaining what motivates these types of killers. (For the latter, see Chapters 3, 4, 5; Arrigo and Purcell, in Chapter 4, for example, trace some of the key determinants to rejection, isolation, and ridicule.) We attempt here to examine how the act of lust homicide is phenomenologically constructed and made meaningful to the

---

1. This chapter is primarily concerned with lust homicide committed by males. We recognize that a nuanced dynamic exists with female crimes in this category (See also Egger 2002; Schechter 2003; Hickey 1997).

killers themselves; that is, we attempt to understand how lust murderers adapt to their perceived frustration and lack, how they construct their predatorial identities, and how they use the seductive features of their offenses to prolong the experience of murder. By doing so, we seek to provide an alternative theoretical framework with which to understand sexual homicides. Drawing on the extant literature, we examine how the subject comes to construct his or her subjectivity through lust homicide. (For other forms of crime, see Halleck 1967; Katz 1988; Salecl 1994; Duncan 1996).[2] We then draw parallels between the ritualistic and ceremonial rites of sacrifice and lust murder, thereby illustrating a killer's drive toward purification and imitation. In the final section, we dissect lust murders as a form of "edgework" (Lyng 2005; Milovanovic 2005).

Modes of Subjectivization and the Creativity of Rule Breaking

Conceptualizing rule breaking as a form of artistic and creative expression entails the reexamination of the deviant subject as an active collaborator (agent) in the production of meaning in the face of normativity (see Williams 2004). Predominant sociological thinking *a la* Durkheim (1964) has foreshadowed the erosion of meaning, solidarity, and norms as a consequence of industrialization and technological advancements. Recent notable works, however, have challenged that logic by demonstrating how individuals actively and creatively resist the anomie of modernity by engaging in illegalities. For instance, Ferrell's (1996) work chronicles the creative expressions of graffiti artists who challenge the capitalistic order through their artistic deviance; Lyng's (1990) ethnography of skydiving illustrates the ephemeral sense of personal control that the skydivers experience as a resistance and antidote to the alienating effects of capitalism and class. In light of these recent developments, it behooves us to reexamine heinous acts such as sexual homicides from an alternative theoretical framework.

Rule breaking is but one of the many ways that an individual can respond to the constraints of social norms (Merton 1938). It represents an innovative way of adapting to the frustrating and adverse conditions that an individual

---

2. Future projects should look at how the first time lust killer becomes committed to further similar crimes and thus graduates to being a serial lust killer. Space limitations here preclude this line of analysis.

might face in economic, social, and emotional spheres of life. Whichever way we conceptualize the source of stress in social life, there will be variance in the way each individual experiences the tension-riddled conditions and creatively adapts to them. Thus, as Merton (1938) posited long ago, conformity, retreatism, ritualization, innovation, and outright rebellion are just some of the established modes of adapting to strain. For Halleck (1967), the two central modes of adaptation are autoplastic and alloplastic. In the former, an "organism" effectuates a change within itself upon confrontation with stress, and alters its internal environment; in the latter an organism effectuates upon the external environment. For Halleck, rule breaking (a criminal act) is "almost always an alloplastic adaptation," since the agents that experience an unpleasant condition maneuver to bring about a change in the external environment.

Creativity and play are two modes of alloplastic adaptation pertinent to this discussion. Creativity here means a "highly prized" form of adaptation. Thus, artistic activities such as painting can be seen as outlets for creative psychic energy, what Freud referred to as "sublimation." Although play can be included in the creativity category, Halleck distinguishes it from creativity because of its essential motoric character. Halleck declares that individuals who are deprived of adequate means of expressing and channeling their creative energy will "strive to create their own." And, as Halleck notes, motoric activity is the "most efficient way in which an individual can gratify or modify the external stresses." The central assumptions latent in Halleck's thesis are that (a) humans are driven toward "fulfilling potentialities" and (b) that an organism, following Freud's lead, strives toward reduction of tension.[3] Humans are seen as desiring freedom from "oppressive control" and domination. Thus, any activity that reduces tension, gratifies needs, and does not provide new stress, serves as the criteria in the determination of the adaptive value of actions, even criminal ones. And any action that situates individuals below their full potential represents an "unnatural and unhealthy state of being."

While Halleck (1967) states that social forces, such as living in poverty and being subjected to discrimination are sources of oppression for many, it can also be subjectively—and idiosyncratically—constructed. This is accomplished through an overbearing super-ego, misunderstood oppression, and fictitiously projecting a lack where none exists. Oppression of both forms has also been traced to rejection, isolation, and ridicule (see Chapters 3, 4, 5). The response to these is a feeling of "helplessness." This feeling of helplessness and

---

3. Since there is a drive toward zero tension, the state at which this becomes so is death; hence the enigmatic, "the purpose of life is death."

powerlessness, Halleck asserts, facilitates rule-breaking behavior since "unreasonable" criminal behavior can be conceptualized as a "direct effort to combat the painful effect of helplessness or as an indirect effort to defend against the emergence of this painful emotional state."

Crime in particular and rule breaking in general—the functionality of crime—is advantageous precisely because it offers individuals an escape from the pain of oppression. Just as significant is the fact that the historical and biographical origins of a subject's oppression do not militate against—is irrelevant to—the psychological and behavioral reality of its repercussions. That is, there is a considerable amount of research that already addresses the "causes" of deviant behavior and the faulty cognitive reasoning processes that precede them (i.e., psychological, physical, sexual abuse; perception of being different); but an inquiry that purports to delineate the causes of behavior is separate and distinct from those that attempt to chronicle and expound on its effects.[4] What is indubitable is that individuals who have experienced developmental and/or psychosexual trauma negotiate that stressful condition in a way that is biographically, historically, and serendipitously structured—sometimes turning that frustration and anger inward, sometimes outward, while still others sublimate and find other avenues of expression (see Chapter 6). How such individuals cope with such psychological schisms leads to the following theoretical conjecture: individuals who face stress can effectuate changes in the self or the environment (Halleck 1967). Sexual deviance, from nuisance behaviors to the more extreme ones, represents a psychic and behavioral adaptation to that stress.

As others have noted, that adaptation process is progressive and incremental in character: before a change is effectuated in the environment, it is enacted in the self. Because the locus of control begins in the self, the changes that occur do so from internal to the external, objects to persons, and fantasy to action (Arrigo and Purcell 2001; Keppel and Birnes 1997). As mentioned in previous chapters, fantasy precedes behavior, and functions as its architectural blueprint for violence; moreover, fantasy is primarily used as a coping mechanism by children as a way of adapting to the perceived sense of help-

---

4. We make no pretenses of being able to explain all the factors that contribute to serial lust homicide—since, in many cases, the very determinants found with these predators also appear with non-predators—and thus specifying why the one and not the other respond as they do is problematic. We can, however, attempt to look at various neglected components that shed light on understanding; this is, again, different from explaining or positing motivation behind such actions. We can, at a minimum, cite stress stemming from being treated abusively or by constructions of the same as perhaps a starting point for a theory focused on explanation, without, however, fully operationalizing it here. This is only an approximation that has been frequently found in the literature.

lessness and powerlessness (Pincus 2001). What has not been addressed in the literature is an examination of how the *body of the crime* serves a similar function. From the physical commission of a crime, a person begins to be active, thus restoring both his sense of "freedom" from oppression (and from the act) and a sense of hope. When cognitive aspects of the crime, such as its planning and execution coincide, Halleck states that rule breaking offers an opportunity for creativity and play: the person's sense of dignity, self-esteem, and identity is maintained. In addition to the existential dimensions of criminal action, crime is construed as both stimulating and exciting, as it breaks from the limiting boundaries of society's normative order. We can thus state that crime, as an adaptive mechanism to the oppressive social forces (objectively defined or subjectively constructed), allows a redefining of the human subject to take place. The criminal passes from an intolerable emotional state to a new and less tension filled mode of existence.

The Ceremonial Aspects of Lust Homicide

Lust homicide can be conceptualized as a gross example of a subject's progressive (autoplastic → alloplastic) adaptation to stress. This is not to say that nonlinear development may not take place where one may remain in one form of adaptation and with little more, "jumps" to another as chaos theory would have it. Forms of adaptation, then, fall along an ever expanding continuum (Keppel and Birnes 1997). Fantasy is an important theme in lust killers' and other criminal actors' motivations in general since it often constitutes the beginning point in the pathological adaptation to stress. When the changes in beliefs and thoughts are no longer sufficient, changes in the environment are sought. Simply put, feelings of "helplessness" are powerful and painful emotional states that compel subjects to overcome that situation either alloplastically (outwardly directed) or autoplasticly (inwardly directed). Alternatively, as we see with Katz (1988), through imaginary play, the person may find escape in fantasy, a conceived "elsewhere" in which deplorable conditions are replaced by fulfilling ones. If there is nowhere else to go, it is to a distorted fantasy that one can seek refuge.[5]

---

5. The critical play of emotional display is developed by Katz (1988). For some law breakers, humiliation—and we add, having some more objective or a distorted source of constructed persecution—serves as a painful state that they try to overcome (Katz 1988). And before acts such as homicide can be brought to fruition, the humiliation must be "turned on its head." For Katz, it is rage and a momentarily constructed notion of self-

For lust killers, the condition that compels them to transcend their painful situation is not only sexual, existential, and moral, but religious as well. As Katz (1988) has shown with the form of homicide he calls "righteous slaughter," one needs to enter the realm of moral transcendence, a crusade against society's defined underclass (e.g., prostitutes, homosexuals, or the homeless) or against those who have offended the moral absolute of the transcendental Good. Consequently, it is with righteousness that the serial killer strikes at society's defined deviants. But to mention only the negative duty (e.g., elimination of evil) as an influential factor in the decision to kill would overlook the constituted duty that undergirds the behavior of lust killers: their desire to imitate the gods and live at the heart of primordial reality, to live life in a sacred state as a religious act (Shon 1999).

There are three behavioral features of signature sexual homicides that recur with regularity that bear a strong resemblance to forms of religious worship: (1) mementos taken from the victims (e.g., clothing, jewelry) serve a totemic function, thus facilitating a killer's autoerotic fantasies whose sexual gratification is brought to fruition at a solitary place and time of his choosing (fetishism/totemism). (2) Victims are often approached, lured, abducted, and killed ritualistically, in a manner that is suggestive of a rite of sacrifice—sacrifice in the pursuit of a transcendental and universal moral good (ritualism/rites of purification) (see Katz 1988). And (3) the disposal sites of victims acquire instrumental and psychic significance in the killer's rationality (sacred space). For necrophiliacs (e.g., Ted Bundy, Gary Ridgeway), these spaces allow material access to corpses where they can fulfill their aberrant sexual desires; but just as significantly, they represent affective planes where offenders are able to vicariously relive the crime through their mere presence. Deleuze and Guattari's (1987, p. 129) notion of "point of subjectification" is useful here since it suggests particular instances in which subjectivity is reconstituted. It is the moment at which a subject begins to progressively re-identify himself as an author by reactivating the resonances, excitation, and mental reality associated with each component and phase of the crime; these points of subjectification represent the constantly revitalized moments at which a sequential development, or reification of subjectivity is initiated anew.

Hence, the affinity for predators often revisiting the sites of their grisly crimes, and/or for their desire to keep souvenirs or trophies which provide ongoing reminders. These are the moments that an "I" emerges, the mythical figure of a

---

righteous behavior to uphold universal values that often abruptly spirals into a righteous slaughter form of homicide.

centered subject in control, overcoming the constant despair of helplessness. Similarly, in a Lacanian approach (see Salecl 1994), these revisitations, souvenirs and trophies represent moments for identity reconstructions and reaffirmations.[6] For Salecl (1994, p. 102), "by committing the crime, the criminal sometimes demands an agent which would recognize him as subject. He wants the Other, the symbolic order, to respond to his crime by giving him an identity he did not have before." The judge and other condemnatory agents inadvertently provide this resource. We appropriate this to also mean that the revisited sites as well as souvenirs and trophies become "agents," the points at which narrative construction can unfold in which the predator can situate himself as an "I," the doer of the deed. Here, Deleuze and Guattari, Lacan, and Salecl converge.

These three features—fetishism, ritualism, and sacred space—are consistently found in the behaviors of signature killers in general and those who have been so successful that they have progressed to the logical end of the violence continuum. And it is these recurring features that conceptually bind lust murders with elementary forms of worship. As an example, Keppel notes that Dahmer's apartment was littered with human bodies in various states of decomposition, skulls that had been severed, cleaned, and painted, and "set atop the victim's two hands, cupped with the palms up" (Keppel and Birnes 1997, p. 266). In essence, Dahmer had kept the victims as totem figures as a way of building a "temple or altar" of sorts in his own apartment. Keppel also notes that Bundy often expressed a desire to operate and live in a crematorium as a way of controlling and living with his victims. Thus, the behavioral features common to killers who have progressed along the scale of violence, as reported by those who have had intimate contact with and knowledge of the killers, attest to the uncanny conceptual linkages between signature murderers and the *homo religiosus* (religious man).

The common thread that links the three recurring features is the presence of dread (awe), hierophoany (appearance of the sacred), and the desire for transcendence through the experience of power (Leeuw 1963). Fetishism and sacred spaces, in addition to their symbolic psychological value, represent a

---

6. Although Salecl's Lacanian psychoanalytic analysis of the site of mutilation is insightful, it does not explicitly address the relations of power present in the process. The repeated cases of ocular mutilations and ingestion are not only the *object petit a*, as Salecl states, but these are also sexual fetishes. A core component of a fetish is its hierophany. In other words, the fetish is a physical manifestation of power; in the case of the homo religiosus, a sacred power. And the ambivalent response exhibited by the religious subject culminates with the subject's experience of impotence before this creature feeling. Other infamous serial killers have attributed their compulsion to kill to this creature feeling (Holmes and Holmes 1994).

distinct power process whereby the sacred (hieros) appears (phonein) and manifests itself in the ordinary, thereby transforming a once ordinary object, space, into something epiphenomenal (Eliade 1957). Thus, ordinary objects (e.g., victim's clothing) and profane spaces (e.g., body dumpsites) transform through the ceremonial murder and elicit both feelings of dread, awe, fear, and attraction (Otto 1928). Furthermore, the ritualism that is involved in sexual homicides *purifies* the perceived evil that the victims represent (Livingston 1989), thereby transforming a sexual killer's anger into righteous slaughter—retribution—of "deserving" symbolic victims (Keppel and Birnes 1997). These types of rituals not only familiarize behavior, but follow the patterns established through a divine revelation. The fetishism, ritualism, and murder themselves are manifestations of honor for the sacred which are objectified in violence, acts of transcendence to live the life of a *homo religiosus*.

All the endeavors of the *homo religiosus* throughout his life serve one central purpose: to live at the heart of primordial reality. That is, the *homo religiosus* seeks to transcend the profane mode of his existence. One way of fulfilling this moral imperative is to live life as a religious act—*imitatio dei*. Simply put, he seeks to imitate the gods in his life. And by reproducing the same acts and gestures of the primordial gods, he attempts to "live close to the gods" (Eliade 1957, p. 91). It is only through imitation that the religious man can endure and transcend his situation in profane space and time. As Eliade (1957, p. 94) observes, it is man's ontological nostalgia, his "wish to return to the presence of the gods, to recover the strong, fresh, pure world that existed *illo tempore*. It is at once thirst for the sacred and the nostalgia and being." Since one of the primary activities of the gods is creation, the *homo religiosus's* preoccupation with recreation of the original creation, its time and space, through rituals and myths, is a way of imitating the gods. Consequently, the *imitatio dei* places a tremendous amount of responsibility on the individual; and since the religious man believes he is imitating the gods, no matter how depraved, mad, or criminal an act may appear, the blood sacrifices find their justification in their existential and religious expression.

The Auto-Alloplasticity of Serial Murder

We have outlined the conceptual linkages between the homo religiosus and the lust killer in the way both categories redefine subjectivity and emerge from an intolerable emotional state to a new and hopeful (be it violent and grisly) mode of existence. To that end, we have relied upon the theoretical insights of Halleck to illustrate how individuals adapt to stresses in life. A detailed exploration into the tactical strategies of lust killers further demonstrates how violent forms of creativity and play manifest in lust homicide. The five-phase model of serial murder put forth by Holmes and Holmes (1994) appears to be a useful approximation of the various moments. It should be noted that not all the phases are present in all serial murders (fantasy, stalk, abduction, kill, disposal). In Ressler et al.'s (1992) study of thirty-six murderers, they noted four analytically distinct phases that overlap those of Holmes and Holmes (1994): "antecedent behavior and planning"; "the act of murder"; "disposing of the body"; and "postcrime behavior."

Holmes and Holmes (1994) write that in their studies, "there is always a fantasy," meaning that there are elements of thoughts, ideas and fantasized scenarios of sexual encounters that catapult the killer into the process (see also, Schechter 2003, p. 259; Ressler et al. 1992, pp. 34, 165, 215). Consider the "BTK killer," Dennis Rader's remarks after his capture:

> I started working out this fantasy in my mind. And once that potential—that person becomes a fantasy, I could just loop it over. I could lay in bed at night and think about this person, the events and how it's gonna happen. And it would become a real, almost like a picture show. You know, I wanted to go ahead and produce it and direct it and go through with it. No matter what the costs were, the consequences. It was gonna happen one way or another. Maybe not that day, but it was gonna happen (cited in Magnus 2005).

With Ressler et al. (1992), this first phase included stress-induced triggering events (i.e., trouble with a significant female, such as wife, mother, girlfriend, female boss, in the offender's life; being fired from a job), the frame of mind, and planning. Their frame of mind, Ressler et al. (1992, p. 48) found, indicated an overall negative emotional state just before the crime was committed: "frustration (fifty percent), hostility and anger (forty-six percent), agitation (forty-three percent), and excitement (forty-one percent)."[7] Along with this, however, was minimal internalized distress: "nervousness (seventeen percent), depression (fourteen and six-tenths percent), fear (ten percent), calm (eight percent), or confusion (seven percent)." In short, evidence suggests that the justifications for the impending crime are already supporting his grisly crime and "there is no emotional reservoir to relate to the vulnerability, pain,

---

7. Similarly, Proulx et al. (2002) found that heightened anger appeared just before the crime.

and fear of the victim" (Ressler et al. 1992, p. 48). For Ressler and colleagues (1992, p. 48), the first phase also includes planning. This crucial phase of serial murder can be synthesized with Halleck's notion of autoplastic adaptation to life stress. The adaptation takes place in the killer's mind through imaginative creations and productions.

The second phase, stalking, combines both autoplastic and alloplastic components of adaptive methods. In this phase, the killer actively pursues his targeted victim, gaining knowledge of the victim's patterns and "organizing the crime scene" (Holmes and Holmes 1994). Consider, at one extreme, the "BTK killer": "[The] stalking stage is when you start learning more about your victims, potential victims. Went to the library, I looked up their names, address, cross reference, called them a couple of times, drove by there whenever I could" (cited in Magnus 2005). During this stage, the killer is already engaged in selecting a site of disposal, possibly even modes of mutilation and murder (see also, Schechter 2003, p. 282). This active part on the killer illustrates alloplastic adaptation. The "depersonalization of the victim" (casted as an "it" or object; an I-it relation), or the mental work that the killer uses to distance himself from the victim, as well as the intricate planning of the crime, can be seen as a form of autoplastic adaptation. The killer is actively engaged in the surveillance and stalking, while mentally restructuring his relationship with the targeted victim. In this phase, both cognitive and behavioral aspects of creativity and "play" are at work. In Ressler et al.'s (1992, p. 49) study, the serial killer often cruises various single and gay bars, gay districts, and parking lots for possible victims (see also Schechter 2003, p. 288; Egger 2002, pp. 11, 93; Egger 2003, pp. 53-54). Often, the predator has certain criteria for the eventual victim and seeks fulfillment of this fantasy (see Egger 2002, p. 11); at times, however, mere opportunity will do. "The murderer," Ressler et al. (1992, p. 51) state, "with a well-rehearsed fantasy of murder kills to preserve the fantasy." Consider, BTK: "In my dreams, I had what they called torture chambers. And to relive your sexual fantasies you have to go to the kill ... I don't think it was actually the person that I was after, I think it was the dream ... I had more satisfaction building up to it and afterwards than I did the actual killing of the person" (cited in Magnus 2005). Often this fantasized target may symbolize someone from his past. In other cases, certain behavior exhibited by the victim would set the homicide in gear; in yet others, certain responses by the target person would do: "someone may remind him of his belief in an unjust world. He may feel unfairly treated, and this sets into motion the justification to kill." In short, fantasies may progress into the next stage by "triggering factors" (Schechter 2003, p. 280).

In the abduction phase, while it appears that only the brute force of alloplasticity is at play, such view would miss the "sensual and moral dynamics" of abduction. While the disorganized types generally prefer a "blitz type attack," the organized types usually employ well-rehearsed conversations, tricks, or some other type of cunning ploy to allure the victim to the killer's comfort zone (Holmes and Holmes 1994). As Katz (1988) has shown, this initial method of approach provides the offender with a moral and ontological feeling of superiority over the victim, a sensuous process of moral domination in its incipience. For the lust killer, this phase is only an introduction to the potential for play in the next phase.

The fourth phase is the murder of the victim. The main motives that consistently appear in the literature for the murder are sexual gratification, power, and revenge (Holmes and Holmes 1994; Keppel and Birnes 1997). The methods by which the victim is killed, mutilated, and ingested all signify the idiosyncratic mode of manifesting his being, his subjectivity. This phase reveals the most gruesome illustration of "creative play" for the lust killer. On occasion, the victim may not succumb according to the previously constructed fantasy; in this scenario, the predator may experience heightened emotional states of fear, excitement, and horror (Ressler et al. 1992, p. 53). For some predators, there may be even more fulfillment than the fantasy had promised: "there is confirmation and reinforcement of the fantasy, and pleasure or triumph in the power of the act" (Ressler et al. 1992, p. 53). Ressler and colleagues, similar to Holmes and Holmes, saw sexual elements as critical in these homicides.

The last phase, disposal of the body (see also Ressler et al. 1992, pp. 57-58; see also Schechter 2003, pp. 331-337), brings the five phases to a full circle. The phases are conceptually represented as a circle rather than a linear progression model since the autoplastic and alloplastic adaptations fuse into a dialectic framework. Ressler and colleagues (1992) noted that in twenty-eight percent of the cases they studied, the body was positioned in a particular way. This indicates meaning for the killer based on some sexually violent fantasies: "by choosing to pose his victim, he revealed a distinct behavioral characteristic relating to his fantasies and premeditation of the crime" (Ressler et al. 1992, p. 60). Similarly, the exact location of the body or body parts has symbolic meaning related to prior fantasies; in some cases, the body or body parts are stored close to the predator and further the excitement connected with the the fantasy and homicide (Ressler et al. 1992, p. 61).

The disposal site is imbued with an aura of sacredness that is tinged with titillating sexuality; furthermore, it is a highly relevant space to the killer since one of the post-offense behavioral characteristics of certain type of lust killers is the tendency to return to the crime scene (Holmes and DeBurger 1988;

Ressler et al. 1992, pp. 62-63). From a linear progression model, the disposal should signify its terminality; however, the behavior of lust murderers demonstrates that this particular homicide transcends the understanding attained in the homicide literature since these types of offenders go beyond death to prolong the pain, humiliation, and suffering of victims, thereby elongating their experience of murder. For example, when these killers are not successful in their hunt, their autoplastic behavior fulfills the requirements during those frustrating periods, providing that his imagination is sufficiently endowed with a propensity for fantasy and imaginative capacity (Halleck 1967).

The site of mutilation not only has existential significance but permeates with religious overtones as well. The human body can be seen as a microcosm of the universe (Eliade 1957). In matters of transcendence, the way in which this is done is through an "opening in the universe, house, temple or the human body" (Eliade 1957). In lust killers, this incursion is typified by "gross assaults ... including body mutilation and displacement of selected body parts that have sexual significance to the killer" (Holmes and Holmes 1994). The fact that knives and edged instruments are often used to forcefully create an opening in the victims is an "attempt to pass through the narrow gate"; the genesis of an ontological mutation (Shon 1999). It's as though the given erogenous zones of the body have been expanded not for the victim, but for the pleasure and fantasy of the lust murderer. Just as those who are denied normative outlets invent new ones, lust killers, in order to arrive at a sacred state, "invent" outlets, initially through fantasy (autoplasticity), then through action (alloplasticity). In other words, it is a twisted example of an "organism" refusing to function below his "healthy" state.

The return to the crime scene is the occasion for such autoplastic adaptive behavior: fantasizing about previous crimes and victims while engaging in autoeroticism is a commonly found activity among lust killers (Olshaker and Douglas 1996). It is an opportunity to continuously relive the fantasy (Ressler et al. 1992, p. 62). In addition, other amulets, totems, trophies, souvenirs, and tokens from the victims serve a similar function for lust killers (Ressler et al. 1992, pp. 63-64; Schechter 2003, p. 328). These fetishes provide sexual stimulation and a continuous reminder of the event and thus provide further fuel for his fantasies; others act as ongoing reminders and symbols of his skill (Ressler et al. 1992, p. 64).[8] According to Keppel and Birnes (1997, p. 191), the

---

8. Schechter (2003, p. 329) makes a distinction between a souvenir and a trophy. The souvenir "serves the same function that a statuette of the Eiffel Tower does for a tourist who has just vacationed in Paris—it reminds the kill of how much fun he had and allows him to relive the experience in fantasy until he can do it again." The trophy, on the other hand,

serial lust murderer "enjoys what he's doing, and he takes such items as clothing or body parts so that he can masturbate later and satisfy himself sexually as an experience separate from the homicide." Lust murderers, therefore, experience the act of murder on several different planes: (1) they rely on fantasy as a rehearsal tool to mentally "practice" their offenses; (2) the physical act of killing provides a palpable satisfaction while concurrently serving as "fodder" for future fantasy; and (3) the use of souvenirs as symbolic representations of victims during their masturbation provides a visceral re-experience of the crime. In this way, the meaning and pleasure of lust murder is phenomenologically constructed and elongated in their quotidian practices. Thus, we can see that the initial process, which began as a form of autoplastic adaptation, progresses along an alloplastic route of adaptation, culminating and coming full circle in the last phase, again finding form in an autoplastic adaptation.

Edgework and Lust Homicide

Along with crime as a mode of adaptation, subjectivization, and ritualistic expression, we can also look to edgework literature (Lyng 2005) for further understanding of lust homicides. This is not to say that all lust homicide includes these dimensions; but it is to say that an important component, missing in the literature, or more often only implicitly developed, is the notion of excitement (Ressler et al. 1992, p. 53; Schechter 2003, pp. 259-262) connected to the approaching and crossing of boundaries. Consider for example, the BTK killer who taunted the police (he sent them poems, letters, a disk, a license of a victim; he tipped the police about a completed homicide, and even provided his identity in a coded form in a poem). Clearly, the BTK killer was playing with the edge between detection and secrecy, a greatly exaggerated "sneaky thrill" type of crime. The key boundary described by a number of key theorists is that between fantasy and the real (i.e., Jacques Lacan and Gilles Deleuze). The work of Jacques Lacan (1977)[9] is useful in so much as it devel-

---

is much like "the mounted moose head or stage antlers that a hunter might proudly display over the fireplace—prideful evidence of the killer's lethal skill."

9. From a Lacanian view, subjectivity is essentially linked to desire and its negative character, that is, desire is linked to "lack," a "manque d'etre." With its entrance into the symbolic order and the castration registered as its cost, the person seeks various objects of desire ("objet petit a") that will fill in this gap-in-being, and hence establish a temporary, but illusory sense of fulfillment (plenitude) which is experienced as jouissance, a heightened emotional state of enjoyment. The male subject wishes to pursue the object of his enjoyment but must negotiate the law-of-the-father, which blocks the subject's direct access to

ops the relation between fantasy and the three orders constitutive of subjectivity: imaginary, symbolic, and the real[10] The work of Deleuze[11], from a competing perspective, focuses on the body, its forces, desires, and intensities (see especially, Delanda 2002; Bonta and Protevi 2004; Milovanovic 2005). Whereas for Lacan the imaginary is distinguishable from the symbolic and real, for Deleuze, all is part of the virtual.[12]

We could gain some guidance by resituating fantasy and excitement associated with lust homicide in a five-dimensional framework (Milovanovic 2005). These dimensions include: in-and-out-of-control; legal/illegal; degree

---

it. In other words, it is an effect of the law, not realized by law (Salecl 1994). Because of the original crime (associated with Oedipus and the overthrow and killing of the father) and the guilt it entails, the subject "perceives himself as a criminal" although no actual crime has taken place. Thus by committing a crime, the subject forces the Other, the symbolic order, the law, or what Freud called the father's deputy, to recognize him as a subject. A new identity begins to form.

10. Salecl (1994) has also addressed crime as a means of reconstituting or subjectivizing from a Lacanian psychoanalytic perspective, using the context of the fall of Socialism in the former Soviet Union and the Chikatilov case (he was convicted of killing 53 people; see Schechter 2003, p. 230). In Lacanian psychoanalysis, the Father is a crucial figure in a subject's life since it is the Father who subordinates the child to the law. This Father is what Lacan calls the paternal metaphor, not the biological father but a universal, generic concept of Father. This Freudian notion of Oedipal father is significant because the father first forbids the subject's incestuous relationship with his mother: the father has to be murdered and for Freud, everyone is guilty of this original crime. The key point is that the father, for Lacan, the Law, the law-of-the-father, regulates the subject's desire, subordinates it. This is a fundamental step in the psychoanalytic construction of subjectivity.

11. Deleuze, on the other hand, focuses on the body and its forces, intensities, assemblages, the Body without Organ, and desire as production, not as inherently tied to lack. The underlying ontology relies on a Nietzschean and Spinozean idea of forces in dynamic movement, out of which some take on more stable form (assemblages, multiplicities), overdetermined by a logic (abstract machine). The body without organs is the plane on which these connections are constituted. Desire is production; it connects up forces and shows itself in subsequent emotional display with varying degrees of intensity (see Deleuze 1983). In this model, it is the will to power (having both affirmative and negative dimensions), that acts in the piloting role in the actualized configuration of forces (active, which allow the subject greater self actualization; or reactive, which separates the body from what it can do). In this view, lust homicide can be seen as a negative will to power connected with reactive forces. Thus, using Deleuze's language, we can identify a lust homicide abstract machine.

12. Deleuze and Guattari (1987, p. 376) have suggested a new field of study, "noology," the "study of images of thought and their historicity." This field would study the emergence of images, their fixity in history, their effects. For an application to law, see Jamie Murray, "Nome Law: Deleuze and Guattari on the Emergence of Law" (2005). See also Deleuze 1994, pp. 129-167; Williams 2003, pp. 111-137.

of emotional intensity; form of jouissance; and socio-historically structured opportunities.

Let us focus on the much explored connection between fantasy, excitation, and the legal-illegal dimension. Much literature indicates that the predator spends much time in his fantasy of killing, which often reaches a crescendo demanding action. Fantasies, too, apparently undergo more refined development as the predator progresses from his first killing to subsequent ones (Ressler et al. 1992, pp. 33-43). For most people, fleeting fantasies do not cross the edge into the real. For the lust homicide predator there seems a more intense and a lengthier period of time engaged in fantasizing sexual homicide.[13] According to Schechter (2003, p. 260), for "many serial killers, the experience of stepping over that line fills them with an intoxicating sense of power, even invincibility. Once they have taken that fateful step, they cannot —and have no wish to—go back." On many occasions, for the would-be-killer, excitation is sufficiently achieved by merely approaching the edge: "trolling" for potential victims in itself suffices; abusing employees at the work place vents sublimated forms of growing urges; engaging in "weird sex" and employing "rough sex" with prostitutes allows expression of built-up urges; diverging into drugs and alcohol for the enhancement and in some cases for the redirecting of the fantasy, and various other opportunities exist whereby fantasy doesn't translate directly into the commission of lust homicide (see Keppel and Birnes 1997, pp. 191-92). On other occasions, an imaginary "elsewhere" tied to the normative order will do to disengage from further movement toward the real (Katz 1988).

If the region between the fantasy and the real represents a psychological embodiment of the dialectics of boundary crossings, then its empirical form finds a corporeal manifestation in the legal/illegal distinction. That's because lust murderers exemplify the evolution of behaviors, from nuisance offenses to downright dangerous ones. Thus, the desire to espy on others in a state of undress or sexual activity, or compelling others to see one's nakedness constitute ocular crossings; however, when that visual medium of penetration is

---

13. According to Schechter (2003, p. 259): " ... mental images of mayhem and rape aren't the stuff of nightmare [for the serial killer]; on the contrary, they form the basis of his favorite daydreams. Far from trying to put such unwholesome thoughts out of his mind, he will cultivate them—wallow in them. The recollection of a real or perceived slight inspires him to envision the most sadistic forms of revenge. The sight of a pretty girl arouses thoughts of abduction, sexual torture, and dismemberment-murder. For days, weeks, months, he will dwell on—and masturbate to—such imagined atrocities." For the development of these fantasies, see also Ressler et al. (1992, pp. 28, 34-45, 165, 215).

escalated into tactile (e.g., frotteurism), spatial (e.g., B&E, cat-burglary), and phallic ones (e.g., rape), then the boundary between fantasy and the real, and legal and illegal has clearly been traversed. Lust homicide can be understood in this translation of fantasy into the real, and as the negotiation—approach and crossing—of boundaries. As Ressler et al. (1992, p. 53) state, "some murderers are exhilarated—they broke the rules, they killed. This feeling will induce some to kill again. ..." The boundary itself has magical properties in the transformation of action and identities. At the boundary, the normative order undergoes dissipation. What abound are singularities and symmetry breaking cascades (Delanda 2002), bifurcations leading to a plethora of relatively uninhibited options (Deleuze and Guattari 1987). It is tinged with excitement, with an intensity that takes hold of the whole body; it is the body-without-organs that has been stripped of its "organs" allowing new organizations, new intensities. The boundary region, in short, is the locus of "lines of flight," acting much like solitons, criss crossing the body-without-organs, putting into higher resonance and often intertwining or coupling relatively stabilized zones of intensity with distinct effects. In short, the whole body comes alive with intense excitement. For the lust murderer, these are line of destruction, activating reactive forces, caught in repetition, underscoring the idea that the boundary region can be a generator of active *or* reactive forces.

A second dimension deals with emotional intensity. We have already seen with Halleck that compared to the often mundane, monotonous, and degrading work of the real world, crime offers an opportunity for alternative outlets of creativity, entrepreneurship, reward, and satisfaction. Lust homicide offers an example of this process at work. According to Keppel and Birnes (1997, p. 188), "the predator's prolonged torture of the victim gratifies him, energizes his fantasy system, and temporarily satisfies his lust for control, domination, and mastery." His targets (Lacan's *objet petit a*; for Deleuze, points of subjectivization) are often selectively chosen for the perceived value as a target of symbolic retribution or as a source of sexual thrill; in this way, fantasy and reality become fused into an amorphous entity, one that exerts a compulsion all its own. The lust homicide predator engages in a transgression of areas of the body considered ultimately private, a crossing of boundaries of civility with unrestrictive and uninhibited exploration and mutilation. The "excitation killer" (Keppel and Birnes 1997, p. 187), draws great thrill in not only drawing out the pain and suffering inflicted on the victim, the subsequent sexual exploitation of the victim's body, the collection of parts of the body as a trophy (Ressler et al. 1992, pp. 61, 63-64), and the return to the victimization site, as a way of elongating excitation—but also in the subsequent opportunities provided by the interest shown by media before and after his capture (Egger 2003, p. 206). This again seems to elongate the act and experience of murder in a way that transcends the structural understanding of the affective dimensions of homicides.

In a Deleuzian framework, the body-without-organs is a surface of folds with vibratory zones of intensity with various degrees of excitation which produce sensations. It is when these zones couple producing resonance that bifurcations or lines of flight are generated with effects (Massumi 1992, pp. 70-73). It is at the boundary, here of civility, where resonance is heightened, sometimes to the pitch that the lust murderer has an inescapable urge to act out his grisly crimes.

A third dimension is in-and-out-of-control. Studies suggest that unlike other edgeworkers who often begin to lose control as they come close to the edge as in Katz's "righteous slaughter," the serial killer stays in control from beginning to the end.[14] In this sense, his status on the continuum is much more like those of enthusiasts of "sneaky thrills" and extreme sports whose thrill is approaching the edge without losing control and experiencing incredibly intense "highs" from these confrontations and opportunities by showing high levels of skill under extreme life-threatening conditions at the edge. The predator takes great satisfaction in realizing his fantasy in an orderly and controllable fashion. The killer "is feeding emotionally and visually from the experience of exerting control and domination over a victim" (Keppel and Birnes 1997 p.192). According to Ressler and colleagues (1992, pp. 165–166), the well-rehearsed fantasy allowed the predator a certain protection from "becoming totally disorganized and psychotic"; it was in fantasy that he felt control, and in the real, anxious at the slightest deviation of his plan. The predator often "felt in control of his fantasy and out of control in the real world" (Ressler et al. 1992, pp. 165–166). The killer takes great pride in avoiding detection and even taunts detectives, playing with the edge between detection and avoidance, in the signatures he leaves at the scene of the crime (Egger 2003, p. 143).[15]

A fourth dimension has to do with the form of jouissance at play. In Lacanian language, jouissance is enjoyment (in the French, having a sexual con-

---

14. This is not to say that there are not instances when offenders are not in control. There are times where the edge is crossed and the predator only later reflects as to his uncontrollable state (e.g., when Bundy realized what he had done and started frantically throwing out a victim's clothes out the window as he was driving down the highway; see Keppel and Birnes 1995). A self-objectification within a fantasized script, however, assures a tendency toward a linear progression toward the ultimate crime.

15. Some have questioned the degree of taunting that has said to take place (Schechter 2002, p. 318).

notation, lost in the English translation). The notion of jouissance has been explained by Jacques Lacan by the use of the borromean knots consisting of three interconnected rings (see Figure 1; see also Milovanovic 2005). Two ex-

Figure 1. Borromean Knot

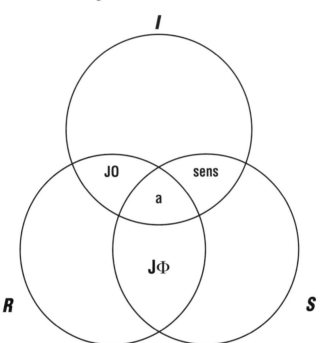

treme form of jouissance are specified: phallic jouissance ($J\Phi$) , constituted at the intersection of the real and symbolic, has everything to do with how culturally defined objects of desire tainted with the law-of-the-father come to fill in the gaps-in-being (*manque d'etre*). Plenitude is the overcoming of these gaps in being. Jouissance is the visceral experiencing of this process as elation.

The other form of jouissance is jouissance of the body (JO) constituted at the intersections of the imaginary with the real, unmediated by the conventional symbolic order, nor directly by the law-of-the-father the very principle providing stability in the unconscious, be it one privileging the male. In the extreme, we have a Lacanian "foreclosure" of the father depicted in his Schema I where there are no bounds to the imagination (Lacan 1977). It is where the Symbolic ring in Figure 1 becomes disconnected from the other two. For Lacanians, it is the "fourth order," *le sinthome*, that reconnects the three rings (Orders), producing a relative stability. Here it could be an implicit, relatively coherent, and idiosyncratic narrative framework ("implicit theory") that tends to construct the other more in terms of an "I-it," than an "I-thou." The jouissance of the body is ineffable and inexpressible in dominant discourse and provides an intense form of jouissance that can only be "comprehended" by the person in visceral ways. It can be the basis of both good and bad consequences. Good, in the sense that novel and more fulfilling opportunities are engendered for self and other; bad, when new structures are destructive of the other and self.

Suggested here is that a boundary region exists between the two forms of jouissance: $J\Phi \rightarrow |\ R\ | \leftarrow JO$. The boundary region can be envisioned as that of the Real; a disorderly world of disconnected images, momentarily connected but unrecognized parts, dissipating forms, a flow of unmediated primordial sensory data, a rush of psychic energy without bounds, an abyss, black hole … Thanatos itself. Here, jouissance (on the left) resulting from stable meaning construction within the dominant symbolic order can be disordered as boundaries are approached, the other side of which represents the domain of what Lecercle (1985) refers to as the idiosyncratic languages of the body (on the right), a déliré (relegated to poets, novelists, the insane; see for example James Joyce's *Finnegan's Wake*). Conversely, languages of the body begin to take on conventionally recognizable form as they cross the boundary (from the right) and become constituted in dominant signifiers. But, in either case, from the left or right, the Real interrupts the crossing of the one into the other; it is where singularities and symmetry breaking cascades are ubiquitous; it is a moment of both terror and new possibilities.

Ultimately, however, for Lacan, it is at the intersection of the imaginary and symbolic orders that "sens" or meaning is established as "fantasy." This is designated by Lacan as $\$ \Diamond a$, which indicates the embodiment of the subject's desire in *objet petit a*. It is an illusory sense of plenitude, more on the side of real and symbolic ($J\Phi$) than the real and imaginary (JO), where *object a* fills in *manque d'etre*, gaps in being and meaning, a gap engendered in the inauguration of the child into the symbolic order with its promise of mastery but with a cost—a castration from the Real. By the intervention of journalists, lawyers, criminologists, detectives, novelists, and psychiatrists, apprehended lust murderer's narratives become codified in dominant narratives for public consumption. For the lust homicide predator, however, personal narratives remain tied to fantasy in idiosyncratic form, by virtue of an "implicit theory," a more hidden narrative framework of reference (Beech et al. 2005; Polaschek and Gannon 2004; Ward et al. 1997; Ward 2000). It is within this context that JO makes its appearance, even though material from dominant discourse is constitutive of the idiosyncratic implicit theory itself.[16] Thus, "sens," for the lust serial murderer, even though ultimately located at the intersections of the imaginary and symbolic, is primarily constituted by reference to the intersections of the imaginary and real order.

Many apprehended predators, too, revel in their celebrity status (see Egger 2003, p. 206; 2002, pp. 100, 235; Schechter 2002, pp. 262, 272-274).[17] The apprehended suspect of lust homicide contributes to the constitutive process of building a narrative explaining his acts. He, too, is taken in by the constructions. This furthers the movement toward subjectivization. The predator is provided a momentary marker, an I, a discursive subject-position within which to take up residence; accordingly, these publicly receptive narrative constructions provide the appearance of a centered subject in control.

The jouissance of the body has been given a different understanding by Deleuze (1983). The body-without-organs is composed of active and reactive forces in some relatively stable configurations producing distinct effects. With the dominance of active forces we see movement toward self-realization, a continuous process of becoming; with the dominance of reactive forces, we witness a body-without-organs caught in destructive repetition, directed toward self (autoplastic) and/or others (alloplastic). The predator's form of jouissance of the body feeds off the extreme suffering of others; its constitutive reactive forces are replenished only with additional homicides and sexual deviations. It's an insatiable drive towards destruction.

In short, the form of jouissance at play can be situated in relation to the boundary region of the Real. We may never know precisely the implicit theory of the serial lust murderer, since he too is often taken in by the attributions of social control agents, the media, criminologists, and the public as well

---

16. See for example research on various rhetorics that construct the other in terms of I-it rather than I-thou ("instrumental and egoistic rhetoric," Schwendinger and Schwendinger 1985; discourses of rationalization and neutralization; Matza 1964; Cressey 1953). See also constructions of narratives of law in everyday usage by a constitutive process (Ewick and Silbey 1998; Henry and Milovanovic 1996).

17. Consider both "Son of Sam" (David Berkowitz) and "BTK" (Dennis Rader) and their taunting of police with more and more audacious messages. Rader, right after he pleaded guilty to the deaths of 10 people said in an interview: "I feel like I'm a star right now" (cited in Magnus 2005). In responding to the question of why the self label, BTK, he said: "I just put it in one of the first letters [to the police/media]. I'm always surprised I put it up there first. I think it was just—Bind, Torture, Kill. Now I had a label on me. It was like the "Green River Killer" and "Son of Sam" and a whole slew of others stuff—"The Boston Strangler" (cited in Magnus 2005).

as by his integration of elements of dominant rhetorics that may then constitutively justify commission of his violent act.

The fifth dimension concerns socio-historical processes that provide the opportunity for, and tacit encouragement of, various forms of crime (see also O'Malley and Mugford 1994). Lust homicide is but one form along a continuum, be it at the extreme end. Salecl (1997), for example, has shown how serial killers are "created" in historical settings (in her example of the Chiaktilo case, at the time of the disintegration of the former Soviet Union). Schechter (2003, Chapter 9) has cited the extensive glorification of violence in the media.[18] At a deeper level, Duncan (1997) has shown how non-law abiding and law abiding live in a symbiotic relationship, each feeding off the other (see also Egger 2002, pp. 100-110; Schechter 2003, pp. 262-265). Law enforcement officers, too, are provided an opportunity "to be where the criminal is, to think like the criminal and think *about* the criminal for years on end—all the while justifying this behavior as required by his fight against criminality." And we implicate society in creating disenfranchised, disempowered, stigmatized, and marginalized groups which are then targeted by predators, who can now readily construct a coherent rhetorical basis, be it exaggerated, of righteousness for their gruesome acts (Matza 1969). Thus, the discovery, manufacture, and at times subtle, be it inadvertent, encouragement of lust homicide is inherently connected with political economy and historical conditions.

Socio-historical change provides not only differential opportunities, forms of oppression, and possible adaptations, but also changing borderlands and internecine spaces ("liminal zones") within which the Symbolic, Imaginary, and Real are unstable. Here, too, "edges" are emergents. They provide both specifications of normative frameworks in their transgressions and an invitation to what is beyond.

In short, the literature on serial lust homicide suggests that one of the most extreme forms of violence to emerge could be understood not only as a mode of subjectivization, ceremonial ritual, mode of adjustment, but also as a form of edgework—approaching boundaries and the experiencing of intense excitement, which all lead to the elongation of murder. This five-dimensional grid provides an orienting tool for further inquiry and an approximation toward a better understanding.

---

18. Schechter (2002, p. 402) has provided some relevant websites: www.crimelibrary.com; www.mayhem.net; www.angelfire.com/oh/yodaspage; www.crimeweb.com; www.sondralondon.com; www.zodiackiller.com; www.casebook.org.

Conclusion

That a rift between the socially prescribed symbols of success and the absence of legitimate opportunities for their attainment adumbrates the adoption of innovative methods of adaptation is a sociological truism (Merton 1938). But rather than defining success with an overly materialist hue, we have broadened it to include the affective facet of social life (see the "introduction" to this book). That is, while crime in general is debilitating to society, unfairly denies the life of another, creating enormous amount of suffering, a discussion of the highly transcendental and creative manifestation of a serial killer's psychic energy need not be conflated with the moral prescriptivism that usually accompanies such discourse. Consequently, we have examined how lust murders function as adaptive mechanisms, a creative force, be it destructive, in the human subject's (offender's) mode of being.

As Halleck noted quite some time ago, the most effective way to reduce tension and stress in one's condition is through motoric activity; and if we apply this conceptual framework to lust murders, we can begin to see their non-material allure. As outlined in this chapter, fantasizing, stalking, conjuring up ruses, abducting, and killing a victim involves a significant investment of one's time, energy, and resources; moreover, it involves a considerable amount of physical action prior to, during, and after the act. That is, once a victim has been selected, killers have to acquire intelligence regarding the victim's habits, routines, and vulnerabilities; furthermore, killers have to determine how such information will ultimately be employed in the pursuit of their retributive and sexual aim. And during this process, the killers actively—physically and mentally—become engrossed in the task at hand.

In lust murders, precipitating factors that often tend toward heightened feelings of anger, a highly noxious and tension producing state, are incrementally transformed into physical action; and it is precisely during this corporeal metamorphosis that an individual senses the tingling sensations of hope, along with a non-negligible heaping of excitement and the possibility of danger (O'Malley and Mugford 1994). But most significantly, these actions provide creative outlets for killers to transform their impotent and frustrated existential situation into an autonomous mode of *being* in the planning, preparing, and execution of their criminal acts (see Halleck 1967, p. 77). But to explain their behavior by declaring their anti-sociality, psychopathy, and self-indulgence merely provides one type of answer at the cost of overlooking another; that is, to view these very types of offenses as the outcome of a diseased mind, as persons lacking "self control" as a result of poor parenting and deficient moral training, overlooks crucial phenomenological, psychological, and empirical observations: that the act is suffused with an unmistakable tinge of existential boundary crossings that are manifested in the corporeal, spatial, emotional, and moral experiences of killers (Katz 1999).

Consequently, we have tentatively—and theoretically—explored lust homicide as a form of "edgework," examining how the serial lust predator is "subjectivized" by his offenses, which in turn ossifies the predatorial identity (Lyng 2005; Milovanovic 2005). Thus, a more troubling—and theoretically titillating—question would be to explore how serial murders present a set of moral and emotional challenges that killers attempt to work through; furthermore, it might be worthwhile to examine how criminals in general "elongate" their rule-breaking experience, thus simulating the intensities and "highs" of their offenses; an exploration into the fantasy of criminal simulacra may yield another notable set of contributions to the literature on rule breaking. As we have conjectured in this chapter, killers use highly innovative methods to respond to their perceived existential dilemmas. It is perhaps the allure of these moral and emotional challenges and gains that is equally, if not more theoretically worthy of further investigation than the material ones.

References

Adams, L., and Dale R. (1999). "Dissecting columbine's cult of the athlete." *The Washington Post*, June 12, p. A1.

Adler, A. (1941). *Understanding Human Nature*. New York: Tower Books.

American Law Institute (1985). *Model Penal Code and Commentaries*. Philadelphia, PA: ALI.

American Psychiatric Association. (1994). *Diagnostic and Statistical Manual of Mental Disorders* (4th ed. revised). Washington DC.

Applebaum, S. (2004) "Hollywood won't touch Columbine." (London) *Sunday Times*, January 18, Features p. 10.

Arrigo, B. A., and Purcell, C. E. (2001). "Explaining paraphilia and lust murder: Towards an integrated model." *International Journal of Offender Therapy and Comparative Criminology* 45: 6-31.

Arrigo, B., and Shipley, S. (2005). *Introduction to Forensic Psychology*. (2nd Ed.). Burlington, MA: Elsevier Academic Press.

Associated Press/MSNBC. (2004). "Forgiveness not needed, say Klebold's parents." May 16, http://www.msnbc.msn.com/id/4990167/.

ATSA (2001). *Practice Standards and Guidelines for Members of the Association for the Treatment of Sexual Offenders*. Beaverton, OR: ATSA.

Avery, S. (1985). "Night of stalker has a thousand eyes." *Los Angles Times*, August 31, p. B1.

Bader, M. J. (2003). *Arousal: The Secret Logic of Sexual Fantasies*. New York: St. Martin's.

Baker, B. (1985). "Psychological profile: Probing killer's mind." *Los Angeles Times*, August 29, p. B1.

Baker, R. (1984). "Some considerations arising from the treatment of a patient with necrophiliac fantasies in late adolescence and young adulthood." *International Journal of Psychoanalysis* 65: 283-294.

Bancroft, J. (1985). *Deviant Sexual Behavior*. New York: Oxford University Press.

Bateson, G. (1978). *Mind and Nature: A Necessary Unity*. New York: Bantam Books.

Bays, L., and Freeman-Longo, R. (1990). *Why did I do It again?: Understanding My Cycle of Problem Behaviors.* Orwell, VT: The Safer Society Press.

"Bearing the cost of prosecution." (1987). *Los Angeles Times,* November 12, p. B2.

Beech, A., Fisher, D., and Ward, T. (2005). "Sexual murders' implicit theories." *Journal of Interpersonal Violence* 20: 1366-1389.

Beech, A.R., and Fisher, D.D. (2002). "The rehabilitation of child sex offenders." *Australian Psychologist,* 37: 206-214.

Belcher, J., and Skeleton, N. (1985). "Neighbors gang up." *Los Angeles Times,* September 1 p. A1.

Bennett, W., and Hess, K. (2004). *Criminal Investigation.* (6th Ed.). Belmont, CA: Wadsworth Publishing.

Bible, The Holy. New International Version. Zondervan.

Bierman, J.S., (1962). "Necrophilia in a thirteen-year old boy." *Psychoanalytic Quarterly* 31: 329-340.

Black, D., and Larson, C. (1999). *Bad Boys, Bad Men.* New York: Oxford University Press.

Black, E. (2005). "Red Lake School Shooting: Measuring the media coverage against Columbine." (Minneapolis) *Star Tribune,* March 26, metro edition, p. 18A.

Blanchard, G. T. (1995). *The Difficult Connection.* Brandon, VT: Safer Society Press.

Block, C. R., and Block, R. (1991). "Beginning with Wolfgang: An agenda for homicide research." *Journal of Crime and Justice* XIV(2): 31-70.

Block, R., and Block, C. R. (1992). "Homicide syndromes and vulnerability: Violence in Chicago community areas over 25 Years." *Studies on Crime and Crime Prevention* 1, 1, National Council for Crime Prevention.

Bonta, M., and Protevi. J. (2004). *Deleuze and Geophilosophy.* Edinburg, UK: Edinburg University Press.

Brandl, S. (2004). *Criminal Investigations: An Analytical Perspective.* Boston: Person Publishing.

Brill, A.A. (1941a). "Necrophilia." *Journal of Criminal Psychopathology* 2: 433-443.

Brill, A.A. (1941b). "Necrophilia." *Journal of Criminal Psychopathology* 3: 50-73.

Brittain, R. P. (1970). "The sadistic murderer." *Medicine, Science, and the Law* 10: 198-207.

Brown, H. "Murder in mind." (London) *Daily Telegraph,* March 12 (2005) Books, p. 2. Online at http://portal.telegraph.co.uk/arts/main.jhtml?xml= /arts/2005/03/13/bomassacre.xml&sSheet=/arts/2005/03/13/bomain.html.

Brown, P. (2003). *Killing For Sport: Inside the Minds of Serial Killers*. New Millenium Press.

Buamann, E., and O'Brien, J. (1990). "Hell's Belle living with the widow Gunness was murder." *Chicago Tribune*, June 1, p. A1.

Bugliosi, V., and Gentry, C. (1974). *Helter Skelter: The True Story of the Manson Murders*. New York: W. W. Norton & Co.

Burg, B. R. (1982). "The sick and the dead: The development of psychological theory on necrophilia from Krafft-Ebing to the present." *Journal of the History of the Behavioral Sciences* 18(3): 242-254.

Burgess, A. W., Hartman, C., Ressler, R. K., Douglas, J., E., and McCormack, A. (1986). "Sexual homicide: A motivational model." *Journal of Interpersonal Violence* 1(3): 251-272.

Byrne, D. (1994). "Talk of death becomes lively topic." *Chicago Sun-Times*, May 5, p. A37.

Calder, M. C. (1999). *Assessing Risk in Adult Males who Sexually Abuse Children*. (eds.). Dorset, England: Russell House Publishing.

Calef, V., and Weinshel, E.M., (1972). "On certain neurotic equivalents of necrophilia." *International Journal of Psychoanalysis* 53:67-75.

"Camera ban at Ramirez hearing to face challenge." (1985). *Los Angeles Times*, December 13, p. B3.

Carich, M. S. (1985). *The Psychology of a Cybernetics View of Family Development as Applied to Therapy*. Unpublished doctoral dissertation, St. Louis University.

Carich, M.S. (1999b). "Evaluation of recovery: 15 common factors or elements." *American Society of Clinical Hypnosis* 40(4): 5, 8.

Carich, M. S. (2000). "The direction of contemporary sex offender treatment: An issue of social constructivism vs. logical positivism." *The Forum* 12(3): 4-5.

Carich, M. S. (2002). "Pros and cons of teaching victim empathy in treatment." *The IL-ATSA Review* Vol. 5(1): p. 5.

Carich, M. S., and Adkerson, D. (1995). *Adult Sexual Offender Packet*. Brandon, VT: The Safer Society Press.

Carich, M. S., and Adkerson, D. (2003). *Adult Sexual Offender Report*. Brandon, VT: The Safer Society Press.

Carich, M. S., and Calder, M. (2003). *A Handbook of Contemporary Sex Offender Treatment*. Dorset, England: Russell House Publishing Ltd.

Carich, M. S., Gray, A., Rombouts, S., Stone, M., and Pithers, W. D. (2001). "Relapse prevention and the sexual assault cycle." Pp. 77-104 in *Handbook of Sexual Abuse Treatment*. Edited by M. S. Carich and S. E. Mussack. Brandon, VT: The Safer Society Press.

Carich, M. S., Jones, R. J., Egger, S. A., and Meyer, C. C. (1996). "Profiling serial killers Part II: A theoretical overview of a serial killer." *Journal of Correctional Research* Vol. 1. (IDOC).

Carich, M. S., and Metzger, C. (1999). "Hypnotherapy." Pp. 43-59 in *Interventions and Strategies in Counseling and Psychotherapy*. Edited by R. E. Watts and J. Carlson. Ann Arbor, MI: Accelerated Development.

Carich, M.S., and Metzger, C. (2004). "Rediscovering and utilizing the concept of the unconscious in contemporary sex offender treatment." *The Forum* XVI (4).

Carich, M. S., and Mussack, S. (2001). *A Handbook for Sexual Abuser Assessment and Treatment*. (Eds.). Brandon, VT: The Safer Society Press.

Carich, M S., and Parwatikar, S. D. (1992). "A mind-body connection: A sex offender switch box: A brief review." *INMAS Newsletter* 5(3): Pp. 2-4.

Carich, M. S., and Parwatikar, S. D. (1996). "Mind-body interaction: Theory and its application to sex offenders." *Journal of Correctional Research* Vol. 1 (IDOC).

Carich, M.S., and Stone, M. (1996). *The Sex Offender Workbook*. Chicago, IL: Adler School of Professional Psychology.

Carich, M.S., and Stone, M. (2001). "Utilizing relapse intervention strategies to treat sexual offenders." *The Journal of Individual Psychology* 57(1): 26-36.

Chen, E. (1989). "Night stalker's guilty." *Los Angeles Times*, September 21p. A1.

CBS News. (2002). "Did Columbine Killer Drop Hints?" Oct. 5. Online at http://www.cbsnews.com/stories/2003/05/09/national/main553075.shtml.

Clarke, J., and Carter, A. J. (2000). "Relapse prevention with sexual murderers." Pp. 389-401 in *Remaking Relapse Prevention with Sex Offenders*. Edited by D. R. Laws, S. M. Hudson, and T. Ward. London: Sage.

CNN. Online at http://www.cnn.com/SPECIALS/2000/columbine.cd/frameset.exclude.html and http://archives.cnn.com/2000/US/05/15/columbine.report.03/index.html.

CourtTV.com (2005). *Court TV's Crime Library: Criminal Minds and Methods*. {Data file}. Available from http://courttv.com

Cullen, D. Slate. April 20, (2004). Online at http://www.slate.com/id/2099203/.

"Death sentence in serial murder case." (1992). *Los Angeles Times*, February 1, p. A25.

"Death sentence in serial murder case." (1992). *St. Petersburg Times*, January 31, p. A25.

DeHart, D., and Mahoney, J. (1994). "The serial murderer's motivations: An interdisciplinary review." *Omega* 29: 29-45.

del Olmo, F. (1985). "Gratitude and a band of 'heroes." *Los Angeles Times*, September 12, p. B5.

Delanda, M. (2002). Intensive Science and Virtual Philosophy. London: Continuum.

Deleuze, G. (1983). *Nietzsche and Philosophy.* New York: Columbia University Press.

Deleuze, G. (1988). *Spinoza: Practical Philosophy.* San Francisco: City Light Books.

Deleuze, G. (1989). *Masochism: Coldness and Cruelty.* New York: Zone Books.

Deleuze, G., and Guattari, F. (1987). *A Thousand Plateaus.* Minneapolis, MIN: University of Minneapolis Press.

DeRiver, J. P. (1949). *The Sexual Criminal: A Psychoanalytic Study.* Springfield, IL: Charles C. Thomas.

Dershowitz, A. (1994). *The Abuse Excuse and Other Copouts, Sob Stories and Evasions of Responsibility.* Boston, MA: Little, Brown.

Diagnostic and Statistical Manual for Mental Disorders (DSM-IV). (1994). (4th Ed.). Washington, DC: American Psychiatric Association.

Dial v State. (2003) WL 352982 (Wash. App.).

Dietz, P. (1986). "Mass, serial, and sensational homicides." *Bulletin of the New York Academy of Medicine* 62(5): 477-497.

Dimock, J., and Smith, S. (1997). "Necrophilia and antisocial acts" Pp. 241-251 in *Sexual Dynamics of Anti-Social Behavior* (2nd Ed.). Edited by L. Schlesinger and E. Revitch. Springfield, IL: Charles C. Thomas Publisher, Ltd

Dix, G. (2002). *Gilbert Law Summaries: Criminal law* (17th Ed.). New York: Harcourt Legal and Professional Publications.

Douglas, J., and Olshaker, M. (1995). *Mindhunter.* NY: Scribner Books.

Douglas, J. E., Burgess, A. W., and Ressler, R. K. (1995). *Sexual Homicide: Patterns and Motives.* NY: the Free Press.

Douglas, J., and Olshaker, M. (1999). *The Anatomy of Motive.* New York: Pocket Books.

Douglas, J., and Olshaker, M. (2000). *The Cases that Haunt Us.* New York: Pocket Books.

Dreikurs, R. (1950). *Fundamentals of Adlerian Psychology.* Chicago, IL: Alfred Adler Institute.

Dreikurs, R. (1967). *Psychodynamics, Psychotherapy and Counseling.* Chicago, IL: Alfred Adler Institute.

Drell, A., and Long, R. (1994). "Gacy's hours dwindle." *Chicago Sun-Times,* May 9, p. A1.

Duncan, M. (1997). *Romantic Outlaws, Beloved Prisons: The Unconscious Meanings of Crime and Punishment.* New York: New York University Press.

Durant, W. (1926). *The Story of Philosophy.* Garden City: Garden City Publishing.

Durkheim, E. (1964). *The Division of Labor in Society*. New York: The Free Press.

Dusky v United States. 362 U.S. 402. (1960).

Egger, S. A. (1984). "A working definition of serial murder and the reduction of linkage blindness." *Journal of Police Science and Administration* 12(3): 348-357.

Egger, S.A. (1990a). *Serial Murder: An Elusive Phenomenon*. (Ed.).New York: Praeger.

Egger, S. A. (1990b). "Serial murder: A synthesis of literature and research." Pp. 3-34 in *Serial Murder: An Elusive Phenomenon*. Edited by S. A. Egger. New York: Praeger.

Egger, S. A. (1998/2002). *The Killers Among Us*. Upper Saddle River, N.J.: Prentice Hall.

Egger, S.A. (2003). *The Need to Kill*. Saddle River, New Jersey: Prentice Hall.

Eliade, M. (1957). *The Sacred and the Profane*. NY: Harper & Row.

English, K. (1998). "The containment approach: An aggressive strategy for the community management of adult sex offenders." *Psychology, Public Policy and Law* 4(1/2): 218-235.

Erickson, M.H., Rossi, E.L., and Rossi, S. (1976). *Hypnotic Realities: The Induction of Clinical Hypnosis and Forms of Indirect Suggestions*. New York: Irington Publishers.

Erikson, E. (1963). *Childhood and Society*. New York: W. W. Norton & Co., Inc.

Ewick, P., and Silbey, S. (1998). *The Common Place of Law*. Chicago: University of Chicago Press.

"Experts differ on suspected mass killer: Some see Ted Bundy as scapegoat in 40 sex slayings." (1978). May 3, *Los Angeles Times*, p. A1.

Feldman, P. (1986). "Chilling stalker testimony turns up few firm links." *Los Angeles Times*, March 24, p. B1.

Feder, R. (1994). "Gacy's execution pulls media circus." *Chicago Sun-Times*, May 5, p. A47

Ferguson, C. J., White, D., Cherry, S., Lorenz, M., and Bhimani, Z. (2003). "Defining and classifying serial murder in the context of perpetrator motivation." *Journal of Criminal Justice* 31: 287-292.

Ferrell, J. (1996). "Style Matters: Criminal identity and Social Control." Pp. 169-189 in *Cultural Criminology*. Edited by J. Ferrell and C. Sanders. Boston: Northeastern University Press.

Fontana, T., Whitesell, S., and Nayar, S. (Writers), and Tobin, J. (Director). (2004). Even the score [Television series episode]. In B. Levinson, T. Fontana, & J. Finnerty (Producers), *Oz: The Complete Fourth Season*. New York: Home Box Office Productions.

Foraker, A.G. (1976). "The romantic necrophiliac of Key West." *Journal of Florida Medical Association* 63(8): 642-645.

Fornek, S. (1994). "Death penalty debate grows." *Chicago Sun-Times,* April 18, p. A1.

Fox, J. A., and Levin, J. (2005). *Extreme Killing.* Thousand Oaks, Calif.: Sage.

Frankl, V.E. (1959). *Man's Search for Meaning.* NY: Washington Square Press.

Freed, D., and McGraw, C. (1985). "Citizens capture stalker fugitive." *Los Angeles Times,* September 1,p. A1.

Freud, S. (1914). *Totem and Taboo: Resemblances Between the Psychic Lives of Savages and Neurotics.* New York: Vintage Books.

Freud, S. (1970). *A General Introduction to Psychoanalysis.* New York: Pocket Books.

Garner, B. (1996). *Black's Law Dictionary.* (Ed.). St. Paul, MN: West Publishing.

Geberth, V. J. (1983). *Practical Homicide Investigation: Tactics, Procedures, and Forensic Techniques.* (1st Ed.). New York: Elsevier.

Geberth, V. J. (1996). *Practical Homicide Investigation: Tactics, Procedures, and Forensic Techniques.* (3rd Ed.). Boca Raton, FL: CRC Press.

Giannangelo, S. J. (1996). *The Psychopathology of Serial Murder: A Theory of Violence.*

Gilbert, J. (2004). *Criminal Investigation.* (6th Ed.). Upper Saddle River, NJ: Prentice Hall.

Glidwell, J. (1998). "Murderous 'hobby' buys little fame." *St. Petersburg Times,* March 24, p. A1.

Grisso, T. (2003). *Evaluating Competencies: Forensic Assessments and Instruments.* (2nd Ed.). New York: Kluwer Academic/Plenum.

Grossman, L. S. (1985). "Research directions in the evaluation and treatment of sex offenders: An analysis." *Behavioral Sciences and the Law* 3: 421.

Grossman, L.S., Martis, B., and Fichtner, C.G. (1999). "Are sex offenders treatable? A research overview." *Psychiatric Services* 50 (3): 349-361.

Grosz, E. (1994). *Volatile Bodies: Toward a Corporeal Feminism.* Bloomington, Indiana: Indiana University Press.

Grubin, D. (1994). "Sexual murder." *British Journal of Psychiatry* 165: 624-629.

Halleck, S. (1967). *Psychiatry and the Dilemmas of Crime.* CA: University of California Press.

Hammel-Zabin, A. (2003). *Conversations with a Pedophile.* Fort Lee, NJ: Barricade Books.

Hansen, J. T. (2005). "The devaluation of inner subjective experiences by the counseling profession: A plea to reclaim the essence of the profession." *Journal of Counseling and Development* 83(4): 406-415.

Hansen, J.T. (2004). "Thoughts on knowing: Epistemic implications of counseling practice." *Journal of Counseling and Development* 82: 131-138.

Hanson, R. K., and Harris, A. J. R. (2001). "A structured approach to evaluating change among sexual offenders." *Sexual Abuse: A Journal of Research and Treatment* 13: 105-122.

Harari, R. (2001). *Lacan's Seminar on 'Anxiety': An Introduction.* New York: Other Press.

Harbort, S., and Mokros, A. (2001). "Serial murderers in Germany from 1945-1995: A descriptive study." *Homicide Studies* 5(4): 311-334.

Hare, R. (1999/1993). *Without conscience: The Disturbing World of the Psychopaths Among Us.* New York: The Guilford Press.

Hazelwood, R., and Douglas, J. (1980). "The lust murderer." *FBI Law Enforcement Bulletin* 49: 1-8.

Hazelwood, R., and Michaud, S. (2001). *Dark Dreams.* New York: St. Martin's Press.

Healy, J. (2006). "The etiology of paraphilia: A dichotomous model." Pp 57-68 in *Sex Crimes and Paraphilia.* (Ed). Upper Saddle River, NJ: Prentice Hall.

Heasman, A., and Jones, E. (2006). "Necrophilia." Pp 273-280 in *Sex Crimes and Paraphilia.* (Ed). Upper Saddle River, NJ: Prentice Hall.

Henry, S., and Milovanovic, D. (1996). *Constitutive Criminology.* London: Sage Publications.

Hensley, C., and Tewksbury, R. (2003). *Sexual Deviance: A Reader.* (Eds.) NY: L. Rienner

Hickey, E. (1997). *Serial Murderers and Their Victims* (2nd Ed.). Belmont, CA: Wadsworth

Hickey, E. (2001). *Serial Murder and Their Victims* (3rd. Ed.). Belmont, CA: Wadsworth.

Hickey, E. (2006a). *Serial Murderers and Their Victims.* (4th Ed.). Belmont, CA: Wadsworth Publishing.

Hickey, E. (2006b). *Sex Crimes and Paraphilia.* (Ed). Upper Saddle River, NJ: Prentice Hall.

Hickey, E. (2006c). "Preface." Pp ix-xiv in *Sex Crimes and Paraphilia.* (Ed). Upper Saddle River, NJ: Prentice Hall.

Hickey, E. (2006d)."Paraphilia and Signatures in Crime Scene Investigation." Pp 95-110 in *Sex Crimes and Paraphilia.* (Ed). Upper Saddle River, NJ: Prentice Hall.

Holley, D. (1985). "Recalling Ramirez: Even friends didn't trust him." *Los Angeles Times,* September 8, p. 1.

Holmes, R.M., and DeBurger, J. (1988). *Serial Murder.* CA: Sage Publications.

Holmes, R.M., and Holmes, S.T. (1994). *Murder in America.* Thousand Oaks, CA: Sage

Holmes, R., and DeBurger, J. (1998). "Profiles in terror: The serial murderer." pp 5-16 in *Contemporary Perspectives on Serial Murder*. Edited by R. Holmes and S. Holmes. Thousand Oaks, CA; Sage Publishing.

Holmes, S., and Holmes, R. (2002). *Sex Crimes* (2nd Edition.). Thousand Oak, CA: Sage

Horgan, J. (1974). *Criminal Investigation*. New York: McGraw Hill.

Huber, Van H. (1962). Nekrophile 16: 564-568.

Hucker, S., and Stermac, L. 1992. "The evaluation and treatment of sexual violence, necrophilia, and asphyxiophilia." *Psychiatric Clinics of North America* 15(3): 703-719.

Jackson v Indiana, 406 U.S. 715 (1972).

Jenkins, P. (1994). *Using Murder: The Social Construction of Serial Homicide*. New York: Aldine de Gruyter.

Jesse, F.T. (1924). *Murder and Its Motive*. New York: Knopf.

Johnson, J. (2006). "Sexual sadism in rapists." Pp 409-418 in *Sex Crimes and Paraphilia*. (Ed). Upper Saddle River, NJ: Prentice Hall.

Jones, A. (1996). *Women Who Kill*. New York: Holt.

"Jury recommends death for Wuornos." (1992). *St. Petersburg Times*, May 8, p. A1.

Kappeler, V., and Potter, G. (2005). *The Mythology of Crime and Criminal Justice*. (4th Edition.) Long Grove, IL: Waveland Press.

Katz, J. (1988). *Seductions of Crime: Moral and Sensual Attractions of Doing Evil*. New York: Basic Books.

Katz, J. (1999). *How Emotions Work*. Chicago: University of Chicago Press.

Keeney, B. P. (1983). *Aesthetics of Change*. New York: The Guilford Press.

Keeney, B. P., and Ross, J.M. (1983). "Cybernetics of brief family therapy." *Journal of Marital and Family Therapy* 9: 375-382.

Kelley, G. (1955). *The Psychology of Personal Constructs*. New York: W.W. Norton & Company.

Kelley, G. (1963). *A Theory of Personality: The Psychology of Personal Constructs*. New York: W. W. Norton & Company.

Kennerley, H. (2000). *Overcoming Childhood Trauma: A Self-Help Guide Using Cognitive Behavioral Techniques*. New York: New York University Press.

Kenworthy, T., and Litton, S. (2006). "Fetishism: Development, personality characteristics, theories, and treatment indicators for the fetishist." pp 155-164 in *Sex Crimes and Paraphilia*. (Ed). Upper Saddle River, NJ: Prentice Hall.

Keppel, R. (1992). *An Analysis of the Effect of Time and Distance Relationships in Murder Investigations*. Ph.D. Dissertation, Special Individual Ph.D. Program, University of Washington.

Keppel, R. (1995). "Signature murders: A report of several related cases." *Journal of Forensic Sciences* 40(4): 670-674.

Keppel, R. (2000). "Signature murders: A report of the 1984 Cranbrook, British Columbia cases." *Journal of Forensic Sciences* 45(2): 500-503.

Keppel, R., and Birnes, W. (1997). *Signature Killers.* New York: Pocket Books.

Keppel, R., and Birnes, W. (2003). *The Psychology of Serial Killer Investigations.* San Diego, CA: Academic Press.

Keppel, R., and Birnes, W. (1995). *The Riverman: Ted Bundy and I Hunt for the Green River Killer.* New York: Pocket Books.

Keppel, R., and Weis, J. (1994). "Time and distance as solvability factors in murder cases." *Journal of Forensic Sciences* 39(2): 386-401.

Keppel, R., and Weis, J. (2004). "The rarity of 'unusual' dispositions of victim bodies: Staging and posing." *Journal of Forensic Sciences* 49(6): 1-5.

"Key testimony to be allowed in murder trial." (1979). *The New York Times,* July 7, p. A6.

Kifner, J. (1994). "Man who killed 33 is executed in Illinois." *The New York Times,* May 10, p. A12.

Kirwin, B. (1997). *The Mad, the Bad, and the Innocent.* New York: HarperTorch.

Klaf, F.S., and Brown, W. (1966). "Necrophilia: brief review and case report." *Psychiatric Quarterly* 32: 645-652.

Kline, P. (1987). "Sexual deviation: Psychoanalytic research and theory." Pp 150-175 in *Variant sexuality: Research and Theory.* Edited by G. D. Wilson; Baltimore, MD: Johns Hopkins University Press.

Kohut, M. (2004a). *Excuse me!* Manuscript submitted for publication.

Kohut, M.(2004b). *Medical Treatment Facility's Response to Sexual Assault.* Ellsworth AFB: United States Air Force.

Kohut, M. R. (2004c). *Who knew? The killers next door.* Manuscript submitted for publication.

Kohut, M. (2005). *What's eating you? Why cannibalistic serial killers do what they do.* Manuscript submitted for publication.

Kozol, R., and Sneed, M. (1978). "Police find 8 more bodies." *Chicago Tribune,* December 28, p. A1.

Kozol, R., and Sneed, M. (1978). "6 bodies put toll at 28." *Chicago Tribune,* December 30, p. A1.

Kurtis, B. (Writer). (2005). *Gary Ridgeway: The Green River Killer* (Television series episode). In B. Kurtis (Producer), *Biography.* New York: Arts and Entertainment Network.

Lacan, J. (1977a). *Four Fundamental Concepts of Psychoanalysis.* New York: W.W Norton

Lacan, J (1977b). *Ecrits.* New York: W.W Norton

Lacan, J (1998). *Encore: The Seminar of Jacques Lacan, Book XX.* Bruce Fink. Trans. New York: W.W. Norton and Company.

Lancaster, N.P. (1978). "Necrophilia, murder and high intelligence: a case report." *British Journal of Psychiatry* 132: 605-608.

Lane, R. (1997). *Murder in America: A History.* Columbus, OH: Ohio State University.

Lanier, M., and Henry, S. (2004). *Essential Criminology.* Boulder, CO: Westview Books.

Lankton, S. R., and Lankton, C. H. (1983). *The Answer Within: A Clinical Framework of Ericksonian Hypnotherapy.* New York: Brunner/Mazel.

Larson, E. (2003). *The Devil in the White City.* New York: Vintage Books.

Lavin, C. (1991). "First woman serial killer." *St. Petersburg Times,* January 18, p. A1.

Lavin, C., and Ross, J. (1992). "Murders, movies and a plea to die." *St. Petersburg Times,* April 20, p. B1.

Laws, D.R. (1995). "Central elements in relapse prevention procedures with sex offenders." *Psychology, Crime and Law* 2: 41-53.

Laws, D.R. (1999). "Relapse prevention: The state of the art." *Journal of Interpersonal Violence* 14(3): 285-302.

Lecercle, J.J. (1985). *Philosophy Through the Looking Glass.* London: Hutchinson.

Leeuw, G. (1963). *Religion in Essence and Manifestation.* New York: Harper & Row.

Lindsey, R. (1984). "Officials cite a rise in killers who roam U.S. for victims" *The New York Times,* January 21, p. A1.

Lindsey, R. (1985) "Man held in coast deaths after capture by citizens." *The New York Times,* September 1, p. A20.

Livingston, J. (1989). *Anatomy of the Sacred: An Introduction to Religion.* New York: Macmillan Publishing Co.

Longo, R.E. (2002). "A holistic integrated approach to treating sexual offenders." *The Sex Offender: Current Treatment Modalities & System Issues* Vol. 4, chapter 21

Lyng, S. (1990). "Edgework: A social-psychological analysis of voluntary risk taking." *American Journal of Sociology* 95(4): 876-921.

Lyng, S. (2005). *Edgework: The Sociology of Risk-Taking.* London: Routledge.

MacCulloch, M.J., Snowden, P.R., Wood, P.J.W., and Mills, H.E., (1983). "Sadistic fantasy, sadistic behavior, and offending". *British Journal of Psychiatry* 143: 20-29.

Macias v Arizona, 293 (1929).

Mahoney, M. (2003). *Constructive Psychotherapy: A Practical Guide.* New York: The Guilford Press.

Magnus, E. (2005). "31 Years of the BTK Killer." http://msnbc.msn.com/id/8916264

Malamuth, N. M., and Brown, L. M. (1994). "Sexually aggressive men's perspectives of women's communications: Testing three explanations." *Journal of Personality and Social Psychology* 67: 699-712.

Manners, T. (1995). *Deadlier Than the Male: Stories of Female Serial Killers.* Trafalgo Square Publishing.

Manson, M. (1999). "Columbine: Whose Fault Is It?" *Rolling Stone*, June 24, Pp. 23-26. Online at http://www.rollingstone.com/news/story/_/id/5923915?rnd=1133205047792&has-player=true&version=6.0.12.1212.

Marshall, W.L. (1996). "Assessment, treatment, and theorizing about sexual offenders: Development over the past 20 years and future directions." *Criminal Justice and Behavior* 23(1): 162-199.

Marshall, W.L. (1999). "Current status of North American assessment and treatment program for sexual offenders." *Journal of Interpersonal Violence* 14(3): 221-239.

Marshall, W.L. (2005). "Therapist style in sexual offender treatment: Influences on indices of change." *Sexual Abuse: A Journal of Research and Treatment* 17(2): 109-116.

Marshall, W.L., Anderson, D., and Fernandez, Y. (1999). *Cognitive-Behavioral Treatment of Sexual Offenders.* Chichester: Wiley.

Marshall, W.L., and Eccles, A. (1991). "Issues in clinical practice with sexual offenders." *Journal of Interpersonal Violence* 6(1): 68-93.

"Mass murder suspect on F.B.I. fugitive list." (1978). *The New York Times,* February 11, p. A8.

Massumi, B. (1992). *A User's Guide to Capitalism and Schizophrenia.* Cambridge, MA: Swerve Edition.

Matza, D. (1969). *Becoming Deviant.* Englewood Cliffs, New Jersey: Prentice-Hall, Inc.

McCorkle, R., and Miethe, T. (2002). *Panic: The Social Construction of the Street Gang Problem.* Upper Saddle, NJ: Prentice Hall.

McCrary, G., and Ramsland, K. (2003). *The Unknown Darkness.* New York: Harpertorch.

McFall (1990). *Social Dimension.* Federal Hearing.

McGuire, R.J., Carlisle, J.M., and Young, B.G., (1965). "Sexual deviations as conditioned behaviors: A hypothesis." *Behavior Research and Therapy* 2: 185-190.

McNamara, J. J., and Morton, R. (2004). "Frequency of serial sexual homicide victimization in Virginia for a ten-year period." *Journal of Forensic Sciences* 49(3): 1-5.

Meadows, R., and Kuehnel, J. (2005). *Evil Minds: Understanding and Responding to Violent Predators*. Upper Saddle River, NJ: Pearson Prentice Hall.

Merton, R. K. (1938). "Social Structure and Anomie." *American Sociological Review* 3: 672-682.

Metzger, C., and Carich, M.S. (1999). "Eleven point comprehensive sex offender treatment plan." Pp 293-311 in *Assessing Risk in Adult Males Who Sexually Abuse Children*. Edited by M. Calder. Dorset, England: Russell House Publishing Ltd.

Michael, M., and C.L. Kelleher. (1998). *Murder Most Rare: The Female Serial Killers*. Praeger Publishers: Westport, CT.

Michaud, S., and Aynesworth, H. (2000). *Ted Bundy: Conversations with a Killer: The Death Row Interviews*. New York: Barnes and Noble Books.

Miller, W., and Rollnick, S. (1991/2002). *Motivational Interviewing: Preparing People to Change Addictive Behavior*. New York: The Guilford Press.

Millon, T. (1997). *Millon Clinical Multiaxial Inventory-III Manual* (2nd Ed.). Minneapolis, MN: National Computer Systems.

Milovanovic, D. (2005). "Edgework: A subjective and structural model of negotiating boundaries." Pp 51-74 in *Edgework: The Sociology of Risk-Taking*. Edited by S. Lyng. London: Routledge.

Milsom, J., Beech, A. R., and Webster, S. (2003). "Emotional loneliness in sexual murderers: A qualitative analysis." *Sexual Abuse: A Journal of Research and Treatment* 15: 285-296.

Money, J. (1990). "Forensic sexology: Paraphiliac serial rape (biastophilia) and lust murder (erotophonophilia)." *American Journal of Psychotherapy* 14(1): 26-36.

Moorman, C. (2003). *Parent Talk: How to Talk to Your Children in Language that Builds Self-Esteem and Encourages Responsibility*. New York: Fireside Edition Books.

Morgan, L., and Nickens, T. (1989). "Bundy goes quietly to death." *St. Petersburg Times*, January 25, p. A1.

Mosak, H. (1979). *Adlerian Psychotherapy. Current Psychotherapies*. Edited by R. Corsini. Itasca, IL: F. E. Peacock, Inc.

Mount, C., and Kozol, R. (1978). "Bodies of 4 boys found." *Chicago Tribune*, December 23, p. A1.

Mulkern, A. C. (2004). "Drug taken by Columbine killer linked to increased mania." *The Denver Post*, September 12, p. A-06.

Myers, W. C., Burgess, A. W., Burgess, A. G., and Douglas, J. E. (1999). "Serial murder and sexual homicide." Pp 153-172 in *Handbook of Psychological Approaches with Violent Offenders: Contemporary Strategies and Issues*.

Edited by V. Van Hasselt & M. Hersen. New York: Kluwer Academic/Plenum Publishers.

Neimeyer, R. A., and Bridges, S. K. (2003). "Postmodern approach to psychotherapy." Pp 271-316 in *Essential Psychotherapies: Theory and Practice.* Edited by A. S. Gurman and S. A. Messer.

Neumann, S., Alley, M., Paclebar, A., Sanchez, C., and Satterthwaite, B. (2006). "Frotteurism, piquerism, and other related paraphilias." Pp 237-248 in *Sex Crimes and Paraphilia.* (ed). Upper Saddle River, NJ: Prentice Hall.

Newton, M. (2000). *The Encyclopedia of Serial Killers.* New York: Checkmark Books.

"Night stalker suspect yells at press." (1989). *Los Angeles Times,* May 8, p. A1.

Nobus, D. (2002). "Over my dead body: On the histories and cultures of necrophilia." Pp. 171-189 in *Inappropriate Relationships: The Unconventional, the Disapproved, and the Forbidden.* Edited by R. Goodwin. Mahwah, NJ, US: Lawrence Erlbaum Associates, Publishers.

Nordheimer, J (1978). "All-american boy on trial." *The New York Times Sunday Magazine,* December 10, p. 46.

Nordheimer, J. (1978). Florida inmate a suspect in killings of 36 women, but police lack decisive evidence. *The New York Times,* March 12, p. A1.

O'Hara, C. (1973). *Fundamentals of Criminal Investigation.* (3rd Ed.). Springfield, IL: Charles Thomas Publisher.

O'Malley, P., and Mugford, S. (1994). "Crime, Excitement, and Modernity." Pp 189-211 in *Varieties of Criminology.* Edited by G. Barak. Westport, CT: Praeger.

Otto, R. (1928). *The Idea of the Holy: An Inquiry into the Non-rational Factor in the Idea of the Divine and its relation to the Rational.* London: Oxford University Press.

Palermo, G. B. (2004). *The Faces of Violence* (2nd Ed.). Springfield, IL: Charles C. Thomas.

Palermo, G. B., and Farkas, M. A. (2001). *The Dilemma of the Sexual Offender.* Springfield, IL: Charles C. Thomas.

Pam, A., and Rivera, J. (1995). "Sexual pathology and dangerousness from a Thematic Apperception Test protocol." *Professional Psychology: Research & Practice* Vol 26(1). Pp. 72-77.

Parsons v State, (1877). 2 So. 854 (Ala.).

Peck, M. (2006). "Somnophilia: A paraphilia sleeping in social science research." Pp 267-272 in *Sex Crimes and Paraphilia.* (Ed). Upper Saddle River, NJ: Prentice Hall.

Peña, M. (2000). *Practical Criminal Investigation.* (5th Ed.). Incline Village, NV: Copperhouse Publishing Co.

Peven, D. E. (1993). "The individual psychological viewpoint of the psycho-sexual disorders." Pp. 429-451 in *Psychopathology and Psychotherapy: From Diagnosis to Treatment.* Edited by L. Sperry & J. Carlson. Philadelphia, PA: Accelerated Development, Inc.

Piaget, J., and Inhelder, B. (1963). *The Psychology of the Child.* New York: Basic Books.

Pincus, J. (2001). *Base Instincts: What Makes Killers Kill?* New York: W.W. Norton.

Polaschek, D.L., and T. Gannon. (2004). "The implicit theories of rapists: What convicted offenders tell us." *Sexual Abuse: A Journal of Research and Treatment* 16: 299-314.

Polaschek, D.L.L., and Gannon, T. (2005). *The implicit theories of rapists: What convicted offenders tell us.* Manuscript submitted for publication.

Polaschek, D. L. L., and Ward, T. (2002). "The implicit theories of rapists: What our questionnaires tell us." *Aggression and Violent Behavior* 7: 385-406.

"Potential jurors are quizzed in highway killings." (1992). *St. Petersburg Times,* January 14, p. B1.

Prins, H. (1985). "Vampirism: A clinical condition." *British Journal of Psychiatry* 146: 666-668.

"Prostitute waives trial in 3 killings." (1992). *St. Petersburg Times,* April 2, p. A10.

Proulx, J., Beauregard, E., and Nichole, A. (2002). "Developmental, personality and situational factors in rapists and sexual murderers of women." Paper presented at the 21st annual conference of the Association for the Behavioral Treatment of Sexual Abusers, Montreal, Canada.

Puckett, J. L., and Lundman, R. J. (2003). "Factors affecting homicide clearances: Multivariate analysis of a more complete conceptual framework." *Journal of Research in Crime and Delinquency* 40(2): 171-193.

Purcell, E. C., and Arrigo, B. A. (2006). *The Psychology of Lust Murder: On Paraphilia, Sexual Homicide and Serial killing.* San Diego, CA: Elsevier/Academic Press.

Rapoport, J. (1942). "A case of necrophilia." *Criminal Psychopathology* 4: 277-289.

Regoeczi, W. C., Kennedy, L. W., and Silverman, R. A. (2000). "Uncleared Homicides: A Canada/United States comparison." *Homicide Studies* 4(2): 135-161.

Reichert, D. (2004). *Chasing the Devil.* New York: Little, Brown, & Company

Ressler, R. (1992). *Whoever Fights Monsters.* New York: St. Martin's Press.

Ressler, R. (1997). *I Have Lived in the Monster.* New York: St. Martin's Press.

Ressler, R. J., Burgess, A. W., Hartman, C. R., Douglas, J. E., and McCormack, A. (1986). "Murderers who rape and mutilate." *Journal of Interpersonal Violence* 1(3): 273-287.

Ressler, R. K., Burgess, A.W., and Douglas, J. (1988/1992). *Sexual Homicide: Patterns and Motives.* New York: Free Press.

Rhodes, R. (1999). *Why They Kill: The Discoveries of a Maverick Criminologist.* New York: Vintage Books.

Roberts, J. V., and Grossman, M. G. (1993). "Sexual homicide in Canada: A descriptive analysis." *Annals of Sex Research* 6: 5-25.

Rocky Mountain Media Watch. Media Overdose Alert April (2000). Columbine Anniversary Media Coverage. Online at http://www.bigmedia.org/texts8.html.

Rosman, J. and Resnick, P. (1989). "Sexual attraction to corpses: A psychiatric review of necrophilia." *Bulletin of the American Academy of Psychiatry & the Law* 17(2): 153-163.

Rosner, R. (2003). *Principles and Practice of Forensic Psychiatry* (Ed.). (2nd Ed.). London:

Ross, J. (1992). "Killer condemned, not contained." *St. Petersburg Times,* May 16, p. B1.

Rossi, E. L. (1993). *The Psychology of Mind-Body Healing: New Concepts of Therapeutic Hypnosis* (2nd Ed.). New York: W. W. Norton & Co.

Rossi, E. L. (2002). *The Psychology of Gene Expression.* New York: W. W. Norton & Co.

Rossi, E. L. (2003). "Gene expression, neurogenesis and healing: Psychosocial genomics of therapeutic hypnosis." *American Journal of Clinical Hypnosis* 45(3): 197-216.

Rossi, E.L. (2000). "Psychobiological principles of creative Ericksonian psychotherapy." Pp 112-153 in *The Handbook of Ericksonian Psychotherapy.* Edited by B.B. Geary and J.K. Zeig. Phoenix, AR: The Milton H. Erickson Foundation Press.

Rychlak, J. (1981). *Introduction to Personality and Psychotherapy.* Boston, MA: Mifflin Houghton.

Safarik, M., and Jarvis, J. (2005). "Examining attributes of homicides: Toward quantifying qualitative values of injury severity." *Homicide Studies* 9(3): 183-203.

Safarik, M., Jarvis, J., and Nussbaum, K. (2002). "Sexual homicide of elderly females: Linking offender characteristics to victim and crime scene attributes." *Journal of Interpersonal Violence* 17(5): 500-525.

Salecl, R. (1994). *The Spoils of Freedom: Psychoanalysis and Feminism After the Fall of Socialism.* NY: Routledge.

Salfati, G. C. and Hratsis, E. (2001). "Greek homicide: A behavioral examination of offender crime-scene actions." *Homicide Studies* 5(4): 335-362.

Salfati, G. C. (2000). "The nature of expressiveness and instrumentality in homicides: Implications for offender profiling." *Homicide Studies* 4(3): 265-293.

Salfati, G. C. (2003). "Offender interaction with victims in homicide: A multidimensional analysis of frequencies in crime scene behaviors." *Journal of Interpersonal Violence* 18(5): 490-512.

Samaha, J. (2005a). *Criminal law* (8th Ed.). Belmont, CA: Wadsworth.

Samaha, J. (2005b). *Criminal procedure* (6th Ed.). Belmont, CA: Wadsworth.

Santtila, P., Canter, D., Elfgren, T., and Häkkänen, H. (2001). "The structure of crime scene actions in Finish homicides." *Homicide Studies* 5(4): 363-387.

"Satanic symbolism reported in homes of 'stalker' victims." (1985). *Los Angeles Times*, September 2, p. A26.

Schechter, H. (2003). *The Serial Killer Files*. New York: Ballantine Books.

Schlesinger, L. B. (2003). *Sexual Murder: Catathymic and Compulsive Homicides*. Boca Raton, FL: CRC Press.

Schwartz, B., and Cellini, H. (1995). *The Sex Offender: Corrections, Treatment and Legal Developments*. (Eds.). Kingston, NJ: Civic Research Institute.

Schwendinger, H., and Schwendinger, J. (1985). *Adolescent Subcultures and Delinquency*. New York: Praeger.

Segal, H. (1951). "A necrophiliac fantasy." *International Journal of Psychoanalysis* 34: 98-101.

Segrave, K. (1990). *Women Serial and Mass Murderers*. McFarland and Co. Inc. Publishers.

"Serial killer movies." (1994). *USA Today Magazine*, Aug94, p. 7.

Shon, P.C.H. (1999). "The sacred and the profane: The transcendental significance of lust murder in the construction of subjectivity." *Humanity & Society* 23 (1): 10-31.

Simon, R. (1996). *Bad Men Do What Good Men Dream*. Washington, DC: American Psychiatric Press Inc.

"Slaying suspect in restraints." (1978). *Los Angeles Times*, December, 29, p. A5.

Smith, S.M., and Braun, C. (1978). "Necrophilia and lust murder: report of a rare occurrence." *Bulletin of American Academy of Psychiatry & Law* 6: 259-268.

Sneed, M., and Kozol, R. (1978). "6 more bodies to Gacy." *Chicago Tribune*, December 26, p. A1.

Sprengelmeyer, M.E., and Ames, M. "Report offers Columbine hindsight." Denver Rocky Mountain News, November 22, (2000). Online at http://denver.rockymountainnews.com/shooting/1122shad1.shtml.

Sunday Magazine, p. 46.

"Supreme court refuses to block Bundy death." (1989). *The New York Times,* January 24 p. A14.

Surette, R. (1998). *Media, Crime, and Criminal Justice: Images and Reality.* Belmont, CA: Wadsworth Publishing Company.

Swanson, C., Chamelin, N., and Territo, L. (1996). *Criminal Investigation.* (6th Ed.). New York: McGraw Hill.

Thornton, D. (2002). "Constructing and testing a framework for dynamic risk assessment." *Sexual Abuse: A Journal of Research and Treatment* 14(2):137-151.

Thornton, D., and Shingler, J. (2001). *"Impact of schema level work on sexual offenders' cognitive distortions."* Paper presented at the 20th annual Research and Treatment Conference, San Antonio, Texas.

Walsh, J. (1997). *Tears of Rage.* New York: Pocket Books.

Ward, T. (2000). "Sexual offender's cognitive distortions as implicit theories." *Aggression and Violent Behavior* 5: 491-500.

Ward, T. and Hudson, S. M. (2000). "Sexual offender's implicit planning: A conceptual model." *Sexual Abuse: A Journal of Research and Treatment* 12(3): 184-202.

Ward, T., and Hudson, S. M. (1998). "A self-regulation model of the relapse process in sexual offenders." *Journal of Interpersonal Violence* 13: 700-725.

Ward, T., and Keenan, T. (1999). "Child molesters' implicit theories." *Journal of Interpersonal Violence* 14: 821-838.

Ward, T., and Stewart, C. A. (2003). "The treatment of sex offenders: Risk management and good lives." *Professional Psychology: Research and Practice* 3(4): 353-360.

Ward, T., Hudson, S. M., Johnston, L., and Marshall, W. L. (1997). "Cognitive distortions in sex offenders: An integrative view." *Clinical Psychology Review* 17: 479-507.

Watkins, J., and Watkins, H. (1997). *Ego States: Theory and Therapy.* New York: W.W. Norton & Co.

Weinberg, M.S., Williams, C.J., and Calhan, C. (1995). "If the shoe fits ... : Exploring male homosexual foot fetishism." *The Journal of Sex Research* 32(1): 17-27.

Weiter v Settle, 193 F. Supp. 318, 321-22 (1961).

Weston, P., and Lushbaugh, C. (2006). *Criminal Investigation: Basic Perspectives.* (10th Ed.). Upper Saddle River, NJ: Prentice Hall.

Wilgoren, J. 2005. "Eerie parallels are seen to shootings at Columbine." *New York Times,* March 23, p. A-12.

Williams, C. (2004). "Reclaiming the expressive subject: Deviance and the art of non-normativity." *Deviant Behavior* 25: 233-254.

Williams, J. (2003). *Gilles Deleuze's Difference and Repetition*. Edinburg, UK: Edinburg University Press.

"Witnesses at sex murder trial: 2 faces of Gacy: 'Beast', 'Nice man.'" (1980). *Los Angeles Times*, February 22, p. A2.

Wolfgang, M. (1958). *Patterns in Criminal Homicide*. Philadelphia, PA: University of Pennsylvania Press.

"Woman guilty in first of seven road slayings." (1992). *Los Angeles Times*, January 28, p. A13.

Wright, R. (1940). *Native Son*. New York: HarperCollins Publishers, Inc.

Wrightsman, L., Nietzel, M., and Fortune, W., (1994). *Psychology and the Legal System* (3rd edition). Burlington, VT: Elsevier, Inc.

Wrightsman, L. (2001). *Forensic Psychology*. Belmont, CA: Wadsworth Publishing.

Yapko, M.D. (1995). *Essentials of Hypnotherapy*. New York: Brunner/Mazel, Inc.

Yapko, M.D. (1984). *Trance Work: An Introduction to Clinical Hypnosis and Psychotherapy*. New York: Irvington Publishers.

Zandt, C. V. (2005). "BTK Killer: Hiding in Plain Sight." http://www.msnbc.msa.com/id/7052887

Biographies of Contributors

Bruce A. Arrigo, Ph.D. is Professor of Crime, Law, and Society within the Department of Criminal Justice at the University of North Carolina-Charlotte. He holds additional faculty appointments in the Psychology Department and the Public Policy Program. He served as Chair of the Department of Criminal Justice at UNC-Charlotte (2001–2004) and as Director of the Institute of Psychology, Law, and Public Policy at the California School of Professional Psychology-Fresno (1996–2001). Dr. Arrigo is the author of more than 125 journal articles, chapters in books, and scholarly essays. In addition, he is the (co)author or editor of 20 volumes published or in press. Recent books include *Psychological Jurisprudence: Critical Explorations in Law, Crime, and Society* (2004), *Police Corruption and Psychological Testing* (2005), *Criminal Behavior* (2006), and *Philosophy, Crime, and Criminology* (2006). Dr. Arrigo is the Editor-in-Chief of the peer-reviewed quarterly the *Journal of Forensic Psychology Practice*, as well as the Book Series Editor for *Criminal Justice and Psychology* (Carolina Academic Press) and *Critical Perspectives in Criminology* (University of Illinois Press). Professor Arrigo is a past recipient of the Criminologist of the Year Award (2000), sponsored by the Division on Critical Criminology of the American Society of Criminology. He is also a Fellow of the American Psychological Association (2002) and a Fellow of the Academy of Criminal Justice Sciences (2005).

Anthony Beech is a Professor in Criminological Psychology at the University of Birmingham, U.K. and a fellow of the British Psychological Society. He has published widely in the field of sexual offender research.

Deanna Cahill is a major in social science education at Indiana State University. She plans on teaching at the college level. She is a member of Alpha Chi Omega.

Dr. Mark S. Carich is currently with Illinois Dept. of Corrections at Big Muddy River CC. He coordinates the sex offender treatment programs and in particular the Sexually Dangerous Person's Assessment & Treatment Program. Dr. Carich is also adjunct faculty with the Adler School of Professional Psychology, in Chicago. He has published extensively including the following books: (1) *Handbook of Sexual Abuser Assessment & Treatment* (2001) co-edited S. Mussack, Safer Press; (2) *Adult Sexual Offender Assessment Packet* (1995), with D. Adkerson, Safer Press; (3) *Sex Offender Relapse Intervention Workbook* (1996) with M. Stone, Adler School; (4) *Adult Sexual Offender Report* (2003) with D. Adkerson, Safer Press; and (5) *Contemporary Treatment of Adult Male Sex Offenders* (2003) with M. Calder, Russell House in England. In conjunction, Dr. Carich provides both national & international training & consulting. His current focus is sex offender assessment & treatment, along with general therapy techniques.

Rachel Dickey is a student at Indiana State University majoring in graphic design. She is interested in creating intriguing art forms. She also has a fascination for criminology.

Dawn Fisher is a Consultant Clinical and Forensic Psychologist and Head of Psychological Services at Llanarth Court Hospital in Wales. She is also an Honorary Senior Research Fellow at the University of Birmingham, U.K.

John Randolph Fuller has been teaching criminology classes at the University of West Georgia for the past 25 years. Dr. Fuller received his graduate education at the School of Criminology at Florida State University. He has worked as a probation and parole officer and a criminal justice planner. He is author of a new textbook; *Criminal Justice: Mainstream and Crosscurrents*. He is presently working on a juvenile delinquency text.

Margaret Kohut has been a Licensed Clinical Social Worker since 1986, and a Licensed Addiction Counselor since 1996. For ten years, Margaret worked with juvenile and adult criminal offenders in her home state of Oklahoma. In 1988, Margaret was commissioned as an officer in the United States Air Force, specializing in the clinical evaluation and treatment of mental health disorders, domestic violence and chemical dependency treatment. Margaret primarily treated active duty members who became involved with the military and civilian criminal justice system. Margaret has written numerous publications on forensic issues for the Department Of Defense. Now retired from the Air Force, Margaret and her husband live in Mapleton, Maine.

Christopher Kudlac has authored a book on capital punishment and the media. His interests include serial killers, the media, capital punishment, religion and police discretion. He received a Ph. D. in Sociology from Fordham University and is an Assistant Professor of Criminal Justice at Westfield State College.

Dragan Milovanovic received his Ph.D. from the School of Criminal Justice, SUNY at Albany. He is Professor of Justice Studies at Northeastern Illinois University. He has authored, co-authored, or edited eighteen books and more than one-hundred-fifty publications. He is the 1993 recipient of the Distinguished Service Award from the Division on Critical Criminology of the American Society of Criminology. He is editor of the *International Journal for the Semiotics of Law*. His recent books include *Critical Criminology at the Edge* (Praeger/Criminal Justice Press), *Lacan: Topologically Speaking* (Other Press), and co-authored *The French Connection in Criminology* (SUNY Press). His forthcoming books are: (co-authored) *Introduction to Social Justice* (Rutgers University Press); *Deleuze and Justice* (Illinois University Press), *The Social Justice Reader* (Routledge), and the two-volume (co-authored) *Semiotics of Law* (Springer).

Catherine E. Purcell, Ph.D. received her Bachelors degree from the University of Redlands, and her doctorate in Forensic Psychology from the Institute of Psychology, Law and Public Policy at the California School of Professional Psychology in Fresno, California. Dr. Purcell has worked for several years as a psychologist at the California Department of Corrections. Her most recent position has been in the capacity of Mental Health Coordinator for the only maximum security juvenile detention facility in Kern County. In addition, she has also taught several classes in both psychology and criminology at National University in Fresno, and for California State University Fresno Campus. Dr. Purcell continues her research endeavors in the area of model and theory development of parpahilic sexual crimes, and has recently been involved in profiling such cases with law enforcement entities, as well as lecturing to audiences on forensic psychology. Along with Bruce A. Arrigo, Ph.D., she is the lead co-author of *the Psychology of Lust Murder: Paraphilia, Sexual Killing, and Serial Homicide* (2006).

Phillip C. Shon, Ph.D. is an Assistant Professor of Criminology at Indiana State University. He holds a bachelor's degree in philosophy, a master's degree in linguistics and criminal justice, and a Ph.D. in criminal justice. His works have appeared in journals such as *International Journal of Law and Psychiatry, Punishment & Society, Critical Criminology, Discourse & Society, Criminology & Social Integration, and Journal for the Psychoanalysis of Culture and Society*.

DeVere D. Woods, Jr. is an Associate Professor in the Department of Criminology and Criminal Justice at Indiana State University. A former police investigator, he received his Ph.D. from Michigan State University where he collaborated with Robert Trojanowicz on research and consulting for the National Center for Community Policing. Along with his continual consultations on community policing, he was recently appointed as a special advisor for the National Police of El Salvador. His current research includes community policing, police management, policy implementation, criminal investigation, and crime analysis. His research has been published by *Law Enforcement Executive Forum*, *Police Studies*, *The Journal of Community Policing*, *Policing in Central and Eastern Europe: Dilemmas of Contemporary Criminal Justice*, the Department of Justice, the Community Policing Consortium, and *Identification News*.

Index

Author Index